Bernd Kappenberg

SETTING SIGNS FOR EUROPE

Why Diacritics Matter for European Integration

With a foreword by Peter Schlobinski

ibidem-Verlag
Stuttgart

Bibliografische Information der Deutschen Nationalbibliothek
Die Deutsche Nationalbibliothek verzeichnet diese Publikation in der Deutschen Nationalbibliografie; detaillierte bibliografische Daten sind im Internet über http://dnb.d-nb.de abrufbar.

Bibliographic information published by the Deutsche Nationalbibliothek
Die Deutsche Nationalbibliothek lists this publication in the Deutsche Nationalbibliografie; detailed bibliographic data are available in the Internet at http://dnb.d-nb.de.

Font: Linux Libertine

∞

Gedruckt auf alterungsbeständigem, säurefreien Papier
Printed on acid-free paper

ISSN: 1614-3515

ISBN-13: 978-3-8382-0663-9

© *ibidem*-Verlag
Stuttgart 2015

Alle Rechte vorbehalten

Das Werk einschließlich aller seiner Teile ist urheberrechtlich geschützt. Jede Verwertung außerhalb der engen Grenzen des Urheberrechtsgesetzes ist ohne Zustimmung des Verlages unzulässig und strafbar. Dies gilt insbesondere für Vervielfältigungen, Übersetzungen, Mikroverfilmungen und elektronische Speicherformen sowie die Einspeicherung und Verarbeitung in elektronischen Systemen.

All rights reserved. No part of this publication may be reproduced, stored in or introduced into a retrieval system, or transmitted, in any form, or by any means (electronic, mechanical, photocopying, recording or otherwise) without the prior written permission of the publisher. Any person who does any unauthorized act in relation to this publication may be liable to criminal prosecution and civil claims for damages.

Printed in the EU

Soviet and Post-Soviet Politics and Society (SPPS)
ISSN 1614-3515

General Editor: Andreas Umland,
Institute for Euro-Atlantic Cooperation, Kyiv, umland@stanfordalumni.org

Commissioning Editor: Max Jakob Horstmann,
London, mjh@ibidem.eu

EDITORIAL COMMITTEE*

DOMESTIC & COMPARATIVE POLITICS
Prof. **Ellen Bos**, *Andrássy University of Budapest*
Dr. **Ingmar Bredies**, *FH Bund, Brühl*
Dr. **Andrey Kazantsev**, *MGIMO (U) MID RF, Moscow*
Prof. **Heiko Pleines**, *University of Bremen*
Prof. **Richard Sakwa**, *University of Kent at Canterbury*
Dr. **Sarah Whitmore**, *Oxford Brookes University*
Dr. **Harald Wydra**, *University of Cambridge*

SOCIETY, CLASS & ETHNICITY
Col. **David Glantz**, *"Journal of Slavic Military Studies"*
Dr. **Marlène Laruelle**, *George Washington University*
Dr. **Stephen Shulman**, *Southern Illinois University*
Prof. **Stefan Troebst**, *University of Leipzig*

POLITICAL ECONOMY & PUBLIC POLICY
Prof. em. **Marshall Goldman**, *Wellesley College, Mass.*
Dr. **Andreas Goldthau**, *Central European University*
Dr. **Robert Kravchuk**, *University of North Carolina*
Dr. **David Lane**, *University of Cambridge*
Dr. **Carol Leonard**, *University of Oxford*
Dr. **Maria Popova**, *McGill University, Montreal*

FOREIGN POLICY & INTERNATIONAL AFFAIRS
Dr. **Peter Duncan**, *University College London*
Dr. **Taras Kuzio**, *Johns Hopkins University*
Prof. **Gerhard Mangott**, *University of Innsbruck*
Dr. **Diana Schmidt-Pfister**, *University of Konstanz*
Dr. **Lisbeth Tarlow**, *Harvard University, Cambridge*
Dr. **Christian Wipperfürth**, *N-Ost Network, Berlin*
Dr. **William Zimmerman**, *University of Michigan*

HISTORY, CULTURE & THOUGHT
Dr. **Catherine Andreyev**, *University of Oxford*
Prof. **Mark Bassin**, *Södertörn University*
Prof. **Karsten Brüggemann**, *Tallinn University*
Dr. **Alexander Etkind**, *University of Cambridge*
Dr. **Gasan Gusejnov**, *Moscow State University*
Prof. em. **Walter Laqueur**, *Georgetown University*
Prof. **Leonid Luks**, *Catholic University of Eichstaett*
Dr. **Olga Malinova**, *Russian Academy of Sciences*
Prof. **Andrei Rogatchevski**, *University of Tromsø*
Dr. **Mark Tauger**, *West Virginia University*
Dr. **Stefan Wiederkehr**, *BBAW, Berlin*

ADVISORY BOARD*

Prof. **Dominique Arel**, *University of Ottawa*
Prof. **Jörg Baberowski**, *Humboldt University of Berlin*
Prof. **Margarita Balmaceda**, *Seton Hall University*
Dr. **John Barber**, *University of Cambridge*
Prof. **Timm Beichelt**, *European University Viadrina*
Dr. **Katrin Boeckh**, *University of Munich*
Prof. em. **Archie Brown**, *University of Oxford*
Dr. **Vyacheslav Bryukhovetsky**, *Kyiv-Mohyla Academy*
Prof. **Timothy Colton**, *Harvard University, Cambridge*
Prof. **Paul D'Anieri**, *University of Florida*
Dr. **Heike Dörrenbächer**, *DGO, Berlin*
Dr. **John Dunlop**, *Hoover Institution, Stanford, California*
Dr. **Sabine Fischer**, *SWP, Berlin*
Dr. **Geir Flikke**, *NUPI, Oslo*
Prof. **David Galbreath**, *University of Aberdeen*
Prof. **Alexander Galkin**, *Russian Academy of Sciences*
Prof. **Frank Golczewski**, *University of Hamburg*
Dr. **Nikolas Gvosdev**, *Naval War College, Newport, RI*
Prof. **Mark von Hagen**, *Arizona State University*
Dr. **Guido Hausmann**, *University of Freiburg i.Br.*
Prof. **Dale Herspring**, *Kansas State University*
Dr. **Stefani Hoffman**, *Hebrew University of Jerusalem*
Prof. **Mikhail Ilyin**, *MGIMO (U) MID RF, Moscow*
Prof. **Vladimir Kantor**, *Higher School of Economics*
Dr. **Ivan Katchanovski**, *University of Ottawa*
Prof. em. **Andrzej Korbonski**, *University of California*
Dr. **Iris Kempe**, *"Caucasus Analytical Digest"*
Prof. **Herbert Küpper**, *Institut für Ostrecht Regensburg*
Dr. **Rainer Lindner**, *CEEER, Berlin*
Dr. **Vladimir Malakhov**, *Russian Academy of Sciences*

Dr. **Luke March**, *University of Edinburgh*
Prof. **Michael McFaul**, *US Embassy at Moscow*
Prof. **Birgit Menzel**, *University of Mainz-Germersheim*
Prof. **Valery Mikhailenko**, *The Urals State University*
Prof. **Emil Pain**, *Higher School of Economics, Moscow*
Dr. **Oleg Podvintsev**, *Russian Academy of Sciences*
Prof. **Olga Popova**, *St. Petersburg State University*
Dr. **Alex Pravda**, *University of Oxford*
Dr. **Erik van Ree**, *University of Amsterdam*
Dr. **Joachim Rogall**, *Robert Bosch Foundation Stuttgart*
Prof. **Peter Rutland**, *Wesleyan University, Middletown*
Prof. **Marat Salikov**, *The Urals State Law Academy*
Dr. **Gwendolyn Sasse**, *University of Oxford*
Prof. **Jutta Scherrer**, *EHESS, Paris*
Prof. **Robert Service**, *University of Oxford*
Mr. **James Sherr**, *RIIA Chatham House London*
Dr. **Oxana Shevel**, *Tufts University, Medford*
Prof. **Eberhard Schneider**, *University of Siegen*
Prof. **Olexander Shnyrkov**, *Shevchenko University, Kyiv*
Prof. **Hans-Henning Schröder**, *SWP, Berlin*
Prof. **Yuri Shapoval**, *Ukrainian Academy of Sciences*
Prof. **Viktor Shnirelman**, *Russian Academy of Sciences*
Dr. **Lisa Sundstrom**, *University of British Columbia*
Dr. **Philip Walters**, *"Religion, State and Society", Oxford*
Prof. **Zenon Wasyliw**, *Ithaca College, New York State*
Dr. **Lucan Way**, *University of Toronto*
Dr. **Markus Wehner**, *"Frankfurter Allgemeine Zeitung"*
Dr. **Andrew Wilson**, *University College London*
Prof. **Jan Zielonka**, *University of Oxford*
Prof. **Andrei Zorin**, *University of Oxford*

* While the Editorial Committee and Advisory Board support the General Editor in the choice and improvement of manuscripts for publication, responsibility for remaining errors and misinterpretations in the series' volumes lies with the books' authors.

Soviet and Post-Soviet Politics and Society (SPPS)
ISSN 1614-3515

Founded in 2004 and refereed since 2007, SPPS makes available affordable English-, German-, and Russian-language studies on the history of the countries of the former Soviet bloc from the late Tsarist period to today. It publishes between 5 and 20 volumes per year and focuses on issues in transitions to and from democracy such as economic crisis, identity formation, civil society development, and constitutional reform in CEE and the NIS. SPPS also aims to highlight so far understudied themes in East European studies such as right-wing radicalism, religious life, higher education, or human rights protection. The authors and titles of all previously published volumes are listed at the end of this book. For a full description of the series and reviews of its books, see
www.ibidem-verlag.de/red/spps.

Editorial correspondence & manuscripts should be sent to: Dr. Andreas Umland, DAAD, German Embassy, vul. Bohdana Khmelnitskoho 25, UA-01901 Kyiv, Ukraine. e-mail: umland@stanfordalumni.org

Business correspondence & review copy requests should be sent to: *ibidem* Press, Leuschnerstr. 40, 30457 Hannover, Germany; tel.: +49 511 2622200; fax: +49 511 2622201; spps@ibidem.eu.

Authors, reviewers, referees, and editors for (as well as all other persons sympathetic to) SPPS are invited to join its networks at
www.facebook.com/group.php?gid=52638198614
www.linkedin.com/groups?about=&gid=103012
www.xing.com/net/spps-ibidem-verlag/

Recent Volumes

131 *Elisa Kriza*
Alexander Solzhenitsyn: Cold War Icon, Gulag Author, Russian Nationalist?
A Study of the Western Reception of his Literary Writings, Historical Interpretations, and Political Ideas
With a foreword by Andrei Rogatchevski
ISBN 978-3-8382-0589-2 (Paperback edition)
ISBN 978-3-8382-0690-5 (Hardcover edition)

132 *Serghei Golunov*
The Elephant in the Room
Corruption and Cheating in Russian Universities
ISBN 978-3-8382-0570-0

133 *Manja Hussner, Rainer Arnold (Hgg.)*
Verfassungsgerichtsbarkeit in Zentralasien I
Sammlung von Verfassungstexten
ISBN 978-3-8382-0595-3

134 *Nikolay Mitrokhin*
Die "Russische Partei"
Die Bewegung der russischen Nationalisten in der UdSSR 1953-1985
Aus dem Russischen übertragen von einem Übersetzerteam unter der Leitung von Larisa Schippel
ISBN 978-3-8382-0024-8

135 *Manja Hussner, Rainer Arnold (Hgg.)*
Verfassungsgerichtsbarkeit in Zentralasien II
Sammlung von Verfassungstexten
ISBN 978-3-8382-0597-7

136 *Manfred Zeller*
Das sowjetische Fieber
Fußballfans im poststalinistischen Vielvölkerreich
Mit einem Vorwort von Nikolaus Katzer
ISBN 978-3-8382-0757-5

137 *Kristin Schreiter*
Stellung und Entwicklungspotential zivilgesellschaftlicher Gruppen in Russland
Menschenrechtsorganisationen im Vergleich
ISBN 978-3-8382-0673-8

138 *David R. Marples, Frederick V. Mills (Eds.)*
Ukraine's Euromaidan
Analyses of a Civil Revolution
ISBN 978-3-8382-0660-8

"Piled Higher and Deeper" by Jorge Cham / www.phdcomics.com

Diacritics matter!

Mi papá tiene 47 años.—My dad is 47 years old.

Mi papa tiene 47 anos.—My potato has 47 anuses.

Contents

1	Introduction	17
1.1	Problem description	17
1.2	Process is running—coordination is missing	20
1.3	Touched policies and policy levels	22
1.4	Definition of terms	24
1.5	How this book is structured	25
2	Definition of the required character repertoire	27
2.1	Narrowing the topic	27
2.2	Basic letters	27
2.3	Variants of letters	29
2.4	Letters from other scripts	31
2.5	Ligatures	32
2.5.1	Ligatures based on handwriting	32
2.5.2	Typographic ligatures	33
2.6	Diacritics	36
2.7	Conclusion	50
3	History of character sets	51
3.1	BAUDOT code	52
3.2	MURRAY code	53

3.3	ASCII	53
3.3.1	ISO 646	54
3.4	8-bit codes (extended ASCII formats)	55
3.4.1	ISO 8859	57
3.4.2	Windows-125x ("ANSI")	60
3.5	EBCDIC	61
3.6	ISO/IEC 10646 (Universal Character Set) and Unicode	62
3.6.1	Unicode transformation formats (UTFs)	65
3.6.2	Windows Glyph List 4 (WGL4)	68
3.7	Success of Unicode	69
3.8	Mojibake	70
4	Unicode-compatible fonts	73
5	State of the "diacritical integration" in the media	83
5.1	Diacritics in news agencies	83
5.2	Examples from selected media	83
5.2.1	Print media	83
5.2.2	Online media	87
5.3	Case study: dpa	88
5.3.1	Problems of limitation to ISO 8859-1	90
5.3.2	The upcoming solution: Unicode-compatible software	90
6	Failure examples	93
6.1	Incompatible character sets	93
6.2	Do-It-Yourself diacritics	94
6.3	Incorrect operation of dead keys	95
6.4	Ignorance of the differences between diacritics	96

6.5	Use of combining diacritics	97
6.6	Replacement by images	98
6.7	Replacement by escape sequences	98
6.8	Conclusion	98
7	Diacritics as style element in brand and product names	99
7.1	Macron as distorted French acute	100
7.2	Macron as distorted French accent	102
7.3	Macron as allusion to a special shape on a shoe's sole	104
7.4	Macron as artistic alienation of the umlaut	104
7.5	Trema points as allusion for bubbles	105
7.6	Dot over character as artistic alienation of the French acute	106
7.7	Scandinavian diacritics	106
7.8	S with haček	107
7.9	Mirrored e	108
7.10	M with acute	109
7.11	Using macrons to convey a phonetic function	109
7.12	Using diacritics to convey dictionary character	111
7.13	Using diacritics to convey exoticism	112
7.14	Using diacritics to convey currency symbolism	113
7.15	Written with diacritics or not?	114
7.16	Conclusion	117

8	How people react to diacritics	121
8.1	Cartoons, sketches and jokes	121
8.2	Decontextualized characters	126
9	Legal basics of using diacritics in personal names	131
9.1	International agreements	131
9.1.1	Charter of the United Nations	131
9.1.2	Universal Declaration of Human Rights	132
9.1.3	European Convention on Human Rights	132
9.1.4	UN International Covenant on Civil and Political Rights	133
9.1.5	Helsinki Final Act	133
9.1.6	Convention on the indication of surnames and forenames in civil status registers	134
9.1.7	Document of the Copenhagen Meeting	136
9.1.8	Charter of Paris for a New Europe	137
9.1.9	UN Declaration on Minority Rights	137
9.1.10	European Charter for Regional or Minority Languages	138
9.1.11	Framework Convention for the Protection of National Minorities	140
9.1.12	Oslo Recommendations Regarding the Linguistic Rights of National Minorities	142
9.1.13	Bilateral agreements	143
9.2	EU law	149
9.3	German law	151
9.3.1	SAGA	151

9.3.2	Civil Status Act	153
9.3.2.1	XPersonenstand—standardization of data interchange formats in civil status information	155
9.3.2.2	Registration office software	156
9.3.3	Regulatory reporting	157
9.3.3.1	Standard dataset for reporting (DSMeld) and XMeld	159
9.3.3.2	Registration software	161
9.3.4	Databases and Unicode	162
9.3.5	Passports and ID cards	167
9.3.5.1	Passports	167
9.3.5.2	ID cards	169
9.3.5.3	Bundesdruckerei	172
9.3.5.4	Electronic data transfer to the Bundesdruckerei using DIGANT	172
9.3.6	Name Change Law	174
9.3.6.1	Practical experience	178
9.4	Austrian law	180
9.4.1	International agreements	180
9.4.2	Civil status law	181
9.4.3	Registration Act and Central residents register	182
9.4.4	E-Government Act	183
9.4.5	Manual diacritics	186
9.4.6	Name Law Amendment Act	192
9.5	Swiss law	192
9.6	United Kingdom law	196
9.6.1	Birth certificates	196

9.6.2	"Disallowed characters" cannot be used in passports and ID cards	197
9.7	European electronic registration information	198
10	Landmark court decisions	201
10.1	International law and European law	201
10.2	Germany	203
10.2.1	German given name must not have a foreign letter	203
10.2.2	Czechoslovakian birth name is to be entered with diacritical marks	204
10.2.3	Registration of Czechoslovak name in civil status registers	205
10.2.4	Diacritical characters cannot be removed by approximation statement	207
10.2.5	Vietnamese names have to be spelled including diacritics	207
10.2.6	Birth registration without the diacritic belonging to it has to be corrected in civil status registers	208
10.2.7	The Turkish first name Yılmaz is to be reproduced with dotless i	209
10.2.8	Turkish letters ı and İ have to be transferred to the civil status registers	210
10.2.9	The Icelandic letter ð is not eligible for registration	211
10.2.10	! is not a letter	216
10.2.11	Conclusion for Germany	216

10.3	Austria	217
10.3.1	In the spelling of a surname, diacritics are also to be taken into account	217
10.3.2	Suppression of diacritical characters is a violation of the right to a name	219
10.3.3	Handwritten or typewritten complement of diacritics is permitted	221
10.3.4	Diacritics in driver's licenses are to complement by hand if required	222
10.3.5	Correct spelling of the family name is constitutionally required	224
10.3.6	Correct spelling of surnames with diacritic characters is a requirement of the Federal Constitution	229
10.3.7	Correct spelling of names on the health insurance card	232
10.3.8	Conclusion for Austria	237
10.4	Netherlands	237
10.4.1	Cases of the national ombudsman	238
10.4.2	Conclusion for the Netherlands	240
10.5	Switzerland	241
10.5.1	Margit Széchényi against Department of the Interior of the Canton of Zurich	241
10.5.2	Conclusion for Switzerland	244
10.6	Outlook	245
11	Diacritics as political symbolism	247

12	Summary and discussion	261
12.1	Technical aspects	261
12.2	Legal Aspects	265
12.3	National implementation	269
12.4	European implementation	273
13	Outlook	277
14	Development of a practical input method for characters	281
14.1	Fundamental considerations	281
14.1.1	Potential conflicts	284
14.2	Escape encodings with diacritics	285
14.3	Escape encodings *without* diacritics	288
14.4	Underscore	292
14.5	Other characters (no compose key)	293
14.6	Dead keys	294
Further readings		295

Peter Schlobinski

A modern society is not possible without writing. The typographic systems—be it the morphosyllabic script in China, the syllabic script systems in Japan, or an alphabetic script such as in Germany—are coding instructions for information storage and distribution in the respective languages. With the development of writing almost synchronized 5000 years ago at the Sumerians and Egyptians, communication becomes storable, and writing is used for commerce, administration and religious practice. By that, a dis-situating process takes place: communication becomes independent of the memory of the individual and the here and now of the interaction participants. It becomes—phrased once aptly by the sociologist Niklas Luhmann—"detached in its social effects from the time of its first occurrence, its formulation", with the consequence that you write for future "situations in which the writer does not need to be present".[1]

But writing systems are more than just storage and distribution systems of information and motors in the process of civilization. They are important factors for the cultural development and cultural identity, be it at the national level or in young small groups. In this case, the sign systems is are great importance.

There are two factors that are generally relevant to note: firstly, writing systems unify and standardize, on the other hand, there are variations that reflect local peculiarities.

---

1   Luhmann, Niklas (1984): *Soziale Systeme. Grundriß einer allgemeinen Theorie*. Frankfurt am Main, p. 128.

- Two examples. The Council for German Orthography[2] allows for the spelling variants *Schmand* and *Schmant* (sour cream), the latter is the Austrian spelling, which is important for the cultural identity of the Austrians and therefore not simply subordinate to the German spelling.
- Example two: the former Bayern player *Hasan Salihamidzic* is from Bosnia, where his name is written in Latin *Salihamidžić*. Is it correct to simply omit the diacritics and (so) to 'Germanize' the spelling of the name? And why not *Salihamidschitch*?

BERND KAPPENBERG explores in his work the problem what the linguistic diversity in Europe means with regard to the sign systems and how linguistic diversity and multialphabetism shall be treated in different perspectives. This raises the central question of how the alphabetic integration in Europe should be, and how in Germany the use of a pan-Latin character set can be enforced as binding. There are four dimensions treated by KAPPENBERG: (a) the legal framework, (b) the political conditions, (c) the technical parameters and (d) the cultural aspects. It is the merit of KAPPENBERG's work to have submitted a foundational work here that discusses all these dimensions knowledgeable and *en détail*, and he presents solutions, down to an improved input method for diacritics. The book is interesting not only for administrators and journalists, civil registry offices and businesses, but for basically anyone who deals with issues of integration in Europe.

---

[2] *Rat für deutsche Rechtschreibung*: http://www.rechtschreibrat.com/

1 Introduction

If I had to do it again, I would begin with culture.

– attributed to Jean Monnet

1.1 Problem description

With the collapse of the Soviet bloc in the late 1980s, People of Western Europe have become more aware of events and people from countries beyond the former "Iron Curtain". In print (and later online) media, but also for documents in administration, a problem arose: most countries in Central, Eastern and South-eastern Europe use *extended* Latin alphabets, which can not be fully displayed with usual Western European character sets (and keyboards), as they contain special diacritics (háček, breve, ogonek, etc.).

Regrettably, no uniform practice for solving this problem in the editorial treatment of extended Latin alphabets has succeeded until today (2015), although the technical requirements have long been fulfilled. I shall illustrate this through the example of the Beneš Decrees, which are of importance for the German-Czech relations. There were different reactions of different German media on the occurrence of the letter š (s with háček):

From "scalping" (Benes) over pseudo-transliteration (Benesch)[3] to switching to an extended Latin character set (Beneš).

On websites, there are further difficulties: depending on the combination of the character set in the HTML source of the page with the Internet browser it is viewed with, often another character is shown instead of the character š (Bene¹, Bene?, BeneΔ, Bene*, Bene , Bene¨, BeneÅ¡) or the š disappears completely (Bene).

If you want to communicate in the pan-European context, you have to deal with linguistic diversity (multilingualism). The European Union (EU), for example, has 24 official languages, into which and out of which has to be interpreted and translated on a daily basis, for example in parliamentary debates and in the publication of EU legislation. Inseparable of linguistic diversity, there is diversity of alphabets (multialphabetism) and of scripts (Latin, Greek, Cyrillic). But multialphabetism is threatened in many ways by the increasing—substandard—digitization of written communication:

- The *character sets* of computer programs are often incompatible with each other and cause—after transmission of the data—the display of the wrong characters (such as Potoènik instead Potočnik or ÐŸÑ€Ð ¸Ð²ÐµÑ‚ instead Привет).
- Standard *fonts* often cover only a small part of the necessary characters, resulting to holes, question marks, or use of glyphs from other fonts in texts.
- Not all *characters* necessary for the pan-European communications are available on standard computer *keyboards*.

---

3   Which is actually wrong (cf. chapter 10.2.9): you can only *transliterate* a word into *another* script, e.g. from Cyrillic into Latin. The correct term here would be "mapping".

- *Alternative input methods* require increased effort (e.g. accessing and browsing a symbols list), expert knowledge (e.g. coding numerical value of a character) or the installation of additional programs (such as virtual keyboards) that may not be free.

- Print and online media spread the names and terms from foreign languages often *without* the necessary diacritics (e.g. Walesa and Solidarnosc instead of Wałęsa and Solidarność). This is partly due to technical problems and time pressure, but in some cases also on cultural chauvinism ("cultured" Romance vs. "wild" Slavonic, Baltic, and Turkic languages).

- Even if diacritics-enabled software is purchased, government employees often refuse customers with a categorical "does not go" when they insist on spelling their name with diacritics.

This dominant state is—not only from a technical point of view—highly unsatisfactory, but it also threatens the cultural identity of many European nations, and the personal rights of individuals: deterred or unnerved by the technical problems and the lack of understanding that meets them from authorities and the private sector ("this little stroke can mean but nothing"), persons with names containing Eastern European diacritics increasingly dispense of their right to correct spelling and assimilate—from a sense of cultural self-censorship—to the *Western* European standard character set as the lowest common denominator. This in turn results frequently in a phonetic mispronunciation. The result is not only a limitation of personal rights of individuals, but also a creeping cultural impoverishment of Europe as a whole, thus contradicting massively the European idea of mutual acceptance and mutual cultural enrichment. Ultimately, this process hinders even European integration, as it confirms fears of EU-sceptical parts of the populations, especially in the smaller ones of the 13 new Member States[4] of the European Union, who fear the loss of their cultural autonomy.

Following the European idea of "unity in diversity", however, it should gradually come to an EU-wide adoption of the diacritics of the respective other countries in the use in writing of administration and media. The European Union would thus prove clearly visible that it respects the personal and cultural identity of its citizens. It would send a signal especially to the people of Central and Eastern European Member States that they are truly welcome in the EU. In this way, it would be easier for the citizens to perceive Europe in its entirety as "home" and the overall project "European Union" would gain in acceptance.

1.2 Process is running— coordination is missing

Approaches for the acquisition of foreign language diacritics reach a long time back: German typewriter keyboards contain since about 1900 French accents (*accent grave* and *accent aigu*, later also the *accent circonflexe*).[5] In the rock music scene, the "heavy metal umlaut" is a popular means of style already for decades (e.g. *Motörhead*).[6] The German national newspapers *Frankfurter Allgemeine Zeitung* and *Die Zeit* (see chapter 5.2.1) have already been converted to extended Latin character sets. Up-scale Polish

---

4   2004: Estonia, Latvia, Lithuania, Poland, Czech Republic, Slovakia, Slovenia, Malta, Cyprus; 2008: Romania, Bulgaria; 2013: Croatia
5   Maria Mayr (type writer museum Peter Mitterhofer, I-39020 Partschins), personal communication (2005-11-22)
6   http://de.wikipedia.org/wiki/Heavy-Metal-Umlaut (2011-11-28)

newspapers use German umlauts.[7] European advertising agencies market the Škoda.[8] The letter x, non-existent in the Lithuanian alphabet, enjoys growing popularity in Lithuanian Internet slang as an alternative notation in words with "ks".[9, 10] The same applies for German sharp ß in text messages in Swiss German (as alternative to "ss") and in Hungarian (as alternative to "sz").[11] And last but not least, so-called "umlaut domains" (*Internationalized Domain Names*, IDNs) with non-US-ASCII-compatible diacritics (for example www.schön.de) are available since March 2004, which were a huge success.[12, 13] Diacritics are now even used as style element in brand and product names (for example Jōvan, Cašmir, see chapter 7).

As you can see, this process of acquisition of foreign language diacritics, technically called *interoperability*, is primarily limited to specific technical or cultural (i.e. non-state) areas. It runs in general slow and without central control or coordination. This is not only due to the mutual technical incompatibility of competing (and often unfortunately outdated "legacy") IT standards, but also in the lack of awareness among political leaders, media and administration of the importance of the topic, and not least in human convenience.

---

7   Bartłomiej Paweł Jesionkiewicz, personal communication (2003-08-07)
8   company website:
     http://www.skoda-auto.com/en (2014-12-06)
9   e.g. kox and tixlas instead of koks und tikslas / Lithuanian Internet provider Liux.lt
10   Petras Kudaras alias moxliukas, personal communication (2005-11-16)
11   http://de.wikipedia.org/wiki/%C3%9F (2006-02-16)
12   list of valid characters for IDNs in Germany:
     http://www.denic.de/domains/internationalized-domain-names/idn-liste.html (2011-11-28)
13   http://www.denic.de/en/denic-in-dialogue/press-releases/press/129.html (2015-01-07)

Figure 1.1: **Correct representation of a Czech diacritic in a German advertisement for the Škoda car brand**

Especially in view of the growing importance of e-government, however, interoperability in the correct processing of personal data containing diacritics, especially with respect to the right to a name, is a central issue.

1.3 Touched policies and policy levels

The question of an EU- or Europe-wide mandatory standard character set represents a complex problem (see table 1.1): the touched *policies* include technical standards and the institutions involved, but also law and administration, economy (media, IT) and education and culture. The touched *policy levels* reach from local and regional level on the national and the EU and European level up to the global level. The responsible institutions are concentrated in the individual policy areas at different levels: education policy in Germany falls into the responsibility of the individual federal states. Media are usually national (e.g. in German) or language-oriented (e.g. in Belgium). Law and administration in turn comprise all levels of policy. Technical standards on the other hand are in the age of globalization increasingly established on EU, European or global level.

Table 1.1: **Touched policies and policy levels**

	Technical standards	Administrative law	Economics	Education
global	• ISO • Unicode • ITU-T • W3C	• International Law • Human Rights • UN	• IT companies	
European	• CEN	• Council of Europe • European Court of Human Rights • *Commission Internationale de l'État Civil*		
EU		• EU law • European Court of Justice • European Commission		• Lisbon objectives
bilateral		• bilateral state treaties		
national	• national standardization body • ASCII standard • language	• Constitutional court • Constitution • Federal administration	• news agencies • national media	• ministry of education
regional	• language	• regional administration	• regional media	• regional ministries of education
local		• local government	• local media	

1.4 Definition of terms

Some important terms will appear frequently in this book. They shall therefore be defined briefly here:

Script: a system to write down spoken languages. Examples are the Latin, Greek, Cyrillic, Arabic, Hebrew, and Chinese script.

Alphabet: the amount of sound-denoting characters (letters) individual to one specific language. Alphabet is often used as a synonym for → script, which is not entirely correct, as for example the Latin *script* is used for a number of *alphabets* which are distinguished by the letters or diacritics used.[14] Examples are the German and the Lithuanian alphabet.

Special characters: all characters that do not denote sounds of a language. These include, for example, punctuation marks (period, comma, question mark, brackets, ...), the degree sign (°), the section sign (§) and → diacritics.

Diacritics: small characters such as dots, lines, hooks, etc. (´ ` ˘ ˆ ¨ ͵ etc.) belonging to letters that indicate a change in pronunciation or stress (from Greek *diakrineîn* [διακρινεῖν] = distinguish).

Repertoire: a set of characters to be encoded.

Character set: an inventory of characters (letters, digits, special characters, control characters, etc.) which are each encoded by a numerical value and are therefore suitable for digital storage and transmission of data.

---

14 Watch this video clip to learn of a drastic example of the difference between Latin *alphabet* and Latin *language* (from *Indiana Jones and the Last Crusade*): https://www.youtube.com/watch?v=XMSK-wq3jlg (2014-12-06)

Font: graphic design of a → character set. It assigns the numerical values to certain forms (glyphs). So the letter A looks in the font *Linux Libertine* different from in the font *Microsoft Sans Serif* (A) or *Everson Mono* (A).

1.5 How this book is structured

The following basic questions have to be asked and hopefully answered in this book:

Is there a **character set** (and **fonts**) that include all necessary characters for pan-European communication?

- The totality of the Latin characters necessary for pan-European communications (see chapter 2) is defined. The available character sets (see chapter 3) and selected fonts (see chapter 4) are presented and compared with the previously defined requirements.

How can you raise **media awareness** for the use of the correct characters?

- The handling of diacritics in media is investigated (see chapter 5), particularly the treatment of diacritics in print and online media. I analysed the obtained data and developed strategies for the different problems that came to light.

How can you encourage **individuals** to stand up for their linguistic rights?

- I have examined the legal requirements in international law, EU law and national law for the question *"Is there a right to diacritics in personal names?"* (see chapter 9) and compiled regard landmark court decisions in this regard (see chapter 10). Particular attention I have directed to the treatment of personal names with diacritics in the German civil status registers and civil registration.

How can you encourage **software engineers** to implement improvements?

How can you raise **government employee's awareness** for the use of the correct characters?

Is there the possibility to make above mentioned character set a **mandatory** European standard?

- With a summary and discussion (see chapter 12), the book is addressing the question how effective approaches for raising awareness in software engineering, media, administration, and employees for the correct handling of diacritics can be created, in order to practically implement a "Europeanized spelling".
- Most favourably, this should happen in the context of European interoperability and/or the multilingualism policy of the European Union.

An outlook (see chapter 13) closes the book.

As an Annex, I dived into the topic how the **input of characters** can be simplified (see chapter 14).

As digressions, I considered how **people react to diacritics** (see chapter 8), how diacritics are used as **stylistic devices** (see chapter 7) and as **political symbolism** (see chapter 11).

2 Definition of the required character repertoire

2.1 Narrowing the topic

A character repertoire shall be defined for the *Latin script*, since it has the most letters with diacritics of all European scripts, and only for *European* languages.

Not subject of this investigation are Asian, American and African languages with Latin alphabets (Vietnamese, Native American, African Reference Alphabet, etc.), transliteration into Latin ("Romanization" of Arabic, Chinese, Cyrillic, etc.), and special diacritics or letters, such as for medieval studies or phonetics. However, I am of the opinion that the results obtained by me can also be applied to these.

2.2 Basic letters

The classic Roman Latin alphabet contained only 20 letters: A B C D E F H I K L M N O P Q R S T V X. To this end, the following should be noted: [15]

---

15 http://de.wikipedia.org/wiki/Lateinisches_Alphabet (2011-11-28)

- G is actually a C with a slash as a diacritical mark and already existed in ancient Roman times. For example, the Roman personal name *Gnaeus* is abbreviated Cn., i.e. based on the archaic spelling dating from the period before the letters C and G were differentiated.[16]
- Y and Z were introduced to write terms taken from the Greek script (e.g. *cycle, zona*; compare French *y grec*).
- The later Roman emperor CLAUDIUS (from 10 BC to 54 AD) introduced during his time as a censor three new characters: Ↄ (for the combinations "PS" and "BS"), Ⅎ (consonantal V, to distinguish it from the "u" sound) and Ⱶ (pronunciation of u and i as *sonus medius* before labial consonants as in *optimus*).[17] They did not succeed in the long term.
- Today's *lowercase* (minuscule) letters were developed during the Carolingian period (8th century).[18]
- The differentiation of I versus J and U versus V only took place during the Renaissance.
- W is actually a ligature of two U/V (compare English *double u*, French *double v*).

The resulting *modern* Latin alphabet has 26 basic letters:
A B C D E F G H I J K L M N O P Q R S T U V W X Y Z.

In the various Latin alphabets of vernacular languages, the basic letters were extended to other variants (ı ĸ ŋ ...), other ligatures (æ ij œ ß ...), other letters from other scripts (e.g. þ and ƿ from the Runic script) and especially by additional letters with diacritics (ö ł ç ...). Further modifications can be

---

16 http://en.wikipedia.org/wiki/Gnaeus_(praenomen) (2015-02.12)
17 Oliver, Revilo P. (1949). "The Claudian Letter Ⱶ". (American Journal of Archaeology, Vol. 53, No. 3), 249–257. doi:10.2307/500662.
http://jstor.org/stable/500662. (2011-11-28)
18 http://de.wikipedia.org/wiki/Karolingische_Minuskel (2011-11-28)

found in non-European Latin alphabets, in phonetic alphabets as well as in special alphabets, e.g. for Medieval Studies or for the Romanization of Oriental and Indian scripts. Their detailed treatment in this book would be too much, but it should be noted that some originally purely phonetic symbols have been incorporated into newly created alphabets, such as for Turkish and African languages.[19]

2.3 Variants of letters

The following variants of the basic letters are of importance for the modern European languages:

Eng (Ŋ ŋ), a "n" with J-shaped hook on the second leg, was originally developed for a proposed spelling reform of the English language (for the [ng] sound as in *singing*).[20] It is used in the Sami languages (Scandinavian minority languages).

Eth (Ð ð), a "d" with stroke, usually refers to a voiced or voiceless [th] sound. It is used in Icelandic, in the Danish regional language Faroese and in the Swedish minority language Elfdalian.

Ezh (Ʒ ʒ), a "z" with bottom loop, used in Scandinavian minority language Skolt Sami and denotes the [dz] sound.

İ and ı. In Turkish, the i with dot has as counterpart a versal İ with dot; vice versa, the I without a dot has as equivalent an ı without a dot.

---

19 http://de.wikipedia.org/wiki/Lateinisches_Alphabet (2011-11-28)
20 Alexander Gill the Elder: *Logonomia Anglica, qua gentis sermo facilius addiscitur*, London, by John Beale, 2nd edit. 1621

Schwa   (Ə ə), an "e" rotated by 180°, denotes in phonetics an unstressed short [e] (as in *taken*). It is used in Azerbaijani (as alternative to Ä ä).

Other variants of letters are used for example in African languages.

Of historical importance are:

Kra   (Kʻ ĸ), a variant of "k" in the Danish regional language Greenlandic. In 1973 it was replaced by a language reform with (Q q).[21]

Long-s   (ſ), a variant of the "s" from Blackletter, remained also conserved in the left arch of the ß ligature and in the integral sign ∫ (from Latin *ſumma*).[22]

Yogh   (Ȝ ȝ), a variant of "g" based on its insular (Irish) form ᵹ), was used in Middle English and Scottish to denote various sound variations of g. It was gradually replaced by the Carolingian g, y or gh (e.g. niȝt → night). Through optical confusion or in the absence of the necessary letter for printing, ȝ was often replaced by z, for example in the Scottish surname Menzies (actually Menȝies, therefore pronounced "Mingis").[23]

and also variants of letters that were used between 1922 and 1940 in various Turkic languages of the former Soviet Union: Gha (Ƣ ƣ), a variant of "q",

---

21 http://en.wikipedia.org/wiki/Kra_(letter) (2011-11-28)
22 http://de.wikipedia.org/wiki/Langes_s (2011-11-28)
23 BBC News: Why is Menzies pronounced Mingis?
    http://news.bbc.co.uk/2/hi/uk_news/magazine/4595228.stm
    (Last Updated: Tuesday, 10 January 2006, 09:40 GMT)

(N n), a "n" with descender, (Ɵ ɵ), a variant of the "ö", (Y y), a variant of the "y", and (Z z), a variant of the "z".²⁴

Even in Roman inscriptions, sometimes variants of letters appear: mirrored F and P (Ⅎ, ꟼ), upside-down M (Ԝ), archaic M (ᴟ) and long I (*I longa*, I, probably formed from Í [I + *apex*]).²⁵

2.4 Letters from other scripts

The following letters from other scripts are of importance for the modern European languages:

Thorn (Þ þ), derived from the Runic letter Thorn (ᚦ), usually denotes a voiced or voiceless [th] sound. It is used in Icelandic.

Theta (Θ θ), from the Greek script, is used in the international standard spelling of Romani. It serves as a "morpho-graph" in declination suffixes, that is, it indicates that the initial sound is realized after vowels as [t] and after nasal consonants as [d].²⁶

Of historical importance are:

Wynn (Ƿ ƿ), derived from the Runic letter Wynn (ᚹ) was used in Old English for the phonetic value [w] (as in *water*) before the ligature W was introduced into the Latin alphabet.

Sig rune (ᛋ), strictly speaking a fantasy product of esoteric GUIDO VON LIST, was loosely based on the runic letter for sun (ᛋ). During the Nazi

---

24 http://upload.wikimedia.org/wikipedia/commons/1/1b/New_Turkic_alphabets.jpg (2011-11-28)
25 The Unicode Standard, Version 6.0 / Latin Extended-D http://unicode.org/charts/PDF/UA720.pdf (2011-11-28)
26 http://en.wikipedia.org/wiki/Romani_orthography → International Standard (2011-11-28)

period, an extra key was added to some German typewriters to enable them to type the double-sig logo (⚡⚡) with a single keystroke. [27, 28, 29]

2.5 Ligatures

2.5.1 Ligatures based on handwriting

Handwritten ligatures were caused mostly by fast spelling of frequently used combinations of letters, a process that ultimately led to various shorthands and *sigla* (abbreviations with additional markings). [30]

- From the shorthand *cto* (from the Italian *cento* = hundred) developed the percent sign (%), from the Latin word *et* developed the ampersand (&), and from *ad/at* developed the commercial at (@). Ampersand is a "Letter honorary"; it was the 27th letter in the alphabet and ended the ABC song "... X Y Z, *and, per se, and*", which led to "ampersand". [31]

- In Ireland, the ⁊ from the Tironian notes (a Roman shorthand system) is often used instead of the ligature & for *et*.

- The pound sign £, the lira sign ₤ and the hash # (pound sign) all go back to the *siglum* ℔ for Latin *librum* (pound), that is, the abbreviation lb, in which the letters are connected by a dash.

---

27 http://typewriterschubert.magix.net/das_makabere_sonderzeichen.42.html → Das makabere Sonderzeichen (2014-12-07)
28 http://en.wikipedia.org/wiki/Runic_insignia_of_the_Schutzstaffel (2014-12-07)
29 http://de.wikipedia.org/wiki/Siegrune (2014-12-07)
30 http://en.wikipedia.org/wiki/Scribal_abbreviation (2011-11-28)
31 http://people.sc.fsu.edu/~jburkardt/fun/wordplay/letter_words.html (2011-11-18)

- The German umlauts ä ö ü emerged from ligatures for ae oe ue where "e" was set above (a̋ ő ű). The "e" in its cursive form (𝓮) degenerated into two slashes (ű) and was finally visually indistinguishable from trema points. However, unlike letters with trema (e.g. in French *Saül* ↛ *Sauel*), it is in German allowed to disassemble umlauts again (Müller → Mueller), e.g. in crossword puzzles or when using inadequate computer technology.[32] Compare umlauts Ä Ö Ü with the trema letters Ä Ö Ü.
- In the æ ligature, "e" was not set above the "a" but merged with it. Æ is now seen in several languages as a full-fledged letter.[33]
- The development of æ continued to ę (*e caudata*, i.e. tailed e).[34]
- In the œ ligature, "e" was not set above the "o" but merged also with it. Œ is in French a full-fledged letter.[35]

2.5.2 Typographic ligatures

The use of ligatures in print comes from the time of hot metal typesetting and has both aesthetic and technical reasons: in order to avoid optical gaps that would disrupt the flow of reading, especially in letters with ascenders such as f i f l and t, there is often a kerning necessary. But in order to indent a "i" under an "f", for example, you would have the upper length of the "f" on its right side protrude over the cone (the "back" of the letter), risking it to break off. As a solution, problematic combinations were moulded onto a common cone, e.g. as a ligature "fi".[36]

---

32 http://de.wikipedia.org/wiki/Umlaut (2011-11-28)
33 http://de.wikipedia.org/wiki/%C3%86 (2011-11-28)
34 http://de.wikipedia.org/wiki/%C3%86(2011-11-28)
35 http://en.wikipedia.org/wiki/%C5%92 (2011-11-28)
36 http://de.wikipedia.org/wiki/Ligatur_%28Typografie%29 (2011-11-28)

The Universal Character Set includes some ligatures (ff fi fl ffi ffl ft st) for compatibility reasons, but typographical ligatures are generally considered as a matter of *presentation* of characters, that is, as a task to be solved by *software*. This book, for example, was created with the typesetting system TeX. It converts a row of letter combinations and characters automatically into ligatures.[37] Optionally, also the ligatures ch, ck and tz (rare) and ct and st (historical) can be reproduced (see below).[38, 39]

The only problem is that when you create a PDF document and copy-paste text from it, you have to stick to the font used in the PDF document (*Linux Libertine* in this case). Otherwise, place holders will appear instead of the Libertine-specific ligatures.

Figure 2.1: **Wrong URL—the fi should be fi.** (own photo)

Figure 2.2: **Rare ligature tz in a beer** (own photo)

---

37 E.g. fb ff ffh ffi ffj ffk ffl fft fh fi fj fk fl ft fz fi fh fl fs ff ft tt Qu Th °C and °F and the characters ... ‼ ⁉ ?! and ??
38 http://www.prospect-magazine.co.uk/ (2014-12-07)
39 www.pinterest.com (2014-04-24)

Figure 2.3: **Historical ligatures ct and st**

- In printed books from the Middle Ages, there are ligatures that are uncommon today (AA N W...).⁴⁰

- In phonetic alphabets, ligatures (ʤ ʣ ʧ ...) are or were used.⁴¹

- The ligature ß evolved presumably from fz (in Blackletter) or from ſs (in roman and italic fonts). It has long been recognized as a separate letter and has since 2008 officially a versal counterpart (ẞ).⁴²

- The ligature W was created specifically (for phonetic delimitation of the [w] sound versus the [v] sound). W is meanwhile seen as a full-fledged letter (in Swedish only since 2006).⁴³

---

40 The Unicode Standard, Version 6.0 / Latin Extended-D
    http://unicode.org/charts/PDF/UA720.pdf (2014-12-07)
41 http://en.wikipedia.org/wiki/Typographic_ligature#Ligatures_in_Unicode_
    .28Latin-derived_alphabets.29 (2011-11-28)
42 SIGNA special issue 2008 on the occasion of the encoding of the *versal Eszett* in Unicode, 32 pages, numerous figures, Edition Wächterpappel 2008, ISBN 978-3-933629-22-5
43 *news.ch: Das «W» wird offizieller Buchstabe in Schweden*
    http://www.news.ch/Das+W+wird+offizieller+Buchstabe+in+Schweden/
    239737/detail.htm (2011-11-28)

- A special case are the Croatian *digraphs*[44] DŽ / Dž / dž, LJ / Lj / lj and NJ / Nj / nj that are used (in contrast to other digraphs not dealt with in this book) as well as ligatures, as they represent each one letter in the Cyrillic Serbian alphabet (Џ џ, Љ љ and Њ њ).[45] The same applies to DZ / Dz / dz, used for Romanization of Macedonian (for S s).[46]
- The Dutch ij is also a digraph. It probably emerged from "ii" in the old writing without dots, with extension of the second "ı"to a "j" to distinguish "ıı" from "u". The "ij" or "ıj" is often rendered as a ligature ("broken U"), which leads to confusion with "ÿ" and "y", respectively. At the beginning of a word, it is usually simply written with two capital letters (Dutch *IJsselmeer*), but in the Universal Character Set there exist also ligatures (IJ ij).[47]

2.6 Diacritics

Some diacritics already existed in ancient Greek script (acute, grave, circumflex, diaeresis). Others were used only from Roman times (sicilicus) or in later Latin alphabets (kreska, haček, apostrophe, double acute, slash, comma, dot) or developed out of character variations (cedilla) and ligatures

---

44 A digraph (from the Greek *dís* [δίς] (double) and gráphō [γράφω] (to write) is a pair of characters used to write one phoneme (distinct sound) or a sequence of phonemes that does not correspond to the normal values of the two characters combined.
    http://en.wikipedia.org/wiki/Digraph_%28orthography%29 (2015-02-20)
45 http://en.wikipedia.org/wiki/Gaj%27s_Latin_Alphabet (2011-11-28)
46 http://en.wikipedia.org/wiki/Romanization_of_Macedonian (2011-11-28)
47 http://de.wikipedia.org/wiki/IJ (2011-11-28)

(umlaut, ogonek, ring, tilde). Macron and breve came from philology and originally designated long and short syllables in verse.[48]

Diacritics serve, as their name says, as *distinctive* signs associated with otherwise identical-looking letters. Diacritics have full orthographic significance. The omission of diacritics can cause slow flow of reading, ambiguities of pronunciation and therefore mislead word meaning (Académie Française).[49]

The following diacritical marks are present in modern European Latin alphabets:

Acute (Latin *acuta* = sharp) goes back to the similar-looking Roman *apex* (tip, priest's hat), which was used to mark long vowels (e.g. PÁLVS = pile, PALV́S = swamp).[50] The term *acuta* is a loan translation of Greek equivalent *oxeîa* [ὀξεῖα] (high, sharp) that designated high-frequency vowels. In modern languages, the acute accent can e.g. show length or pitch of a *vowel* or a vocalic consonant (l r w), serve to distinguish between words that are written the same (e.g. Dutch *een* = article "a" or numeral "one", *één* = one), or highlight a word within a sentence.[51]

---

48 Isidorus Hispalensis: *Etymologiarum libri XX / Liber I: De grammatica, Caput XVII.* In: Lindemann, F., *Corpus Grammaticorum Latinorum Veterum*, Bd. 3, *sumptibus* B.G. Teubneri *et* F. Claudii, Leipzig 1833, http://books.google.be/books?id=YzU_AAAAcAAJ (2011-11-28)

49 *Académie Française: Questions courantes / Accentuation des majuscules* http://www.academie-francaise.fr/la-langue-francaise/questions-de-langue#5_strong-em-accentuation-des-majuscules-em-strong (2014-04-16)

50 Johannes Kramer: *Die Verwendung des Apex und P.Vindob. L 1 c – Zeitschrift für Papyrologie und Epigraphik Bd. 88, (1991), pp. 141–150 –* Published by: Dr. Rudolf Habelt GmbH, Bonn (Germany) – Stable URL: http://www.jstor.org/stable/20187544 (2014-12-07)

51 http://en.wikipedia.org/wiki/Acute_accent (2011-11-28)

Kreska   (Polish *kreska* = line), an acute-like character but used in *consonants* where it indicates a palatalisation. The kreska over lower-case letters should be actually steeper and leading more to the right than the acute (typographically correct e.g. in *Palatino Linotype*: ć ń ś ź). In the Universal Character Set, however, it was unified with the acute; therefore a distinction is only possible at the level of the font. Over ó (which shows the pronunciation as [u]) stood in Polish originally an → acute, but the shape turned with the time kreska-like.[52] A sign with palatalising function also exists in Bosnian, Croatian and Serbian (ć). In the Romanization of Macedonian, ǵ and ḱ represent the Cyrillic letters ѓ [gj] and ќ.[53]

Gravis   (Latin *gravis* = heavy) is a loan translation of the ancient Greek equivalent *bareîa* (βαρεῖα) = gravity. In modern languages, the gravis denotes e.g. emphasis (Italian *caffè* = coffee), pitch (French è → German ä), length of a vowel or a vocalic consonant (Welsh *mwg* = smoke / *mẁg* = cup) or distinguishes between words that are written the same (French *ou* = or / *où* = where).[54]

Circumflex (Latin *circumflexus* ≈ bent) is derived from the ancient Greek diacritic *perispoméne* [περισπωμένη]. In modern languages, the circumflex can show e.g. length or pitch of a vowel or a vocalic consonant (ŵ) or serve to distinguish between words that are written the same.[55] In French, it usually indicates the omission

---

52 Adam Twardoch: kreska: not exactly acute
    http://www.twardoch.com/download/polishhowto/kreska.html (2011-11-28)
53 http://en.wikipedia.org/wiki/Acute_accent (2011-11-28)
54 http://en.wikipedia.org/wiki/Grave_accent (2011-11-29)
55 http://en.wikipedia.org/wiki/Circumflex (2011-11-29)

of one or more letters, mainly "s" (Latin *fenestra* → French *fenêtre*).[56]

Trema (Greek *trêma* [τρῆμα] = hole) usually indicates a diaeresis, that is, the separate pronunciation of two consecutive vowels (as in French *Noël*). In Catalan, Spanish, Galician, Occitan, French and Brazilian Portuguese, the diaeresis indicates that a "u" between g/q and e/i is not silent (e.g. Catalan *Parc Güell*). In Albanian and Luxembourgish, however, ë stands for the schwa sound, and in Kurdish (Kurmanji), ḧ and ẍ denote two fricatives.[57, 58, 59]

Umlaut See chapter 2.5.1.

Macron (Greek *makrón* [μακρόν] = long) indicates a long vowel. It is used in Latvian (ā ē ī ū and in texts from before the spelling reform of 1946 ō), in Lithuanian (ū), in Livonian (ā ǟ ē ī ō ȱ ȫ ȭ ū ȳ) and in some orthographies of Cornish (ē ō ū ȳ).[60, 61, 62]

Breve (Latin *brevis* = short) originally pointed to a short vowel and was thus the counterpart to → macron. In Romanian (ă), it shows the pronunciation as [ə]. In Turkish (ğ), it was originally pronounced as a fricative, but is now silent and extends only the vowel that stands before it (as in ERDOĞAN). The ğ also occurs in Azerbaijani, Tatar and Crimean Tatar.

---

56 http://en.wikipedia.org/wiki/Use_of_the_circumflex_in_French (2011-11-29)
57 http://en.wikipedia.org/wiki/Kurdish_alphabet (2011-11-29)
58 http://de.wikipedia.org/wiki/Trema (2011-11-29)
59 http://en.wikipedia.org/wiki/Trema_%28diacritic%29 (2011-11-29)
60 http://de.wikipedia.org/wiki/%C5%8C (2011-11-29)
61 http://de.wikipedia.org/wiki/Livisch (2011-11-29)
62 http://en.wikipedia.org/wiki/Cornish_language#Comparison_tables (2011-11-29)

	In Esperanto (ŭ), the breve shows the pronunciation as semi-vowel [w] or the belonging to a diphthong (aŭ eŭ), respectively.[63] It has the shape of a horizontal semicircle (in contrast to the angled → caron).
Caron	(maybe *portmanteau* of caret and → macron), more scientifically haček (Czech *háček* = tick), replaced the original → dot about palatalized consonants (č ň ř š ž) and ě (only in Polish, there is still the form ż).[64] It goes back to the work *De orthographia bohemica* from the year 1406, which is attributed to JAN HUS. It is also used in other West Slavic languages as well as in South Slavic, Baltic, Sami and Romani languages and also in Finnish and Estonian in loan words.[65]
	The haček is angled, in contrast to the semi-circular → breve.
Apostrophe	is used in Czech and Slovak as allographic variant of the → haček in letters with ascenders d, l and t. In contrast to the real apostrophe, the apostrophe-shaped haček sits closer to the letters (*kerning*, compare ď ľ ť compared to d' l' t').[66]
	In Afrikaans, there is a lowercase ʼn for the indefinite article (but its use is depreciated).[67]
Cedilla	(Spanish *cedilla* = small z) arose from a letter variant, the Visigothic z (ʒ). The upper loop was reinterpreted as "c" and the actual "z" (the lower loop) was reduced to a mere appendage. The resulting characters ç is used e.g. in Portuguese, Catalan,

---

63 http://de.wikipedia.org/wiki/Breve_(Zeichen) (2011-11-29)
64 http://en.wikipedia.org/wiki/Caron (2011-11-29)
65 http://de.wikipedia.org/wiki/Hatschek (2011-11-29)
66 http://de.wikipedia.org/wiki/Hatschek (2011-11-29)
67 http://de.wikipedia.org/wiki/%C5%89 (2011-11-29)

Basque, French and Albanian.[68] For the Latin spelling of Turkic languages such as Turkish and Azeri, the character ş was created.[69] Both ç and ş are also used in Kurdish.[70]

In contrast to the free-floating → comma, the cedilla is always connected directly to the letter.

Comma (Romanian *virgulița*) is derived from a "z" added below the letter d (historical), s and t (= dz sz tz). In Latvian (ģ ķ ļ ņ and until 1957 ŗ) in contrast, the comma shows palatalisation.[71]

The comma is often confused with the → cedilla, which leads to persistent confusion (up to false designation in international standards). Often, the Turkish ş (with cedilla) and the (linguistically non-existent) ţ are used for Romanian ș and ț. Only upon pressure from the EU on the occasion of the accession of Romania (2007), the software manufacturer Microsoft updated some of his fonts and corrected the Romanian keyboard driver (from Windows Vista on).[72, 73, 74]

---

68 http://eu.wikipedia.org/wiki/Euskal_alfabetoa (2011-11-29)
69 http://en.wikipedia.org/wiki/Cedilla (2011-11-29)
70 http://en.wikipedia.org/wiki/Cedilla (2011-11-29)
71 http://en.wikipedia.org/wiki/Latvian_language#Standard_orthography (2011-11-29)
72 http://www.microsoft.com/en-us/download/details.aspx?displaylang=en&id=16083 (2015-05-21)
73 http://en.wikipedia.org/wiki/Comma#Diacritical_usage (2011-11-29)
74 http://en.wikipedia.org/wiki/Romanian_alphabet (2011-11-29)

Figure 2.4: **Font with a hodgepodge of comma and cedilla** (own photo)

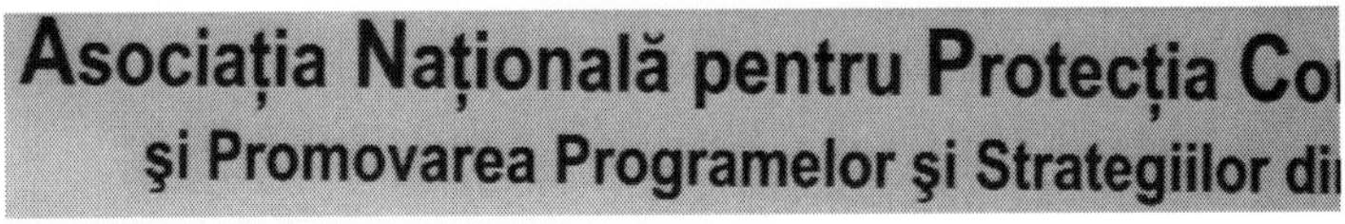

> Asociaţia Naţională pentru Protecţia Co
> şi Promovarea Programelor şi Strategiilor di

Dot set above is used in Lithuanian (ė), Maltese (ċ ġ ż), Polish (ż), Livonian (ȯ ȱ) and Turkish (İ as capital letter to i). In the old orthography of Irish, the dot (*ponc séimhithe*) shows the lenition of consonants (ḃ ċ ḋ/ð ḟ/ɟ ġ/ʒ ṁ ṗ ṡ/ɾ ṫ/ć). This notation is, however, used only in the Irish (insular) variant of the Latin alphabet, while in the standard form the dot is replaced by a trailing "h", e.g. ṡamlaiġ → samhlaigh (to imagine), leaċċúpla → leathchúpla (a twin).[75]

Dot set in centre (Catalan *punt volat* = flown point) is used in Catalan, a regional language in Spain and France, (e.g. in *paral·lel* = parallel) to indicate a → diaeresis.

Typographically, the use of the prearranged "l" in the geminated l is preferable to the insertion of a middle dot (·, 00B7), since with the latter the kerning does not work automatically (L·L l·l compared to ĿL ŀl),[76] along with some search engine and other problems.[77] Unfortunately, Unicode meanwhile concerns the character as depreciated. So this seems to be only solvable with a

---

75 http://en.wikipedia.org/wiki/Dot_(diacritic) (2011-11-29)
76 http://www.raco.cat/index.php/LlenguaUs/article/view/128012/177352 (p.27f and footnotes) (2015-05-30)
77 www.l·l.cat/info/the-geminated-el, slide 22 (2015-05-14, copy the link)

good font where the letter is moved to the privat use area (for the price of compatibility).

Figure 2.5: **Dot set in centre: wrong kerning**

CARAMBEL·LA

Dot set below is used in Europe only as ḥ and as digraph l·l in some dialects of the Spanish regional language Asturian.⁷⁸

Slash   (Latin *solidus*) is used in Danish, Norwegian and Faroese (ø), in Icelandic, Faroese and Elfdalian (ð) and in Polish, Kashubian and Sorbian (ł). The origin of the slash in the ø is not clear; it could be the remaining bar of an OE ligature or an OI ligature (to identify an i umlaut).⁷⁹ The ł (phonetic distinction from l) was suggested by Polish linguists and spread during the 16ᵗʰ century.⁸⁰

In Latvian, the letters ġ, ķ, ļ, ņ and ŗ were written with slash (g k ł ꞑ ɍ) until 1921, as well as s/ſ (s̄) when they stood for sharp s, as well as in sch/fch and tsch/tfch (š and č in modern writing). The s/ſ with slash was used also in Lower Sorbian.⁸¹, ⁸²

Dash   is used in Maltese (ħ), in Croatian, Bosnian, Serbian and Montenegrin (đ) and the Sami (g ŧ).

The capital letters to ð and d are both written with dash (Ð Đ), but have different Unicode numbers (00D0 and 0110). Also—ideally—,

---

78 http://ast.wikipedia.org/wiki/Asturianu#Graf.C3.ADes_dialectales (2011-11-29)
79 http://en.wikipedia.org/wiki/%C3%98 (2011-11-29)
80 http://en.wikipedia.org/wiki/%C5%81 (2011-11-29)
81 DIN: Proposal to encode 10 Latin letters for pre-1921 Latvian orthography http://std.dkuug.dk/jtc1/sc2/wg2/docs/n3587.pdf (2011-11-29)
82 http://www.unicode.org/charts/PDF/UA720.pdf (2014-12-07)

in the (ð Ð) pair, the dash in the capital letter forms an even cross with the stem, whereas in the (đ Ð) pair, it is slightly leans to the right side.

Ogonek (Polish *ogonek* = tail, Lithuanian *nosinė* = nasal), derived from æ over ę (*e caudata*) and from Old Norse ǫ (*o caudata*). It is used in Lithuanian (ą ę į ų), in Polish (ą ę), in the Polish regional language Kashubian (ą), in the Swedish regional language Elfdalian (ą ę į ų ą̊ y̨) and in the regional language Megleno-Romanian (ǫ).[83, 84, 85, 86] In contrast to the cedilla which is curved to the *left*, the ogonek is curved to the *right*.

The Polish typographer ADAM TWARDOCH is of the opinion that the Ogonek is not a diacritic in the strict sense, but rather a *style element* (as a serif or a descender), because appearance and starting point of ogoneks must be carefully matched to the shape of the base character in the respective font.[87] This problem becomes apparent at the composite character y̨ in which the descender and the ogonek overlap in *Linux Libertine* (better *Times New Roman*: y̨).

Ring occurs as *kroužek* (= small ring) in Czech (ů, from the diphthong uo → ů) and as å (from aa → å) in Danish, Norwegian and

---

83 http://en.wikipedia.org/wiki/Kashubian_alphabet (2011-11-29)
84 http://en.wikipedia.org/wiki/Elfdalian_language (2011-11-29)
85 Th. Capidan: *Meglenoromânii III - Dicționar Meglenoromân* http://www.unibuc.ro/CLASSICA/megl3/cuprins.htm (e.g. *Adžilǫchi*) (2011-11-29)
86 http://en.wikipedia.org/wiki/Ogonek (2011-11-29)
87 http://www.twardoch.com/download/polishhowto/ogonek.html (2011-11-29)

	Swedish as well as in the regional languages Elfdalian, Walloon and Emilian. [88, 89, 90, 91]
Tilde	(Latin *titulus* = title) was originally a medieval abbreviation and was placed over vowels to indicate a lack of "m" or "n" (e.g. *fabricātur* for *fabricantur*). In parallel, the tilde also rose as nasalization sign from an set-above "n", for example Portuguese (*mão* = hand, from Latin *manus*) and Breton, and as palatalisation sign ñ (Spanish *anno* → año), also in the regional languages Asturian and Basque. [92]
	The ñ is considered in Spanish as an independent letter, as well as the õ in Estonian. [93]

Figure 2.6: **Church inscription from 1573 in German with macron-shaped tilde (ā/ē for an/en), ring (ů) and ſs instead of ß** (own photo)

---

88 http://cs.wikipedia.org/wiki/%C5%AE (2011-11-28)
89 http://de.wikipedia.org/wiki/%C3%85 (2011-11-28)
90 http://en.wikipedia.org/wiki/Walloon_language (2011-11-29)
91 http://de.wikipedia.org/wiki/Emilianische_Sprache (2011-11-29)
92 http://de.wikipedia.org/wiki/%C3%91 (2011-11-28)
93 http://en.wikipedia.org/wiki/Tilde (2011-11-29)

Of historical importance is

Sicilicus (Latin for "small crescent"), occasionally occurs in Roman inscriptions and marks the doubling of consonants (e.g. SERͅA for SERRA).[94]

The above diacritics occur also in non-European languages (e.g. Vietnamese, Hawaiian, creole languages) or their Romanization (e.g. Japanese, Indian languages). In addition, you will find in these languages diacritics placed *under* characters (e.g. ḅ ḥ ḍ ẹ ạ ụ), and in Vietnamese the horn (as in ơ) and the hook (as in ả).

In Serbo-Croatian phonology, also the inverted breve (â) and the double gravis (ȁ) are used, and in the Lithuanian dialectology a vertical tilde (e.g. in kuɼ̃).[95, 96]

Before the Spanish Civil War, Basque was written in "a bizarre and impractical orthography employing a blizzard of pointless diacritics" (mostly with combining diacritics: d̄ l̄ ñ r̄ t̄, plus the regulars ń ŕ ś).[97] In 1964, the Royal Basque Language Academy promulgated a new standard orthography, leaving only ñ (and ç for loan words) as diacritics.[98]

Next three pages: **Combinations of diacritics**

(letters in brackets means not used in European languages or Vietnamese)

---

94 http://en.wikipedia.org/wiki/Sicilicus (2014-12-07)
95 http://en.wikipedia.org/wiki/Serbo-Croatian_phonology (2011-11-29)
96 http://en.wikipedia.org/wiki/Tilde#Other_uses (2011-11-29)
97 http://bvpb.mcu.es/es/catalogo_imagenes/grupo.cmd?posicion=35&path=11350&forma=&presentacion=pagina (2015-05-23)
98 http://www.omniglot.com/writing/basque.htm (2015-05-23)

Combinations of two diacritics

										Σ
a	ā̇	ǻ	(ā̀)					ã̊ å̊ ā̊ å̌ ā̆	ã́ å̂ ā̀ ā́ â̧		12
c	(ć̣)										–
e	(ḝ)			(é̄) (è̄)				ẽ̊ ê̊ è̊ ế ȩ̂			5
i	(í̇)										–
l	(ḹ)										–
o	ō̇	ȯ́	ø	(ọ̄)	(ó̄) (ò̄)	(ȫ) (ő̄) ō̃			õ̊ ô̊ ò̊ ǫ̋ ộ	ớ ỡ ở ố ọ́	14
n	(ṅ)										–
r	(r̄̇)										–
u	(ú̇)	(ü̇)			(ǚ) (ǔ̇) (ǘ) (ṻ)			ũ̊ ū̊ ù̊ ų́			5
s	(ṩ)	(ṧ)	(š̆)								–
											36

Other letters plus diacritic

										Σ
æ	ǽ	(ǣ)									1
ʒ	ǯ										1
(dz)	(dž)										–
											2

48 BERND KAPPENBERG

	´	˝	`	˶	ˆ	ˆ̣	¨	¨̣	¯	¯̣	˘	˘̣	^	ˇ	˛
A a	á		à	(ä̀)	â		ä		ā		ă		(â)	(ǎ)	
B b									(ḇ)						
C c	ć				ĉ									č	ç
D d					(ḓ)				(ḏ)					ď	
E e	é		è	(ề)	ê	(ẹ)	ë		ē		ĕ		(ê)	ě	(ę)
F f															
G g	(ǵ)				ĝ				(ḡ)		ğ			ǧ	
H h					ĥ		ḧ				(ẖ)		(ẖ)	ȟ	(ḥ)
I i	í		ì	(ì̀)	î		ï		ī		ĭ		(î)	(ǐ)	
J j					ĵ									(ǰ)	
K k	(ḱ)								(k̠)					ǩ	
L l	ĺ						(ḻ)				(ḻ)			ľ	
M m	(ḿ)														
N n	ń		ǹ		(ṉ)						(ṉ)			ň	
O o	ó	ő	ò	(ö̀)	ô		ö		ō	(θ)	ŏ		(ô)	(ǒ)	
P p	(ṕ)														
Q q															
R r	ŕ			(r̀)					(ṟ)				(r̂)	ř	
S s ſ	ś				ŝ									š	ş
T t					(ṱ)		(ẗ)		(ṯ)					ť	(ṭ)
U u	ú	ű	ù	(ù̀)	û	(ụ)	ü	(ṳ)	ū		ŭ		(û)	(ǔ)	
V v															
W w	ẃ		ẁ		ŵ		ẅ								
X x							ẍ								
Y y	ý		ỳ		ŷ		ÿ		ȳ						
Z z	ź				ẑ						(ẕ)			ž	
Σ	13	2	8	–	13	–	9	–	6	–	–	6	–	–	12	2

SETTING SIGNS FOR EUROPE

ʼ	·	.	/ /	-	͟	°	̦	~	˜	˷	ʼ	ʼ			Σ
	ȧ	a̦	(a)		ą	å	(a̦)	ã			å̊				12
	(b)	(b̦)	(b)											(ɓ)	–
		ċ		(ɛ)											5
ḍ	(d)	(d̦)		đ										(d)	3
	ė	e̦	(ɛ)		ę			ẽ		(e̦)	ė				12
	(ḟ)														–
ġ	ġ		(g)	g											6
	(ḥ)	ḥ		ħ								(h)			5
	İ	i̦	(i)		i̧			ĩ		(i̦)	î				11
			(j)												1
ḳ		(ḳ)	(k)	(k)								(k)			2
ḷ		ɫ	ḷ	ł	(ł)				(ł)					(ł)	6
	(ṁ)	(m̦)													–
ṇ	ṅ	(n̦)	(ɴ)					ñ				(n)			6
	ȯ	o̦	ø		o̧			õ			o̊	ơ			14
	(ṗ)			(p)											–
			(ɋ)	(q)											–
ṛ	(ṙ)	(r̦)	(ɾ)	(ɾ)											3
ṣ	(ṡ ḟ)	(ș)	(s f)	(ʃ)											5
ṭ	(ṫ)	(ț)	(t)	ŧ											3
		(u̦)			u̧	ů		(ũ)		(u̦)	ů	ư			11
		(v̇)	(v̦)					(ṽ)							–
	(ẇ)	(w̦)			(ẘ)										4
	ẋ														2
	(ẏ)	(y̦)		(y)	(ẙ)			ỹ			ẙ				7
	ż	(z̦)		(z)								(z)			4
8	9	1	6	2	4	5	2	–	6	–	–	6	2	–	–	–	122

There are also so-called *Named Sequences*, sequences with combining diacritics that were not included as separate Unicode characters:[99]

Lithuanian dictionaries etc.	diverse*
ą̄ ą̃	(à)
ę̄ ę̃ é ẽ	(ē) (ě)
ì ĩ į́ į̃	(ī) (í)
j̃	
ĩ	
m̃	
	(ñg)
r̃	
ų́ ų̃ ú ũ	(ù)

(*apparently not used in European languages)

2.7 Conclusion

When we count them together—26 basic letters, 5 variants of letters, 2 letters from other scripts, combinations of one (122) or two (36) diacritics, the typographic ligatures æ ij œ ß plus ǽ and ȝ, all times two (for upper and lower case)—we arrive at 394 characters, so roughly 400.

Now let us see which character set is able to hold them.

---

[99] http://unicode.org/Public/UNIDATA/NamedSequences.txt (2012-02-11)

3 History of character sets

Character set: Designation for a specific number and configuration of characters. As it is well-known that electronics knows no boundaries, more and more character sets are developed, so that an adjustment between computer and printer is always an adventure and less and less likely.
– Klaus Möller [100]

In order to understand why the computer-aided transmission and processing of letters with diacritics—regardless of the issue of cultural awareness and legal requirements—still represent a problem that big that those responsible for a solution usually shy away from it, a technology-historical review is necessary. This chapter also gives guidance which standard character set covers the pan-European character set defined in the previous chapter.

---

[100] Klaus Möller: *Fröhliches Mini-Wörterbuch Computeritis*, Tomus Verlag GmbH, München 1993, ISBN 3-8231-0411-X

3.1 BAUDOT code

The history of digitally coded character sets goes back even beyond computers, to the beginnings of *telegraph* technology. Telegraphs first used a 5-bit code, developed by the French engineer JEAN-MAURICE-ÉMILE BAUDOT in 1870 (BAUDOT code, ITA1, CCITT-1). [101, 102]

Since each bit can have two different values (0 or 1), a 5-bit code could encode only 32 characters (2^5), including the resting position of the keyboard, which would not even have been enough for 26 letters and ten digits, not to mention punctuation marks, parentheses, mathematical symbols, etc. For this reason, BAUDOT introduced two *control characters* with a switching function (LTRS/FIGS, i.e. *lettres* and *figures*), by which the following code could be interpreted either as a letter or a digit/character. Thus, the number of displayable characters extended to $2 \times (32 - 4) = 56$ characters (i.e. minus rest position, cancel button and the two control characters). The first telegraphs used a piano-like keyboard, on which the 5 bits have been entered directly via the five keys.

BAUDOT's telegraph system spread during the following decades throughout Europe and even Russia and Argentina. [103] Since the available stock of characters did not satisfy the needs of other telecommunications administrations, it came to individual national allocations of codes. [104]

> *The Pandora's box of incompatibility had been opened.*

---

101 International Telegraph Alphabet No. 1
102 *Comité Consultatif International Téléphonique et Télégraphique*, today ITU-T (ITU Telecommunication Standardization Sector)
103 http://de.wikipedia.org/wiki/Jean-Maurice-%C3%89mile_Baudot (2011-11-29)
104 http://de.wikipedia.org/wiki/Baudot-Code (2011-11-29)

3.2 MURRAY code

Around 1901, DONALD MURRAY developed a revised version of BAUDOT's code for use with a *typewriter*-like (alpha-numeric) keyboard. The MURRAY code contained additional control characters (including *carriage return* and *line feed* for printing on sheets of paper instead of paper tape, and the possibility to trigger a bell). In 1932 it became standardized by the CCITT as *International Telegraph Alphabet No. 2* (short CCITT-2) and developed into the standard code in telex networks. Five positions were reserved for national extensions. The possibility to use the free code positions for the German umlauts, however, was never realized in German telex network.

MURRAY's CCITT-2 code has been also changed many times (in the area outside letters and numbers) in order to satisfy local needs. In other countries, the code has been expanded: to allow for the representation of also Greek or Cyrillic characters, a third switching function was introduced (for example in 1963 in the USSR character set MTK-2), for use in typography even more.[105, 106]

3.3 ASCII

ASCII *(American Standard Code for Information Interchange)* is a 7-bit code that was originally developed in 1963 for certain US telegraph models with alphanumeric keyboard. Using ASCII, one can already encode $2^7 = 128$ characters. That sounds a lot, but 32 codes account alone for control characters. There are also ten digits, the 26 letters in upper and (new) lower case, 32

---

[105] MTK-2 without Ё, and 4 doubling in for Ч:
http://ru.wikipedia.org/wiki/%D0%9C%D0%A2%D0%9A-2 (2011-11-29)
[106] http://de.wikipedia.org/wiki/Baudot-Code (2011-11-29)

other characters (punctuation marks, parentheses, mathematical symbols, etc.) as well as the space and the delete key. For diacritics was no room.[107] However, ASCII was introduced in 1968 by ROBERT WILLIAM BEMER as the default character set for *electronic data processing*.

If the task of electronic data processing had been limited to programming commands, this character set would have been sufficient.

> **But when multilingual text processing was added, the character set was not extended — with serious consequences for the future.**

> Had a Czech rather than an American invented our common word processing programs, there would be no problems.
> – HEINZ DIETER POHL[108]

3.3.1 ISO 646

The first attempt to address the lack of ability to adapt to country-specific alphabets and diacritics (localization) was in 1972 the international standard ISO 646 (still 7-bit). It was a code in which up to twelve defined ASCII characters could be replaced by characters from the respective national language (see table 3.1).[109]

For example, the closing square bracket] was replaced in the German version ISO-646-DE[110] by Ü, in the Danish version ISO-646-DK by Å and so on.

---

107 http://de.wikipedia.org/wiki/ASCII (2011-11-29)
108 http://www.kominform.at/article.php/20050513174424617 (2015-02-01)
109 Roman Czyborra, Unix administrator, newspaper taz: ISO 646 (Good ole' ASCII) http://czyborra.com/charsets/iso646.html (2011-11-29)
110 DIN 66003, see DIN pocket book No. 166 *Informationsverarbeitung 4*, Beuth-Verlag GmbH, Berlin/Cologne.

This practice, however, led to *compatibility problems*, as some of the characters to replace occurred in many programming languages.[111]

Table 3.1: **Some national variants of ISO 646**

Code point	23	24	40	5B	5C	5D	5E	60	7B	7C	7D	7E
ISO-646-IRV[112]	#	¤	@	[	\	]	^	`	{	|	}	~
Germany	#	$	§	Ä	Ö	Ü	^	`	ä	ö	ü	ß
Switzerland	ù	$	à	é	ç	ê	î	ô	ä	ö	ü	û
USA (ASCII)	#	$	@	[	\	]	^	`	{	|	}	~
UK	£	$	@	[	\	]	^	`	{	|	}	~
France	£	$	à	°	ç	§	^	`	é	ù	è	¨
Canada	#	$	à	â	ç	ê	î	ô	é	ù	è	û
Finland	#	$	@	Ä	Ö	Å	Ü	é	ä	ö	å	ü
Norway	#	$	@	Æ	Ø	Å	^	`	æ	ø	å	~
Sweden	#	$	É	Ä	Ö	Å	Ü	é	ä	ö	å	ü
Italy	£	$	§	°	ç	é	^	ù	à	ò	ù	ì
Netherlands	£	$	¾	ÿ	½	|	^	`	¨	ƒ	¼	´
Spain	£	$	§	¡	Ñ	¿	^	`	°	ñ	ç	~
Portugal	#	$	@	Ã	Ç	Õ	^	`	ã	ç	õ	~

3.4 8-bit codes (extended ASCII formats)

In the 1980s, the original ASCII format was extended from 7 to 8 bits, so 2^8 = 256 characters could be represented. The 8th bit had been so far a parity

---

111 http://de.wikipedia.org/wiki/ISO_646 (2011-11-29)

bit for error control of data transmission. Now it served to encode 128 additional characters.[113]

Examples include the MS DOS character sets of the IBM PC, the → ISO 8859 character sets used under Linux and MS Windows, the → Windows-125x character sets, Macintosh character sets, and HP Roman8.

Unlike the national variants of → ISO 646, these standards were all based on the *unchanged* 7-bit ASCII character set, i.e. the additional characters needed were no longer *replacing* ASCII characters but were *added* to them. Consequently, the interchangeability of data (interoperability) between computers of different countries was improved. Also for programmers outside the US, life became easier because characters necessary for programming were not missing any more.[114]

However, even these 8-bit codes with their 128 additional memory locations still were not enough to accommodate all of the ≈ 400 letters of the European character repertoire *simultaneously*. As a result, memories were used *differently* in each country and for each computer manufacturer. The result is the *diacritics massacre* (DIETER E. ZIMMER)[115] in data transmission we suffer from to this day:

If one e.g. transmits "Potočnik" from a Slovenian computer, a German computer will interpret this as "Potoènik" because their 8-bit character sets used in each case are not mutually fully compatible beyond the 7-bit ASCII range.

---

113 http://www.rz.e-technik.fh-kiel.de/~dispert/digital/digital8/dig008_8.htm (2014-12-07)
114 http://de.wikipedia.org/wiki/ISO_646 (2011-11-29)
115 Dieter E. Zimmer: *ASCII oder das Sonderzeichenmassaker* (*Die Zeit*, 1996-05-24)

3.4.1 ISO 8859

The ISO/IEC 8859 family of standards consists of a total of 15 different extensions (see table 3.2).[116, 117] Parts 1, 2, 3, and 4 were originally Ecma[118] International standard ECMA-94[119] ("Bohn code").[120] The first 128 characters are again identical for all standards (= 7-bit ASCII). Next are 32 (unused) control characters, so 12.5 % of potential storage space is lost. Only the last 96 positions encode symbols and diacritics.[121] In this area, the ISO 8859 character sets are *not* compatible with each other, which often results in display errors in pan-European communication (e.g. the mentioned Potočnik vs. Potoènik).

Again, none of the ten Latin-script extensions include *all* European diacritics. With ISO 8859-1 (Latin-1), the standardization bodies tried to include as many letters with diacritics for *Western* European languages as possible, which in turn meant excluding the Eastern and Southern European languages. As for completeness, even for Western European languages some characters were missing (especially for French but also the € symbol). Therefore later ISO 8859-15 (Latin-9) was created. Latin-X encodings are next to ASCII and Universal Character Set / Unicode the most frequently used character set on the internet (see figure 3.3).

For writing at least the following 34 national and regional languages, Latin-1 (ISO 8859-1) is sufficient:

---

116 http://en.wikipedia.org/wiki/ISO_8859 (2011-11-29)
117 http://en.wikipedia.org/wiki/ISO/IEC_8859 (2014-12-08)
118 European Computer Manufacturers Association
119 http://en.wikipedia.org/wiki/ISO/IEC_8859 (2015-05-13)
120 http://www.norasoft.de/tt-fonts.html (2015-07-20)
121 http://de.wikipedia.org/wiki/ISO_8859 (2011-11-29)

Afrikaans (without deprecated ṅ), Albanian, Asturian, Basque, Breton (without Œ/œ ligature and uppercase Ÿ), Danish (without Œ/œ ligature and accents Ǽ/ǽ, Ǿ/ǿ and Ǻ/ǻ), German (without long ſ), English (without Œ/œ ligature), Estonian (without Š/š and Ž/ž in foreign words), Faroese, Finnish (without Š/š and Ž/ž in foreign words), French (without Œ/œ ligature and uppercase Ÿ), Frisian, Greenlandic (new orthography), Galician, Irish Gaelic (new orthography), Icelandic (modern), Italian, Catalan (without Ŀ/ŀ), Cornish (general and modern), Corsican, Luxembourgish (modern), Manx, Dutch (without IJ/ij ligature and uppercase Ÿ), Norwegian (Bokmål and Nynorsk), Occitan, Portuguese (including Brazilian), Rhaeto-Romanic, southern Sami, Lule Sami (without ń), Scottish Gaelic, Swedish, Spanish (Castilian), Swahili and Walloon.

Since these are the most used languages nowadays in Western Europe, America and Australia, it is logical that ISO 8859-1 was the dominant character set in these locations until a few years.[122] ISO 8859-1 was the default character set for HTML4.[123]

However, the ISO 8859 standards are no longer actively developed by ISO/IEC, as for the future a progressive replacement of such character sets by ISO/IEC 10646 (→ Universal Character Set, see chapter 3.6) is expected.[124] In HTML5 (2014), the Universal Character Set / Unicode (UTF-8) is the default encoding.[125]

---

[122] http://de.wikipedia.org/wiki/ISO-8859-1 (2011-11-29)
[123] http://www.w3schools.com/html/html_charset.asp (2014-12-08)
[124] http://de.wikipedia.org/wiki/ISO_8859 (2011-11-29)
[125] http://www.w3.org/TR/html5/document-metadata.html#charset (2014-12-08)

Table 3.2: **Latin extensions to ISO/IEC 8859**

-1	Latin-1	Western European, Latin America (detailed list above)
-2	Latin-2	Middle and Eastern European (German, Croatian, Polish, Slovak, Slovenian, Sorbian, Czech, Hungarian)
-3	Latin-3	Southern European (Turkish, Galician, Maltese, Esperanto)
-4	Latin-4	Baltic (Estonian, Latvian, Lithuanian), Scandinavian (Greenlandic, Sami)
-9	Latin-5	Turkish, Kurdish (replaced Icelandic from Latin-1)
-10	Latin-6	Nordic (reordered version of Latin-4, convenient for Nordic languages, also contains the previously missing characters from Greenlandic and Sami)
-13	Latin-7	Baltic (Latvian with characters that are missing in Latin-4 and -6)
-14	Latin-8	Celtic (Breton, Gaelic [Old Irish orthography], Welsh)
-15	Latin-9	**Western European (improved version of Latin-1 with Euro symbol € and Š/š Ž/ž, Œ/œ and Ÿ)**
-16	Latin-10	South-east European (Albanian, Croatian, Italian, Polish, Romanian, Slovenian, Hungarian), but also German, Finnish, French and Irish Gaelic (new orthography)

3.4.2 Windows-125x ("ANSI")

The standard Windows-1252 (CP 1252) by Microsoft ("ANSI Code Page", which is a misnomer) largely corresponds to the standard ISO-8859-1, but 27 of the 32 aforementioned unused control characters are replaced by characters, including those that were only added in ISO 8859-15 (€, Š/š, Ž/ž, Œ/œ, Ÿ).[126] Thus, the available memory space is better utilized than in the ISO 8859 family, but again at the expense of compatibility: the 128 additional memory locations were filled with symbols and diacritics, but not according to the *de facto* standard of the DOS character set. Therefore, DOS text files are no longer readily readable under MS Windows.[127]

Figure 3.1: **DOS character set (Code page 850) vs. "ANSI" character set**

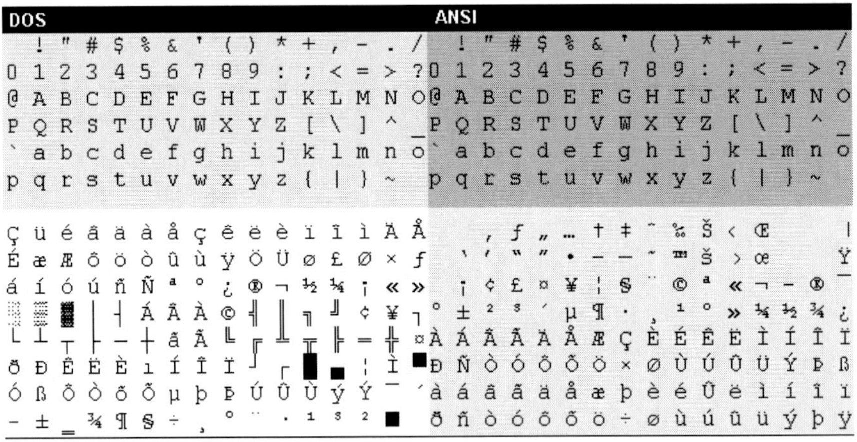

---

126 http://de.wikipedia.org/wiki/ISO-8859-1 (2011-11-29)
127 graphic: http://www.validome.org/doc/HTML_ge/inter/dos_windows.gif (2015-05-23)

Windows-1250 is based on ISO 8859-2 and contains diacritics for Eastern European languages such as Albanian, Croatian, Czech, Hungarian, Polish, Romanian, Serbian (Latin), Slovak, Slovenian, and Belarusian (Latin).[128]

Windows-1254 is based on ISO 8859-9 (Latin-5) and supports Turkish and most Western European languages.[129]

Windows-1257 for Baltic languages (Estonian, Latvian, Lithuanian) is compatible with ISO 8859-13.[130]

3.5 EBCDIC

EBCDIC *(Extended Binary Coded Decimal Interchange Code)* is an 8-bit code developed by IBM and is used primarily on mainframe computers. It descended from the code used with punched cards.[131] Of the possible 256 memory locations, 96 are not occupied in the standard version (37.5 % loss).[132] Furthermore, since *first* the letters and *then* the numbers are encoded, EBCDIC is incompatible to ASCII (and all character sets that are building upon ASCII). There are also different regional and national variants of EBCDIC (filling up the 96 memory locations, thus leading to the same compatibility problems as with extended ASCII character sets). There is even an → Unicode Transformation Format (UTF-EBCDIC).[133]

---

[128] Central & Eastern European Characters
http://code.cside.com/3rdpage/us/windows/windows-1250.html (2011-11-29)
[129] http://en.wikipedia.org/wiki/Windows-1254 (2011-11-29)
[130] http://en.wikipedia.org/wiki/Windows-1257 (2011-11-29)
[131] http://en.wikipedia.org/wiki/EBCDIC (2014-12-08)
[132] http://unicode.e-workers.de/ebcdic.php (2014-12-08)
[133] Unicode Technical Report #16 / UTF-EBCDIC
http://www.unicode.org/unicode/reports/tr16/ (2011-11-29)

3.6 ISO/IEC 10646 (Universal Character Set) and Unicode

Already in the early 1980s, an ISO work group was established which should work on the standard ISO/IEC 10646 (as further development of → ISO 646), a globally valid 32-bit code corresponding to 2^{32} = 4.3 trillion encodable characters. Their work, however, did not make progress for a long time.

In 1988, JOSEPH D. BECKER from Xerox Research together with colleagues proposed the basic architecture of a 16-bit code (corresponding to 2^{16} = 65,536 encodable characters) for multilingual computer applications (primarily for Han Chinese with its abundance of characters).[134] This "unique, universal and uniform character encoding" he called *Unicode*.[135] Unicode is now an international industry standard under the supervision of a non-profit consortium (established 1991),[136] which should once and for all eliminate the problem of countless (mutually incompatible) encodings in different countries of the world (and the resulting obstruction of international data exchange). In the long term, a digital code should be set for each sense-bearing character or text element of all known living and defunct systems of signs.[137]

ISO and the Unicode consortium work closely together. In 1992, the standard ISO/IEC 10646 (called *Universal Character Set* [UCS] by ISO) was finally passed, but with one change: since even the 65,536 characters of Unicode

---

134 Chronology of Unicode Version 1.0
 http://www.unicode.org/history/versionone.html (2011-11-29)
135 http://www.unicode.org/history/earlyyears.html (2014-12-08)
136 Chronology of Unicode Version 1.0
 http://www.unicode.org/history/versionone.html (2011-11-29)
137 http://de.wikipedia.org/wiki/Unicode (2011-11-29)

were not enough if you wanted to consider the wishes of academics for special characters and historical alphabets, the code would be extended to 20 bit. This meant in addition to Unicode, 16 separate 16-bit subsets (so-called *supplementary planes*) of a total of 2^{20} = 1,048,576 characters would be added via the UTF-16 surrogate mechanism (see next chapter).[138]

Since 1993, the Unicode standard and the Universal Character Set are identical in character encoding.[139, 140] While the Universal Character Set only specifies the actual character encoding part, the Unicode standard is a substantial corpus which defines for each character important additional properties such as sorting order (collation), direction of writing, and rules for combining characters.

When the cornerstone was laid for the Universal Character Set / Unicode, it had to be taken into account that a variety of different encodings were already widespread. But UCS-/Unicode-based systems should be able to handle already encoded data with little effort. To this end, for the first 256 characters the ASCII-based ISO 8859-1 encoding (Latin-1, Western European) were retained.[141] The characters of already established codes (industry standards—called code pages—, national and ISO standards) were subsumed into the Universal Character Set / Unicode, even if it meant lowering the standard (e.g. precomposed letter-diacritics combinations). However, this has proved to be an advantage, because even today many word

---

[138] Matt Neuburg: Two Bytes of the Cherry: Unicode and Mac OS X, Part 1, TidBITS 624, 01.04.2002,
http://db.tidbits.com/getbits.acgi?tbart=06774 (2011-11-29)
[139] http://de.wikipedia.org/wiki/Unicode (2011-11-29)
[140] Steven J. Searle (Webmaster, TRON Web): Unicode Revisited
http://tronweb.super-nova.co.jp/unicoderevisited.html (2011-11-29)
[141] http://de.wikipedia.org/wiki/Unicode (2011-11-29)

processors still lack the ability to assemble letters with *combining* diacritics properly (see figure 3.2).[142]

Figure 3.2: **Software mistake trying to assemble letters with combining diacritics: e with trailing ogonek, u with trailing macron** (European Commission, own photo)

Compared to other standards, the special feature of the UCS/Unicode is that once encoded characters are *never removed*, in order to ensure the longevity of digital data. If the encoding of a character subsequently proves as a mistake, (e.g. T/t with cedilla instead of comma), it is merely added "depreciated". Therefore the introduction of a new character in the standard requires a very careful examination which can drag on for years. Currently, we see new Unicode versions approximately at a distance of one and a half years, with about annually 1,000 new characters encoded. The European (modern)

---

142 http://de.wikipedia.org/wiki/Unicode (2011-11-29)

Latin characters, however, are already in the standard since a long time (see table 4.1).[143]

3.6.1 Unicode transformation formats (UTFs)

There are various transformation formats for the representation of Unicode characters for the purposes of electronic data processing. In each of the formats, all 1,114,112 ($2^{16} + 2^{20}$) characters can be accessed, and they convert lossless to another UTF.[144] But they differ in their memory footprint, their encoding/decoding complexity (runtime behaviour) and their compatibility with the older types of encodings with 7 or 8 bits.[145, 146]

UCS-2 is the oldest Unicode Transformation Format. It always uses 16 bits (2 bytes) to encode characters. Thus, it can represent all the 65,536 characters within the first Unicode subset (BMP, *basic major plane*).[147] The file management systems NTFS[148] and the older FAT32[149] already supported file names in UCS-2, as well as the operating system Windows NT 4.0 (newer versions use

---

143 http://de.wikipedia.org/wiki/Unicode (2011-11-29)
144 http://de.wikipedia.org/wiki/UTF-8 (2011-11-29)
145 http://de.wikipedia.org/wiki/Unicode_Transformation_Format (2011-11-29)
146 Kumaran, A. / Haritsa, Jayant R.: On the Costs of Multilingualism in Database Systems. In: Johann-Christoph Freytag, Peter Lockemann, Serge Abiteboul, Michael Carey, Patricia Selinger and Andreas Heuer, Editors, Proceedings 2003 VLDB Conference, Morgan Kaufmann, San Francisco, 2003, Pages 105-116 http://portal.acm.org/ft_gateway.cfm?id=1315462&type=pdf&coll=&dl= &CFID=32457463&CFTOKEN=35654172
147 http://en.wikipedia.org/wiki/Universal_Character_Set (2011-11-29)
148 http://de.wikipedia.org/wiki/ASCII (2011-11-29)
149 http://de.wikipedia.org/wiki/FAT32 (2011-11-29)

          → UTF-16). In UNIX operating systems, however, UCS-2 cause problems because 8-bit encoding is expected (see → UTF-8).[150]

UTF-16   (UCS-2E for *extended*)[151] uses as well always 16 bits to encode characters, but can display a maximum of 1,114,112 characters by "cheating": 2 × 1024 unassigned codes of the BMP[152, 153] are summed to so-called *surrogate pairs* which correspond to 1024 × 1024 characters from the supplementary planes.[154] This "pseudo-32-bit encoding" is necessary, for example, for Chinese characters.[155] UTF-16 is used for internal text representation by the operating systems Windows 2000[156] and beyond, Mac OS X, the Java programming language and the platform Microsoft.NET.[157]

UCS-4   always uses 32 bits (4 bytes) for the coding of characters and thus avoid the use of surrogate pairs. It is the simplest type of encoding, but uses up to four times more storage than other UTFs.[158] The ISO 10646 work group has agreed to reduce the allowable

---

150 Markus Kuhn: UTF-8 and Unicode FAQ for Unix/Linux / What is UTF-8?
http://www.cl.cam.ac.uk/~mgk25/unicode.html#utf-8 (2011-11-29)
151 TERENA (Trans-European Research and Education Networking Association): Extended UCS-2 Encoding Form (UTF-16)
http://www.terena.nl/library/multiling/unicode/utf16.html (2011-11-29)
152 hexadecimal D800-DBFF and DC00-DFFF
153 http://en.wikipedia.org/wiki/Basic_Multilingual_Plane#Basic_Multilingual_Plane (2011-11-29)
154 Markus Kuhn: UTF-8 and Unicode FAQ for Unix/Linux / What different encodings are there?
http://www.cl.cam.ac.uk/~mgk25/unicode.html#ucsutf (2011-11-29)
155 http://de.wikipedia.org/wiki/Unicode_Transformation_Format (2011-11-29)
156 http://en.wikipedia.org/wiki/Unicode_in_Microsoft_Windows (2014-04-23)
157 http://en.wikipedia.org/wiki/UTF-16 (2011-11-29)
158 http://de.wikipedia.org/wiki/Unicode_Transformation_Format (2011-11-29)

SETTING SIGNS FOR EUROPE   67

values range from 0 to 2^{21} to 0 to 1,114,111,[159] making UCS-4 and → UTF-32 virtually identical.[160]

UTF-32　corresponds to UCS-4, but uses for backward compatibility with → UTF-16 only the value range 0 to 1,114,111. This is (currently) not a major limitation, since the range of values in question is currently only occupied by 10 %.[161]

UTF-8　(developed 1992 by ROB PIKE and KEN THOMPSON) is in many areas the most popular transformation format for Unicode. It can use theoretically up to six bytes to encode characters.[162] The great advantage of UTF-8 relative to all other formats is that all ASCII characters (7 bit plus parity bit) are still valid. Applications that use only the ASCII character set (e.g. UNIX) work unchanged with UTF-8. For all Latin alphabet-based documents, UTF-8 is the most space-saving method for mapping of Unicode characters.[163]

ACE strings　(ASCII-Compatible Encoding, 1996 by MARTIN DÜRST as UTF-5 developed)[164] are a transformation format specifically for so-called "umlaut domains", also known as Multilingual or *Internationalized Domain Names* (IDNs): in addition to the previously permitted characters (26 Latin letters, ten digits and the

---

159　0 to 1,114,111 makes 1,114,112 characters
160　Markus Kuhn: UTF-8 and Unicode FAQ for Unix/Linux / What different encodings are there?
http://www.cl.cam.ac.uk/~mgk25/unicode.html#ucsutf (2011-11-29)
161　http://de.wikipedia.org/wiki/Unicode_Transformation_Format (2011-11-29)
162　http://de.wikipedia.org/wiki/UTF-8 (2011-11-29)
163　http://de.wikipedia.org/wiki/Unicode_Transformation_Format (2011-11-29)
164　Original text at W3C:
http://www.w3.org/International/1996/draft-duerst-dns-i18n-00.txt
(2011-11-29)

hyphen[165]), up to 92 additional characters are available for use in Internet addresses since March 2004 in Europe.[166] It involves the Unicode blocks *Latin-1 Supplement* (except the ligature ß, which is automatically broken down at the upstream normalization in "ss") and *Latin Extension A* (decimal Unicode range 224 to 382). In other countries, IDNs are awarded e.g. in Greek, Cyrillic, Korean and Chinese characters.[167] Since management of the Internet is still based on 7-bit ASCII, domain names with diacritics have to be converted internally in the so-called *punycode* method (using a complex algorithm) into an ASCII-compatible character string and are then processed. www.schön.de would so become www.xn--schn-7qa.de.[168, 169]

3.6.2 Windows Glyph List 4 (WGL4)

Microsoft, in agreement with Adobe, has defined a (unfortunately still incomplete) pan-European repertoire of 652 characters which is known under the name *Windows Glyph List 4* (WGL4). It contains diacritics for Western, Central and Eastern European languages (Extensions 1 and A, but only

---

165 not in a Java name: Zigurd Mednieks, Laird Dornin, G. Blake Meike, Masumi Nakamura: Programming Android, p. 141
166 http://de.wikipedia.org/wiki/IDNA (2011-11-29)
167 List with examples of existing IDNs:
http://www.domainregistry.de/sonderzeichen.html (2011-11-29)
168 list of valid characters for IDNs in Germany:
http://www.denic.de/de/domains/internationalized-domain-names/idn-liste.html (2011-11-29)
169 Original text of the memos (March 2003):
ftp://ftp.rfc-editor.org/in-notes/rfc3492.txt (2011-11-29)

rudiments of Extensions B and Additional) and for Cyrillic and Greek. The numbering is according to Unicode. [170, 171]

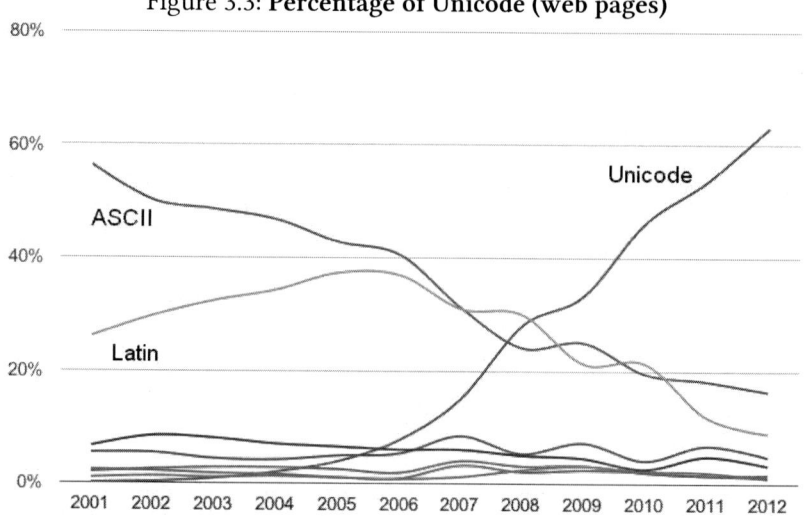

Figure 3.3: **Percentage of Unicode (web pages)**

3.7 Success of Unicode

In the figure 3.3,[172] it can be seen that the ASCII curve drops from 60 % to below 20 % while the curve of Latin-X encodings first increases from approximately 24 % to 34 % and would have made it probably to 50 % by 2012

---

170 Alan Wood: Character Sets / Using special characters from Windows Glyph List 4 (WGL4) in HTML
http://www.alanwood.net/demos/wgl4.html (2011-11-29)
171 Windows Glyph List 4.0 (WGL4)
http://unicode.e-workers.de/wgl4.php (2011-11-29)
172 http://googleblog.blogspot.be/2012/02/unicode-over-60-percent-of-web.html (2014-04-23)

(extrapolated) if it had not been for Unicode. Instead, Latin-X drops to below 10 % while the curve of Unicode increases from 0 % to over 60 % (note also the steeper curve slope of the latter).

Table 3.3: **Examples for jumble of characters (mojibake)**

Initial coding	Web browser setting	Display in the web browser
UTF-8	UTF-8	Falsches Üben von Xylophonmusik quält jeden größeren Zwerg.
UTF-8	ISO 8859-1	Falsches Ãœben von Xylophonmusik quÃ¤lt jeden grÃ¶ÃŸeren Zwerg.
ISO 8859-1	ISO 8859-1	Falsches Üben von Xylophonmusik quält jeden größeren Zwerg.
ISO 8859-1	UTF-8	Falsches �ben von Xylophonmusik qu�lt jeden gr��eren Zwerg.

3.8 Mojibake

When fonts are not properly decoded, a jumble of characters (Japanese *mojibake*) will be the result (see table 3.3). During the early days of the Internet, this condition could occur in all languages that used character sets beyond pure ASCII. A technical solution was found to settle the problem with the introduction of Unicode, but "unclean" websites (not meeting the W3C standards)[173] still create problems.[174] Also the web server may *not* be

---

173 World Wide Web Consortium: http://www.w3.org
174 http://de.wikipedia.org/wiki/Zeichensalat (2011-11-14)

instructed to override the character set of the website,[175] or at least it must be instructed to set it to UTF-8 by default (see also the *manual diacritics*, chapter 9.4.5).

Figure 3.4: "**Everyone knows the problem: wrong encoding.**"

[from www.getdigital.eu/scheiss-encoding.html (2014-04-21)]

---

175 e.g. Apache directive *AddDefaultCharset*

4 Unicode-compatible fonts

But even when using the Universal Character Set / Unicode as encoding, one is not protected from "strange" effects: because of insufficient *fonts*, holes or glyphs from different fonts will appear.

> One example is the case of the *Ludwig Maximilians University* of Munich. It chose the font *LMUCompatilFact* for its corporate design, without first checking for the (Latin) Unicode compatibility. When the University later wanted to present itself in a leaflet to Polish students, the rude awakening followed: the necessary Polish characters were not available, and the leaflet turned into an illegible cloze.
>
> Later, the text was corrected, but the characters in question were inevitably set in a different font (typeface Serif instead of Sans Serif). [176]

To display Latin characters on computer screens (or to print Latin characters on paper), an authority or a printery needs a font that contains *all* the characters required. The Latin characters in Unicode are, as already mentioned, spread over several areas (see table 4.1). Most fonts, however, cover only characters from the basic ASCII and *Latin-1 Supplement*, that is, they are again only tailored to English or the Western European languages, while the characters of other regions are missing.

---

[176] http://www.uni-muenchen.de/studium/administratives/formulare/hinw_beschei_ausl_pl.pdf (2011-11-19, link no longer active)

Table 4.1: **Latin in Unicode**

Area	decimal	hexadecimal
Basic Latin (= ASCII)	0–127	0000–007F
Latin-1 Supplement (= ISO 8859-1)	128–255	0080–00FF
Latin Extended-A	256–383	0100–017F
Latin Extended-B	384–591	0180–024F
• Latin Extended-B in stricter sense	384–451	0180–01C3
• Croatian digraphs for Serbian Cyrillic	452–460	01C4–01CC
• Diacritic vowel combinations for Pinyin	461–476	01CD–01DC
• Additions	477–511	01DD–01FF
• Slovenian additions for Croatian	512–535	0200–0217
• Additions for Romanian	536–539	0218–021B
• Other additions	540–553	021C–0229
• Additions for Livonian	554–563	022A–0233
• Other additions	564–591	0233–024F
IPA extensions (phonetic characters)	592–687	0250–02AF
...		
Latin Extended Additional	7680–7935	1E00–1EFF
• Latin extensions for general use	7680–7835	1E00–1E9B
• uppercase ẞ (sharp s)	7838	1E9E
• Latin extensions for Vietnamese	7840–7921	1EA0–1EF1
• General extensions / extensions for medieval studies	7922–7935	1EF2–1EFF

Extensions C (2C60-2C7F) and D (A720-A7FF) are not important for modern European languages.
Under Extension D, we find the Visigothic z from which the c with cedilla has developed.

Latin-1 Supplement corresponds to ISO 8859-1 and allows the representation of the 34 mainly *Western* European national and regional languages listed in Section 3.4.1.

Latin Extended-A allows also the representation of the 20 mainly *Eastern* European national and regional languages Bosnian, Karelian, Kashubian, Croatian, Kurdish (Kurmanji), Serbian, Latvian, Lithuanian, Maltese, Polish, Northern Sami, Inari Sami, Slovak, Slovenian, Lower Sorbian, Upper Sorbian, Czech, Hungarian and Turkish as well as the artificial language Esperanto.

Also Latin Extended-A allows the complete representation of Afrikaans (with the deprecated ṅ), French and Breton (with ligature Œ/œ and capital Ÿ), Danish (with ligature Œ/œ but without accents in Ǽ/ǽ, Ø̌/ø̌ and Å̌/å̌), English (with ligature Œ/œ),[177] Estonian and Finnish (with Š/š and Ž/ž in foreign words), Greenlandic (old orthography with ĩ, κ [kra] and ũ), Catalan (with L/ŀ), Dutch (ligature IJ/ij and capital Ÿ), Lule Sami (with allographic ń for Latin-1 ñ)[178] and Swedish (with Eastern European diacritics in foreign words).

Latin Extended-B is composed of several subdivisions (see table 4.1) of which, unfortunately, usually not all are available in one font.

From the Extension B in the strict sense, only ǝ [Schwa] for Azerbaijani and Ʒ [Ezh] for Skolt Sami and the Croatian digraphs (DŽ, Lj, nj, etc.) are interesting. Pinyin is Romanization for Chinese and therefore not important in this book. The "additions" include the characters Ā/ā for Livonian, Ǯ/ǯ, G/g, Ǧ/ǧ and Ǩ/ǩ for Skolt Sami, Q/ǫ for Sami and Megleno-Romanian, Ǵ/ǵ for Romani (former Yugoslavia), and Å̌/å̌, Ǽ/ǽ and Ø̌/ø̌ for Danish.

---

177 http://en.wiktionary.org/wiki/Category:English_terms_spelled_with_%C5%92 (2014-05-10)

178 http://en.wikipedia.org/wiki/Lule_Sami_language (2014-05-18)

The Slovenian additions for Croatian (characters with double gravis or inverted breve) do not appear in official alphabets. What is important is the Romanian extension (Ș/ș and Ț/ț), since otherwise one has to use the typographically incorrect characters with cedilla instead of a comma (Ş/ş, Ţ/ţ) from Latin Extended-A. From the "other additions", Ħ/ħ is required for Finnish Romani. The Livonian language (almost extinct) uses Ȫ/ȫ, Ō/ō, Ȯ/ȯ and Ȱ/ȱ,[179] but Ȳ/ȳ from the Livonian addition is also needed for Cornish (*Unified Cornish Revised* orthography).

If Latin Extended-B is entirely present in a font, it allows the representation of Arumanian, Istro-Romanian, Cornish, Megleno-Romanian, Romani (international transcription and former Yugoslavia), Romanian and the presentation of accents in Danish.

If one adds the *IPA extension* (International Phonetic Alphabet), also Azerbaijani (with ə [schwa]) and Skolt Sami (with ʒ [ezh]) can be completely represented.

To complete the representation of European languages written with the Latin script, also the area *Latin Extended Additional* is necessary.

This area contains the characters Ẁ/ẁ, Ẃ/ẃ and Ẅ/ẅ for Welsh, Ḍ/ḍ for Livonian, Ḥ/ḥ and X̌/x̌ for Kurdish (modern Romanization), uppercase ẞ (sharp s) for German and in the section "Vietnamese" the character Ẏ/ẏ for Welsh.

In many fonts, however, the designers have limited themselves to the three "W" characters (Ẁ, Ẃ, Ẅ).

---

179 http://en.wikipedia.org/wiki/Livonian_language (2011-11-30)

SETTING SIGNS FOR EUROPE 77

Fonts that have definitely all of the above mentioned characters are for example *Code2000*,[180] *Everson Mono*,[181] *FreeSerif*,[182] *Gentium Plus*,[183] and *GNU Unifont*[184] (see next two pages[185]).

Also *Arial*,[186] *the Brill*[187] (not in the table), *Calibri*[188] (not in the table), *Charis SIL*,[189] *DejaVu fonts*,[190] *Doulos SIL*,[191] *Junicode*,[192] *Microsoft Sans Serif*,[193]

---

[180] http://web.archive.org/web/20101122142710/http://code2000.net/code2000_page.htm, version 1.171 from 2008 (2014-05-23)
[181] http://www.evertype.com/emono/ version 7 from 2014-12-04 (2015-05-24)
[182] http://ftp.gnu.org/gnu/freefont/ version from 2012-05-03 (2014-05-19)
[183] http://scripts.sil.org/cms/scripts/page.php?item_id=Gentium_download version 5 from 2014-10-28 (2015-05-24)
[184] http://unifoundry.com/unifont.html version 7.0.06 from 2014-10-23 (2015-05-24)
[185] adapted from http://en.wikipedia.org/wiki/Unicode_font (2015-05-25)
[186] sold with Microsoft products: https://www.microsoft.com/typography/fonts/font.aspx?FMID=1081 version 1.01 (2007) (2015-05-25)
[187] http://www.brill.com/about/brill-fonts version 2.06, 2014-10-31 (2015-05-24)
[188] sold with Microsoft products: https://www.microsoft.com/typography/fonts/font.aspx?FMID=1914 version 5.62 (Windows 7), version 5.72 (Windows 8) (2015-05-25)
[189] http://scripts.sil.org/cms/scripts/page.php?item_id=CharisSIL_download version 5 from 2014-10-28 (2015-05-24)
[190] http://sourceforge.net/projects/dejavu/ version 2.35 from 2015-05-17 (2015-05-24)
[191] http://scripts.sil.org/cms/scripts/page.php?item_id=DoulosSIL_download version 5 from 2014-10-28 (2015-05-24)
[192] http://sourceforge.net/projects/junicode/files/ version 0.7.8 from 2012-12-30 (2014-05-23)
[193] sold with Microsoft products: https://www.microsoft.com/typography/fonts/font.aspx?FMID=1936 version 5.02 (Windows 7), version 5.10 (Windows 8) (2015-05-25)

RomanCyrillic Std,[194] *Segoe UI*[195] (not in the table), *Tahoma,*[196] *Times New Roman*[197] proved to have all characters.[198]

But only *Brill* (Serif: ì ī į į̄ j̄) and *Calibri* (Sans Serif: ì ī į į̄ j̄) handled also the composed diacritics in the *Named Sequences* (see chapter 2.6) correctly (standard: ì ī į į̄ j̄).

For texts with characters that include the full Latin Unicode range, the use of (Serif:) *Brill, Doulos, Times New Roman, RomanCyrillic Std, Gentium, Charis* (Sans Serif:) *Calibri, Segoe* or (Monospaced:) *Everson Mono* is advisable.

> Unfortunately, with *Tahoma,* the German quotation mark is turned to the wrong side (" instead of „). Since Windows 7 / Microsoft Office 2007, *Segoe UI* (User Interface) is supposed to take over from *Tahoma.*

This book is set in *Linux Libertine,* because the harmonious typeface and the possibility to set different slopes (n *n* ɴ) and variants of characters (Open-Type, e.g. st/st, Ö/Ö.) have convinced me.

> "Real" italics can also be set in *Charis, DejaVu Serif, FreeSerif, Gentium, Junicode, Times New Roman, Arial* and *DejaVu Sans*; "real" small capitals can also be set in *FreeSerif* and *Junicode*; trema letters can be set in *Charis* and *Code2000*.

---

194 http://kodeks.uni-bamberg.de/aksl/schrift/romancyrillicstd.htm Unicode 6.0 (2011-12-31)

195 sold with Microsoft products: https://www.microsoft.com/typography/fonts/font.aspx?FMID=1941 version 5.01 (Windows 7), version 5.28 (Windows 8) (2015-05-25)

196 sold with Microsoft products: https://www.microsoft.com/typography/fonts/font.aspx?FMID=1951 version 5.06 (Windows 7), version 5.25 (Windows 8) (2015-05-25)

197 sold with Microsoft products: https://www.microsoft.com/typography/fonts/font.aspx?FMID=1953 version 5.05 in Windows 7 (2008), version 6.80 in Windows 8 (2012) (2015-05-25)

198 ClearlyU and Lucida Grande (Facebook font) were not checked because they are OS X-specific.

Table 4.2: **Latin Unicode fonts**

(**bold** numbers = complete block,
lean numbers = characters missing)

	Basic Latin	Latin-1 Supplement	Latin Extended-A	Latin Extended-B	IPA extension	Latin Extended Add.	Latin Extended-C	Latin Extended-D
Arial	95	94	**128**	**208**	96	247	21	7
Charis	95	96	**128**	188	96	**256**	12	28
ClearlyU	95	95	**128**	178	94	246	-	-
Code2000	95	96	**128**	**208**	96	**256**	29	**114**
DejaVu	95	96	**128**	**208**	96	252	31	57
Doulos	95	96	**128**	188	96	**256**	12	28
Everson	95	96	**128**	**208**	96	**256**	32	**114**
FreeSerif	95	96	**128**	**208**	96	**256**	29	81
Gentium	95	96	**128**	**208**	96	**256**	12	28
Unifont	95	96	**128**	**208**	96	**256**	32	**114**
Junicode	95	96	**128**	182	94	**256**	5	97
Libertine	95	96	**128**	194	96	**256**	17	3
Grande	95	96	**128**	183	96	246	-	-
Lucida	95	96	**128**	119	89	8	-	-
Microsoft	95	94	**128**	**208**	96	247	21	7
Tahoma	95	94	**128**	**208**	96	247	21	7
TNR	95	94	**128**	**208**	96	247	21	7
Cyberbit	95	96	**128**	183	96	247	-	-

Table 4.3: **Font choice:**

a) Serif (last version tested):	Remarks:
Code2000 (2008)	Czech/Slovak d, l, t with haček instead of apostrophe, there are two characters T/t with comma
Times New Roman (2008)	may have problems with printing the diacritics on Ǻ
RomanCyrillic Std (2011)	may have problems with printing the diacritics on Ǻ
FreeSerif (2012)	Livonian d is with cedilla instead of with comma
Junicode (2012)	Latvian/Livonian letters are with cedilla instead of with comma
Linux Libertine (2012)	Livonian characters with double diacritics are odd, problems with printing the diacritics on Ǻ
Gentium Plus (2014)	–
Charis SIL (2014)	–
Doulos SIL (2014)	–
the Brill (2014)	–
DejaVu Serif (2015)	Livonian d is with cedilla instead of with comma, diacritics in Ǻ are not separated

b) Sans Serif (last version tested):	Remarks:
Arial (2007)	Latvian letters are with cedilla instead of with comma
Calibri (2009)	–
Microsoft Sans Serif (2009)	Latvian/Livonian letters are with cedilla instead of with comma
Segoe UI (2009)	–
Tahoma (2009)	German quotation mark turns to the wrong side
DejaVu Sans (2015)	Livonian d is with cedilla instead of with comma

c) Monospaced (last version tested):	Remarks:
Everson Mono (2014)	may have problems with printing the diacritics on Ǻ
GNU Unifont (2014)	very pixeled, Czech/Slovak d, l, t with haček instead of apostrophe, characters S/s/T/t with comma are very difficult to distinguish from those with cedilla

A special only-Latin (compatibe to String.Latin, see chapter 9.3) cross-platform font called *UnicodeDoc* is available to (only) the German authorities for issuing ID documents since summer 2012.[199, 200] It also includes characters for transliteration of names from other scripts into Latin.

Figure 4.1: **Detail of a German ID document with the font *UnicodeDoc***

---

199 Olaf Sinnigen, Bundesministerium des Innern, personal communication (2014-05-22)

200 http://www1.osci.de/sixcms/media.php/13/130301_RdSchrTTF_Version1-001.pdf (2015-01-03)

5 State of the "diacritical integration" in the media

5.1 Diacritics in news agencies

The majority of the reports of European and international events reaches the individual newspaper on wire services (historically often referred to as "ticker") of the various news agencies and is used under more or less large changes. Therefore, the practice of using diacritics in news agencies is of particular interest.

5.2 Examples from selected media

As mentioned in the introduction of this book, the individual print and online media have reacted very differently to the increasing confrontation with names and terms containing (Eastern European) diacritics.

5.2.1 Print media

The news magazine *Der Spiegel*, and the newspapers *Frankfurter Allgemeine Zeitung* (F.A.Z.) and *Die Zeit* have already been converted to an extended

Latin character set, as can be seen in these Serbian or Turkish names (MILOŠEVIĆ,[201] KARADŽIĆ / MLADIĆ,[202] and ERDOĞAN[203]).

> Each article goes through several instances within the house [...] The documentation is responsible for the correct spelling of the names of persons and gives corrections to the author or to final editing. For diacritics, there is a »glyph« box available by which unusual characters can be added to a text. *(Der Spiegel)*[204]

> It is in fact so that the news agencies provide the names of Eastern European politicians without diacritics. Most of the texts in our newspaper, however, are delivered by our own correspondents who know the correct spelling of course. (F.A.Z.)[205]

> The fact that e.g. Mr Erdoğan is written in *Die Zeit* mostly accurate lies generally in an attentive proofreading. There is actually a type of specialized dictionary: a list of all relevant persons who are easily misspelled. Not only names containing diacritics, but also about such nit-pickings as Günther/Gunter. So if a text says Erdogan, then an employee of proofreading transforms it with the search-and-replace function into Erdoğan. *(Die Zeit)*[206]

At *Financial Times Deutschland* (FTD, defunct), however, correct spelling was rather a mistake:[207]

---

201 Der Spiegel, „*Ziemlich nahe bei de Gaulle*", Der Spiegel 46/2000, p. 214 ff.
202 FAZ, „*Die Attacken des Mittelstürmers*", FAZ No. 59, 2004-03-11, p. 3
203 Die Zeit, „*Ein Anflug von Leichtsinn*", Die Zeit No. 22, 2005-05-25, p. 76
204 Jörg Rehder, reader service, SPIEGEL publishing house, personal communication (2012-02-08)
205 Reinhard Veser, F.A.Z., personal communication (2012-01-26)
206 Thomas Worthmann, ZEIT proofreading, personal communication (2012-04-19)
207 Astrid Froese, Team Leader editing, G+J Business Media AG & Co. KG, personal communication (2012-03-01)

> If you have discovered at one point of the newspaper the spelling Erdoğan [sic!], then that is, to be honest, a mistake. It is envisaged that we use accents in living Romance languages, trema and cedilla. Other diacritical marks, for example, from the Slavic and Scandinavian languages, we so far do not use. But we are talking about to change this to reflect an increasingly shrinking world. Here it is important to weigh costs and benefits in the context of the time-tight corsets of daily production.
> Differences of spellings by the news agencies are made by hand or over the search-and-replace function.

In the *Hannoversche Allgemeine Zeitung* (HAZ), characters outside ISO 8859-1 are on principle "scalped" (MILOŠEVIĆ, WAŁĘSA, ERDOĞAN → MILOSEVIC, WALESA, ERDOGAN), except the arts section (see chapter 6.2) and sometimes the obituaries. There, for example, the names ANTUNOVIĆ,[208] BLAGOJEVIĆ,[209] BLAŽ and PAROŚKI[210] are found in the correct spelling. Maybe this resort is especially sensitive to the families' wishes.

The use of the Turkish letter "ı" in the term "Ramazan Bayramı"[211] by the HAZ in a single case, however, had probably political reasons: the Turkish Muslims Hanover should be shown cultural respect, given the tensions in the Middle East.

The *Süddeutsche Zeitung* argues in 2005:[212]

> We are well aware of the problem, but there are two aspects which unfortunately speak against setting these accents in our newspaper. One is a purely technical: we do not have the fonts available that would accomplish, for example, the horizontal [sic] line through the Polish l or the diacritics for all

---

208 Obituary Karin Antunović, HAZ No. 36 (2006-02-11)
209 Obituary Petar Blagojević, HAZ No. 149 (2005-06-29)
210 Obituary Svetozar Paroški, HAZ No. 27 (2006-02-01)
211 „Ein bisschen wie Weihnachten", HAZ No. 258 (2005-11-04)
212 Fritz Elster, Süddeutsche Zeitung, personal communication (2005-11-10)

Czech and Turkish accents. Your argument that we as a »serious newspaper« should be able to write the Eastern European names correctly, though true in principle, but pushes on this technical barrier on the one hand. Secondly, there is the problem that we here do not have the language expertise in the final editing to provide all the Eastern European words with the correct accents.

In 2013(!), the *Süddeutsche Zeitung* reported enthusiastically: "Kılıçdaroğlu, Vrančić, Miłos—finally written correctly"[213] and said it proved voices wrong that thought that missing diacritics were a hint that Slavic and Turkic people were not or less respected.

In an advertisement of the *Allianz* insurance company in a university magazine, a young employee can be seen whose apparently Yugoslav surname TOMAŠIĆ is rendered in the correct spelling with diacritics.[214] The Allianz as an employer wants maybe to prove that the individual needs of employees will be respected.

The *Guardian*, an English(!) newspaper, says on the subject:[215]

> In general our policy is to use accents and diacritical marks on foreign words, particularly proper names: the Guardian has an international audience of many millions these days and the least we can do is spell people's names correctly, in whatever language

---

213 http://www.genios.de/presse-archiv/artikel/SZ/20131230/k-inodot-l-inodot-daro-gbreve-lu-vr/A56163904.html (2014-12-13)
214 from an advertisement of the Allianz insurance company in the *Hochschulanzeiger* of the *Frankfurter Allgemeine*, issue 61 (June 2002)
215 http://www.guardian.co.uk/commentisfree/2009/jun/29/language-umlauts-marsh (2011-11-07)

5.2.2 Online media

In their Croatian internet service,[216] *Deutsche Welle* uses Croatian diacritics (unmasked letters in UTF-8 encoded HTML). In its German Internet service,[217] however, they omit any non-German diacritics. In the Polish example text, the words WAŁĘSA and Solidarność[218] and in the Serbian example text the proper name MILOŠEVIĆ[219] were written without diacritics, although the UTF-8 source code would allow the representation of Polish or Serbian diacritics easily. Here, the use of the correct character is not hindered by technology, but apparently by the lack of language skills of the editorial team.

Only recently (2012), the editors tried to represent also South-east European characters correctly.[220]

Sometime it gets really ridiculous:[221]

> We do not use diacritics in tagesschau.de (except in French and Spanish). Therefore yesterday I deleted[!] all [Hungarian] diacritics.
> *(tagesschau.de)*

---

216 http://www2.dw-world.de/croatian/ (2006-02-20)
217 http://www.dw.de/themen/s-9377 (2015-05-29)
218 *"Solidarnosc"-Bewegung mit Folgen*, DW 31.08.2005
    http://www.dw-world.de/dw/article/0,1564,1691118,00.html (2011-11-30)
219 *Milosevic-Prozess vertagt*, DW 06.07.2004
    http://www.dw-world.de/dw/article/0,1564,1255662,00.html (2011-11-30)
220 http://www.dw.de/dw/article/0,,15918267,00.html Rațiu (2012-05-07)
221 Britta Reinke, editing team tagesschau.de, personal communication (2008-06-19)

5.3 Case study: dpa

The German market leader (*Deutsche Presseagentur*, dpa) uses most ISO 8859-15-displayable diacritics. These theoretically allow the representation of the 34 mainly *Western* European national and regional languages listed in chapter 3.4.1, but only 16 of them are actually used.[222] Other ISO 8859-15-displayable diacritics such as Š/š and Ž/ž occurring in many Eastern European languages and also Ÿ/ÿ are not used by the dpa. The news agency justifies that by saying that their customers could not process these diacritics in their content management systems (which presumably are still based on ISO 8859-1). But also the Icelandic letters Ð/ð (Eth) and Þ/þ (Thorn) are waived the dpa, although they can be represented with ISO 8859-1. Likewise argues the news agency *Deutscher Depeschendienst* (ddp, now defunct) that the "politically desired implementation of exact transcription of Eastern European languages into German" is slowed down by the customer with the lowest standard.

On my question whether it would be possible to switch the entire ticker system gradually to Unicode, they replied in all seriousness: "[Unicode] recognizes not our umlauts (ü, ß, etc.) and is therefore not the appropriate common denominator." But even after I had corrected this error (probably caused by an experience with → mojibake), they said that it was not being considered at the moment and they would probably stay at ISO 8859-15 level.[223]

---

[222] Albanian, Danish, German, English, Faroese, Finnish, French, Gaelic, Icelandic, Italian, Catalan, Dutch, Norwegian, Portuguese, Spanish and Swedish.
Source: Michael Jobst, dpa, documentation, department standards, personal communication (2005-09-19)

[223] Andrea Hellmich, dpa, personal communication (2005-11-16)

Table 5.1: **Through ISO 8859-1 disadvantaged European languages with the Latin alphabet, modern orthography**
(bold: official EU languages)

Azerbaijani (ə, ğ, İ, ı, ş)
Bosnian (ć, č, đ, š, ž)
Breton (œ, Ÿ)
Catalan (ŀ)
Cornish (ā, ē, ī, ō, ū, ű, ȳ)
Croatian (ć, č, đ, š, ž)
Czech (č, ď, ě, ň, ř, š, ť, ů, ž)
Danish (æ, å, ø)
Dutch (ij, Ÿ)
English (œ)
Estonian (š, ž in foreign words)
Esperanto (ĉ, ĝ, ĥ, ĵ, ŝ, ŭ)
Faroese (ð)
Finnish (š, ž in foreign words)
French (œ, Ÿ)
German (capital ẞ)
Hungarian (ő, ű)
Icelandic (ð, þ)
Karelian (č, š, ž)
Kashubian (ą, ę, ł, ń, ś, ż)
Kurdish (Kurmanji) (ş) / (Latin) (ă, ā, ě, ē, ĭ, ī, ŏ, ō, ŭ, ū) / (modern Roman.) (ş, ḥ, ẍ)
Latvian (ā, č, ē, ģ, ī, ķ, ļ, ņ, š, ū, ž; sometimes ŗ)
Lithuanian (ą, č, ę, ė, į, š, ū, ų, ž)
Livonian (ā, ǟ, č, ḍ, ē, ģ, ī, ķ, ļ, ņ, ō, ȯ, ȱ, ȭ, ŗ, š, ț, ū, ȳ, ž)
Maltese (ċ, ġ, ħ, ż)
Polish (ą, ć, ę, ł, ń, ś, ź, ż)
Romani (international standard) (ć, ś, ź, θ, ʒ, ŏ, ă) / scientific alphabet (č, ř, š, ž, ə) / Yugoslavia (ć, č, ģ, š, ž) / Finland (ḧ)
Romanian (ă, ş, ţ) / Arumanian (ă, ľ, ń, ş, ţ) / Istro-Romanian (ă, ľ, ń, ş, ţ) / Megleno-Romanian (ă, ľ, ń, ọ, ş, ţ)
Sami (Northern) (ć, č, ð, ŋ, ś, š, ŧ, ź, ž) / (Inari Sami) (č, ð, š, ž) / (Lule Sami) (ń) / (Skolt Sami) (č, ð, ʒ, ǯ, ǧ, g, ǩ, ŋ, š, ž)
Serbian (Latin) (ć, č, đ, š, ž)
Slovak (č, ď, ĺ, ľ, ň, ŕ, š, ť, ž)
Slovenian (č, š, ž)
Sorbian (Lower Sorbian) (ć, č, ě, ł, ń, ŕ, ś, š, ź, ž) / (Upper Sorbian) (ć, č, ě, ł, ń, š, ź, ž)
Swedish (with Eastern European diacritics in foreign words).
Turkish (ğ, İ, ı, ş)
Welsh (ẃ, ẁ, ẅ, ŵ, ỳ, ŷ)

5.3.1 Problems of limitation to ISO 8859-1

If one compares ISO 8859-1-displayable diacritics (while keeping in mind the practice of waiving Ð/ð and Þ/þ) with a list of necessary diacritics to write all European languages (chapter 2.6, table 5.1), it is found that at least the following 37 European languages are more or less strongly disadvantaged, including 18 of the 24 official languages of the European Union (marked in bold).

This means that the entire Central Eastern and South Eastern European region is "diacritical-wise" not covered—including Poland and the Czech Republic, two direct neighbours of Germany! In view of the EU enlargement in the years 2004/2007/2013 and possible future enlargement steps, the coverage of this region will increase more and more, so there is an urgent need to come to a single technical solution for this problem as quickly as possible.

In general, the increased sensitivity to correct spelling of the names of foreign people and places improves the quality of editorial work, and the multiplier effect would be enormous due to the fact that we are daily dealing with print and online media.

5.3.2 The upcoming solution: Unicode-compatible software

The best solution would be, of course, the mandatory or *de facto* conversion of all computer systems of the news agencies, editing offices, and printeries to Unicode-compatible software. This is, however, hindered by the costs involved. Nor is it clear which institution could make (and enforce) such a binding change—after all, this is the free economy. Moreover, it is not expected that the conversion will take place synchronously, that is, there will be compatibility issues, as is already the case between content management systems with ISO 8859-15 and those with ISO 8859-1. The question is how to reduce the compatibility issues between the news agencies and the editing offices to a minimum *in the meantime*.

In 2006, I suggested the introduction of a standardized ticker annex for every word containing non-ISO-8859-1-compliant diacritics,[224] but it was not taken up.

In 2014, I asked dpa again. Their answer: "In the meantime, indeed a lot has moved. We have [now] different XML formats in which we use UTF-8."[225] The XML format *NewsML™-G2* (current version 2.15) was developed by the *International Press Telecommunications Council* (IPTC) and is also used by e.g. *Associated Press* (AP), *Reuters*, and *Austria Presse Agentur* (APA).[226]

---

224 Kappenberg, Bernd: *Zeichen setzen für Europa. Der Gebrauch europäischer lateinischer Sonderzeichen in der deutschen Öffentlichkeit.* In: Networx. No. 49. Rev. 2007-02-18. ISSN: 1619-1021
http://www.mediensprache.net/networx/networx-49.pdf
225 Thomas Steege, dpa, personal communication (2014-05-27)
226 https://iptc.org/standards/newsml-g2/whos-using-newsml-g2/ (2015-05-29)

6 Failure examples

Even when the author of a text made an effort to use the necessary diacritics, it still can sometimes come to technical glitches—partly for reasons of incompatibility, partly because people are ignorant how the setting of diacritic marks work. The analysis of these errors helps to understand what to change in the training of typists and journalists and which technical assistance should be offered.

6.1 Incompatible character sets

In the magazine "Laborjournal",[227] an é was printed instead of a č in the name of EU Commissioner POTOČNIK ("**Potoènik**"), also in a different typeface (see example in chapter 4). This error was most likely caused by the use of incompatible 8-bit character sets, because memory space number 232 is taken by the character č in ISO 8859-2 (and -4, -10, -13) whereas it is the character é in ISO-8859-1 (and -3, -9, -14, -16). To avoid such mishaps, Unicode should be used as the character set, both in the editorial office and in the printery.

---

227 *Info Kompakt,* Laborjournal 09/2004

In two other cases, Code page 437 (MS-DOS Latin US; see also chapter 3.4.2) was used instead of ISO-8859-x (ⁿ for ü and ╔ for É in position 252 and 201, respectively) in McDonalds cash machines in Germany and Belgium (own photos):[228]

6.2 Do-It-Yourself diacritics

Unlike the rest of the *Hannoversche Allgemeine Zeitung*, people in the arts section try to correctly reproduce characters that are not included in ISO 8859-1. Frequently the composer DVOŘÁK is mentioned, next to e.g. his colleague LEOŠ JANÁČEK,[229] the philosopher ŽIŽEK,[230] the painters JIŘÍ NAČERADSKÝ and MILOŠ ENGELBERTH and photographer JIŘÍ MACHT.[231] The culturally competent editorial team of the arts section has somehow managed to synthesize the necessary diacritics in č , ř , š and ž—with one flaw: instead of a haček, they used a breve ("Dvořák", the rounding is clearly visible). Despite this one flaw, the initiative is very commendable. Of course

---

228 https://en.wikipedia.org/wiki/Code_page_437 (2015-08-02)
229 Volker Hagedorn: *Dreihundert Jahre Einsamkeit / Luk Perceval probt in Hannover Janáčeks „Die Sache Makropoulos"*, HAZ No. 33 (2005-02-09)
230 Stefan Arndt: *Aus der Tiefe des Raums / Slovoj Žižek bei den Theaterformen in Braunschweig*, HAZ (date unknown)
231 Michael Wolfson: *Unbekannt – oder? / Arbeiten tschechischer Künstler im hannoverschen Kubus*, HAZ No. 131 (2004-06-08)

SETTING SIGNS FOR EUROPE 95

here the solution lies also in the conversion of the computer systems of the editing and printing department to Unicode.

6.3 Incorrect operation of dead keys

For technical reasons, accent key on typewriters work in such a way that *first* the accent key and *then* the base character to be modified has to be pressed (therefore the moniker *dead keys*: there is no character feed, and the subsequently typed character is marked with the diacritic).

For historical reasons—most likely to facilitate the training of secretaries to computer keyboards—the accent keys taken over from West European typewriters (´ ` ˆ) act *still* as dead keys! Unfortunately, this does no longer work with the vowels ẏ, ŷ and the consonants ć, ń, ź, ẇ, ĝ, ŝ, etc.

Nevertheless, some authors still try to produce e.g. the character ć by typing the combination ´c (Kova´c) or even c´ (Plazanic´).[232, 233] Many typos of diacritics are resulting from the confusion of that order (see figure 6.2).

Figure 6.1: **Failed attempt to assemble the Croatian ć** (own photo)

---

232 Merten, Martina: *Gesundheitssysteme Osteuropas (Teil 3): Slowakische Republik – Zwei Seiten einer Reform / Deutsches Ärzteblatt 102, Ausgabe 11 vom 18.03.2005, Seite A-737 / B-620 / C-578 THEMEN DER ZEIT*
http://www.aerzteblatt.de/v4/archiv/artikel.asp?id=45934 (2006-04-22)

233 Birth announcement Lea and Dominik Plazanić, HAZ No. 138 (2008-06-14)

Figure 6.2: **Typo of *Deutsche Bahn* of Italian à** (own photo)

> Ogni abuso verra˙ punito

6.4 Ignorance of the differences between diacritics

In an example from *ScienceDirect online*, it was attempted to assemble the ę (e with ogonek) in the Polish proper name Węgrzyn from an e and an isolated cedilla (We ̧grzyn). [234]
Besides the fact that they should have used a *combining* cedilla (Unicode character 0327 instead of 00B8) or better a stand-alone character, the difference between cedilla (turned to the left) and ogonek (turned to the right) was ignored.

In Catalan, there is the digraph ŀl, with a dot in the centre (for phonetic distinction of ll, which is pronounced as [j]). In the Castilian-dominated administration, often a normal point (.) or hyphen (-) is used erroneously. [235]

Figure 6.3: **Use of a hyphen instead of the Catalan dot in the centre.**
Traffic sign (own photo).

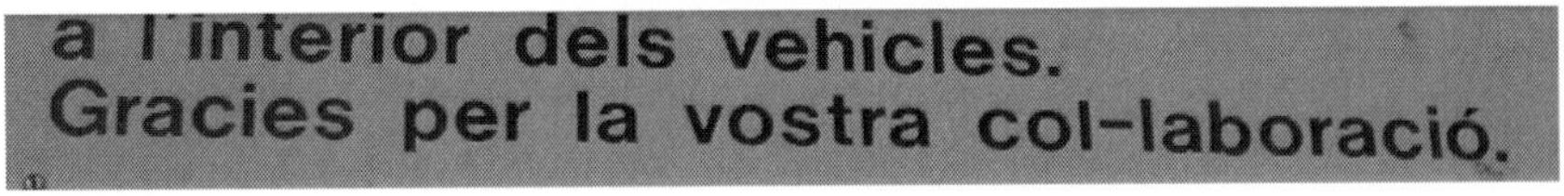

> a l'interior dels vehicles.
> Gracies per la vostra col-laboració.

---

234 doi:10.1016/j.bioorg.2005.07.004
235 http://www.raco.cat/index.php/LlenguaUs/article/view/128012/177352 (p.27f and footnotes) (2015-05-30)

Figure 6.4: **Lithuanian ė is sometimes replaced or confused with é (and sometimes è).**
Text at visitor's centre, European Parliament (own photo).

LANKYTOJŲ GRUPĖS

Figure 6.5: **Icelandic Þ is often mistaken for a P.**
Photo exhibition in Brussels (own photo).

La rivière Pjorsa (ou Thjorsa)

6.5 Use of combining diacritics

In an example from *Science Direct online*, it was attempted to assemble the í in the Czech proper names Jírová and Mezuláníková from the Turkish letter ı and a combining acute (Unicode character 0301, Jı́rová/Mezulánı́ková).[236] Many applications do not display combined diacritics properly, as shown in figure 3.2), and there can be also problems with search functions, so their use should be avoided. All European modern Latin characters with diacritics are also available as stand-alone Unicode characters.

---

236 doi:10.1016/j.tiv.2005.06.013

6.6 Replacement by images

Especially in scientific search engines, diacritics are sometimes represented by images (see screen copies below), which may be lost if the file is saved. Hyphenation may also not be correct (see second example, "Żylicz"):

> SEARCH PUBMED FOR
> ▸ Miodrag Sremč evi ć

> independently is still alien to many of the old guard. "It's unbelievable sometimes — these professors are treated like gods," says Maciej Ż
> ylicz, president of the Foundation for Polish Science in Warsaw and head

6.7 Replacement by escape sequences

Some of the texts are due to the turmoil of the HTML- or e-mail forwarding (see chapter 3.8) encoded as *escape sequences*, e.g. "[mdash]"[237] or "[kappa]".[238]

6.8 Conclusion

In chapter 14 (development of a practical input method for characters), it is made sure that there are fail-safe differences between diacritics, and correct operation of (extended) dead keys, so that neither replacement by images nor by escape sequences is necessary. The use of combining diacritics is still possible, but depreciated.

---

237 Nature Biotechnology Contents: Volume 29 pp. 1055–1150
http://mabsj2.blogspot.be/2011/12/nature-biotechnology-contents-volume-29.html (2014-12-31)

238 doi:10.1038/nm.2586

7 Diacritics as style element in brand and product names

Diacritics are not folkloristic or moribund relics of European language culture that must give way to the dominance of English spelling sooner or later: the appearance of *heavy metal umlauts* aka "röck döts" has long been known (1969).[239] It is a special form of *foreign branding*.

> See TV show *Simpsons*, season 8, episode 10: when Homer wants to drink on a Friday evening something very special and rejects a common Duff Beer, barkeeper Moe quickly turns around and paints an umlaut above the 'u' on the label of an ordinary Duff Bottle and offers it to Homer as "Swedish beer". Homer is delighted.[240]

But here we (generally) concentrate on diacritics *outside* Latin-1. An interesting recent development is the increasing use of foreign language diacritics in English, French, and Spanish products / brand names.[241, 242]

---

239 http://en.wikipedia.org/wiki/Metal_umlaut (2011-11-18)
240 http://simpsonspedia.net/index.php?title=D%C3%BCff (2015-01-07)
241 http://shop.bronny.de/img_central/produktbilder_260/260_shop_inneov_400.jpg (2006-01-20, link no longer active)
242 logo_estee_lauder_navy.png (2011-12-02)

7.1 Macron as distorted French acute

The spelling *ESTĒE* (with macron, see figure 7.1) in place of ESTÉE (with an acute) in the logo of the cosmetics manufacturer Estée Lauder is merely based on "aesthetic considerations"[243]—probably the acute (especially in uppercase letters) would clearly stand out from the word and disturb the harmonious appearance of the logo. Also in the spelling *innēov* (see figure 7.1) in the logo of the dietary supplement manufacturer innéov or with the spelling *CORNĒ* for the chocolate brand Corné Port-Royal,[244] the macron is a distorted French acute. In texts, the manufacturers always write themselves with acute accent.

---

243 Rosa Herzberger, Marketing Assistant, Estée Lauder Companies GmbH, personal communication (2006-01-25)
244 http://www.corneportroyal.be/index.php (2011-11-19)

Figure 7.1: **Macron as style element in the logos Estée Lauder and innéov**

ESTĒE LAUDER

Figure 7.2: **Adoption of the style element into the body text of an internet pharmacy**

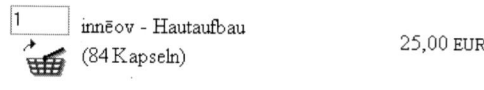

In a single case (see figure 7.2), there was an online pharmacy advertisement for innéov products employing actually a real ē, thanks to the thoroughness of the responsible webmaster. [245, 246, 247]

---

245 hexadecimal coding ē
246 http://www.dr-hagen.de/fwa/schoen/nahrungsergaenzung/inneov/hautaufbau/ (2006-01-20, shopping basket no longer there)
247 Kay Wischkony, webmaster dr-hagen.de, personal communication (2006-01-20)

7.2 Macron as distorted French accent

A macron can stand not only for an acute, proven by the spelling *extē* in the logo for the fashion clothing brand extè,[248] *perlēge* in the chocolate bar Perlège,[249] *Pranarōm* in the logo of the essential oil maker Pranarôm,[250] *Hōpital* for Hôpital in the logo of a Belgian hospital,[251] and *bāton* for bâton in a vintage fashion label.[252]

Figure 7.3: **Macron instead of accent grave**

extē

Figure 7.4: **Macron instead of circumflex**

---

248 http://www.globalvillagedirectory.info/Uploads/Images/-1_Ext%C3%A9-logo.gif (2014-12-13)
249 Nadia Nicholls, chocandco.com, personal communication (2014-12-16)
250 http://www.pranarom.com/ (2014-12-13)
251 http://www.erasme.ulb.ac.be/page.asp?id=214&langue=FR (2014-12-13)
252 https://fr.wikipedia.org/wiki/B%C3%A2ton-Rouge (2015-08-05)

The name *Jōvan*[253] shall suggest a French origin of US products.[254] It is unclear whether the original spelling should maybe have read Jóvan, Jòvan or Jôvan (all three founders are deceased); maybe the spelling was intentionally similar to the cosmetics brand Lancôme (since 1935).[255] Advertisements from the 1970s show consistently the spelling with macron (see figure 7.5). Also on the official website of Jōvan, the character "o with macron" is used.[256, 257]

Figure 7.5: **Macron in the body text of a Jōvan advertisement** (detail)

---

253 Advertising Educational Foundation
http://www.aef.com/images/book_covers/jovan1.jpg (2011-12-02)
254 Advertising Educational Foundation: The Erotic History of Advertising
http://www.aef.com/on_campus/classroom/book_excerpts/data/2476
(2011-12-02)
255 http://perfumeshrine.blogspot.be/2006/12/miracle-forever-by-lancome-fragrance.html (2015-05-30) Originally Lanco**s**me; the circumflex was used to make the brand look "more French".
256 decimal coding ō
257 Company website: http://www.jovansexy.com/ (2011-12-02)

7.3 Macron as allusion to a special shape on a shoe's sole

The brand "YOURS Footwear" is written YŌURS (O with macron), an allusion to the macron-shaped outlines on the shoe's sole:[258]

7.4 Macron as artistic alienation of the umlaut

The fashion sale Sörens used in its logo an o with a macron *(Sōrens)* instead of the spelling with o-umlaut. This is an artistic alienation of the umlaut; a reference to the letter "o with macron" in the Latvian language does not exist. However, one would have to pronounce the name actually [Soorens] because of the macron, which would not have been the case with the available alternatives (Soerens, Sœrens, Sørens, Sőrens).

It is noteworthy that Sörens uses as only one of the investigated manufacturers a single accent-marked character (here the ō, see figure 7.6) as trademark.

---

258 https://www.behance.net/gallery/28318629/YOURS-Footwear (2015-08-05)

Figure 7.6: **Macron as style element in the logo Sörens**

7.5 Trema points as allusion for bubbles

In the advertisement, we see an ï with two differently coloured trema points (white and encircled black). They continue in the drawing in kind of the same way, making it clear that the drink is sparkling. In addition, the words "fines bulles" (fine bubbles) show up.[259]

Figure 7.7: **Ï in an advertisement** (own photo)

---

259 https://www.cocacolabelgium.be/nl/merk-category/finley/ (2015-07-29)

7.6 Dot over character as artistic alienation of the French acute

In this fashion sale Saké, an e with dot above is used instead.[260] This is again an artistic alienation of the of the French acute; a reference to the letter "e with dot above" in the Lithuanian language does not exist.[261]

SAKĖ

7.7 Scandinavian diacritics

The name *Nørdic Mist*[262] shall suggest a Northern European origin of US products, but it is pronounced "Nerdic" in Norwegian and Danish. This is probably the reason why it never was launched in actual 'Nordic' countries.[263]

Figure 7.8: O with stroke in the logo of Nordic Mist

---

260 https://scontent-ams2-1.xx.fbcdn.net/hphotos-xfp1/v/t1.0-9/ 10952058_859833814073032_65444171936264262_n.jpg?oh= 27b07ad9c4ac566a4976bb6663cd0994&oe=564AE08C (2015-07-29)
261 Sakė, personal communication (2015-08-05)
262 http://mixologia.files.wordpress.com/2011/10/wpid-photo-15102011-20451. jpg?w=585&h=654 (2014-12-13)
263 http://en.wikipedia.org/wiki/Nordic_Mist (2014-12-13)

Figure 7.9: **A café in Brussels featuring Å and Ø. Purportedly, the manager wants a 'Nordic flavour'.** (own photo)

The writing *Bågl* for bagel, on the other hand, is an allusion on the hole in the middle of this food item. In addition, there is a word play with whole and hole:

Figure 7.10: "a (w)hole lot of [bagel]" (own photo)

7.8 S with haček

In the perfumery articles *Cašmir*[264] and *Cašran*,[265] the reasons for the choice of notation with š (instead of sh) lie in the dark. No one in the Lancaster Group remembers, and the responsible advertising agency does not exist any more.[266] Therefore, one can only speculate. Cašmir came on the market in 1991, at the time of the collapse of the Eastern Bloc. Perhaps the increased

---

264 https://www.douglas.de/douglas/Pflege-K%C3%B6rper-Pflege-Chopard-Ca%C5%A1mir_productbrand_3000021194.html?sourceRef=u_eAwP2V0 (2015-05-30)
265 http://www.parfumo.de/Parfums/Chopard/Casran (2015-05-30)
266 Phone call with Ms Meier, Lancaster Group (2006-01-31)

contact of the Western European public with Eastern European diacritics triggered by this has played a role in this choice of notation.

Figure 7.11: **Haček as style element in the perfume brand Chopard**

7.9 Mirrored e

The Spanish telephone company *amena* used in its logo a mirrored e (see figure 7.12).[267] Whether this was only a visual gimmick or whether it actually served phonetic purposes, for example as a replacement of a schwa, is unknown.
Meanwhile the operator Orange bought amena.

Figure 7.12: **Mirrored e as a style element in the logo of provider amena**

---

[267] http://www.movilinvasion.es/wp-content/uploads/2010/10/logo-amena-300x194.jpg (2015-05-30)

7.10 M with acute

A Californian fruit company uses "Nacirema" as brand name (a word play, spelling "American" backwards),²⁶⁸ but with an acute on the m (NACIREḾA, see figure 7.13).²⁶⁹ This fruit company seems to have Korean ties.²⁷⁰ Maybe they wanted to recreate the Spanish ñ but ended up with ḿ, used in Romanization of Chinese.²⁷¹

Figure 7.13: **M with acute on the packaging of fruits** (own photo)

7.11 Using macrons to convey a phonetic function

In the logos of the muesli bar *nākd*,²⁷² the consulting firm *thē Corporation*,²⁷³ the alarm clock *snūzNlūz*,²⁷⁴ the audio equipment series *Xplōd*,²⁷⁵ *Mondelēz*

---

268 http://en.wikipedia.org/wiki/Nacirema (2015-01-25)
269 http://www.simonianfruit.com/pomes.html (2015-01-25)
270 http://www.simonianfruit.com/pomes_korean.html (2015-01-25)
271 http://en.wikipedia.org/wiki/%E1%B8%BE (2015-01-25)
272 http://www.nakd.fr/ (2015-05-30)
273 http://www.youtube.com/watch?v=1xOKgwirXK4 (2012-04-19)
274 http://www.thinkgeek.com/stuff/41/snuznluz.shtml (2014-12-13)
275 http://store.sony.com/xplod-cd-radio-cassette-recorder-zid27-CFDG700CP/
cat-27-catid-EOL-Small-Home_Electronics (2015-05-30)

(former Kraft foods)[276] and textiles producer *Eckō*,[277] macrons are not only used as a style element but also fulfil a phonetic function:

Figure 7.14: **Macron as style element in the logos of the Corporation, Xplod** (own photo) **nakd, and *ecko unltd.**

- The term nākd is derived from the word naked (/ˈneɪkɪd/), but the shortening of -ed to -d would mean the pronunciation of short "a" (/ˈnekd/). However, the macron indicates a length, so the resulting pronunciation is long "a" again (/ˈneɪkd/).
- "Thē" instead of "the" means determining pronunciation /ðiː/ instead of /ðə/.

---

276 http://www.businessweek.com/articles/2012-03-21/
kraft-mondelez-and-the-art-of-rebranding (2014-12-13)

277 http://www.eckounltd.com/promos/stores/ecko_retail_coupon_banner.gif
(2006-01-18, link no longer active)

- The term snūzNlūz is derived from the words snooze (/snuːz/), but the shortening to snuz would mean a shortening of the "u" sound (/snuz/) if the macron would not indicates a length.
- The term Xplōd is derived from the verb to explode (/ɪkˈspləʊd/), but the shortening of -de to -d would mean the pronunciation of an open "o" (/ɪkˈsplɒd/). However, the macron indicates a length, so the resulting pronunciation is again a closed "o" (/ɪkˈsploːd/, /ɪkˈspləʊd/).
- The name Mondelēz is derived from "delicious world". The macron indicates a long "e" (instead of "ayse"). Also, it is another way to make the name more "ownable" (see also the perfume bacōn).[278]
- The logo *eckō unltd. derives from a sprayed graffiti signature (tag, see right half of figure 7.14), which goes back again to the nickname "echo" of the textile designer MARC MILECOFSKY (better known as Marc Ecko).[279] The macron here has probably the function of indicating a long vowel. More information could not be obtained from the manufacturer.

7.12 Using diacritics to convey dictionary character

In *Wĕbopēdia*[280] (*portmanteau* of web and encyclopaedia), the risk of phonetically wrong pronunciation is relatively low. The specification of brevity and length by breve and macron shall probably emphasize the dictionary character of this internet service. In fact, Wĕbopēdia had a pronunciation

---

278 http://www.fargginay.com/ (2014-12-14)
279 Rob Walker: Cul-de-sac Cred, New York Times 2005-07-10
   http://www.nytimes.com/2005/07/10/magazine/10ECKO.html (2011-12-02)
280 http://www.theinternetresource.info/graphics/webopedia.gif (2015-05-30)

aid[281] that included characters with diacritics (ā, ä, â, ã, ē, ë, ī, ō, ô, û and ū) but was not used in practice.
Between 2006 and 2011, the logo was redesigned without diacritics.

Figure 7.15: **Breve and macron as style elements in the logo of the internet service Webopedia**

7.13 Using diacritics to convey exoticism

Molvanîa (A Land Untouched by Modern Dentistry)[282] and the sequel *Phaic Tăn* (Sunstroke on a Shoestring; translated as *Phaic Tăn* [sic] into German)[283] are both fictional travel guides. Here, diacritics mean (planned) exoticism.

In the journal *The Economist*, the logo of the Eastern approaches section features Eastern European diacritics:[284]

---

281 http://www.webopedia.com/pronunciationguide.html (2006-01-20, link no longer active)
282 http://de.wikipedia.org/wiki/Molwan%C3%AEen._Land_des_schadhaften_L%C3%A4chelns (2011-11-19)
283 http://de.wikipedia.org/wiki/Phaic_T%C7%8En._Land_des_krampfhaften_L%C3%A4chelns (2011-11-19)
284 http://www.economist.com/blogs/easternapproaches (2014-06-07)

The *Theaterwerkstatt Hannover* drove this to the maximum when they advertised "Īt̃ȟḁ̊k̬ă—or coming home" (with an overkill of diacritics), a play about foreignness and migration.[285]

7.14 Using diacritics to convey currency symbolism

Bitcoin, Litecoin, Peercoin and *Dogecoin*, all cryptocurrencies, are abbreviated by Ƀ (B with stroke), by the Polish letter Ł (L with slash), by the Icelandic letter Ð (Eth) or by Ᵽ (P with stroke), respectively.[286, 287, 288, 289] The aim is probably to make them look like "real" currency symbols (€, $, etc.), probably to raise trust.

---

285 http://www.theaterwerkstatt-hannover.de/?Repertoire:Ithaka_-_oder_nach_Hause_kommen (2011-11-19)
286 http://www.coindesk.com/industry-website-advocate-bitcoins-unicode-symbol/ (2015-01-05)
287 http://en.wikipedia.org/wiki/Litecoin (2014-06-07)
288 http://en.wikipedia.org/wiki/Peercoin (2015-01-05)
289 http://en.wikipedia.org/wiki/Dogecoin (2015-01-05)

7.15 Written with diacritics or not?

- The notation "eckō" provided in the Google search 106,000 results (2012: 203,000; 2006: 59). Here, a change seems to have taken place: the use of macrons based initially on individual initiative, its use is now commonplace.
- The Google search for "Xplōd" yielded about 15,800 hits (2012: 177,000; 2006: 810, so quite a lot). The 2006 results are largely based on a Sony-sponsored racing event. Fearing a phonetic mispronunciation, Sony made the correct spelling with a macron to a condition of the contract.[290] The organizer NHRA installed on the web server a script (search/replace function in Visual Basic)[291] that would automatically change the spelling to Xplōd each time a visitor accessed the expression Xplod.[292] Some of the hits are Latvian sides, which is maybe explained by the fact that the letter ō was in the Latvian alphabet (until 1946).
- Cašmir is marketed since 1991, Cašran since 2000. As I conducted this investigation eight years ago for the first time, I found only on a few

---

[290] Phil Burgess, Editorial Director, NHRA Publications, personal communication (2006-01-20)
[291] <%=Response.Write Replace(rs("StoryText"), "Xplod", " Xpl&#333d ")%>
[292] Jade Davidson, Webmaster NHRA.com, personal communication (2006-01-20)

internet sites with the correct spelling. Exceptions included perfumery Douglas (although not consistently), the internet perfumery Rubion [293, 294] (now defunct) and the internet retailer sweetillusions.com. [295] Correctly spelled, the names appear 2006 on some Czech sites. That makes sense, since š occurs in the Czech alphabet.

Douglas informed me that the correct representation of the product name is part of the respective distribution agreements issued by the manufacturer. After consultation with the company's own internet department, they found out that the diacritics are relatively easy to implement in the design of the internet shop. [296]

Between 2012 and 2014, the frequency dropped from 78,700 to 12,700 entries for ["Cašmir" Chopard] and from 17,300 to 5,010 entries for ["Cašran" Chopard / "Cašran"].

- The Google search for ["Jōvan"] yielded 6,270 hits (2012: 8,460 for ["Jōvan" musk]), so a slight decrease. The quotient "with/without" diacritics slightly rose from 0.5 % to 1 %. So despite the head start in 1972, the spelling with macron has still not been able to enforce itself.

Innēov, nākd and the book Phaic Tăn will be to watch for the next years.

---

293 http://www.rubion.de/10_Casmir.html (2006-01-20, link no longer active)
294 http://www.rubion.de/10_Casran.html (2006-01-20, link no longer active)
295 Sweet Illusions: Cašmir by Chopard Paris
   http://www.sweetillusions.com/w-casmir.html (2011-12-02)
296 Thomas Lau, Perfumery Douglas, personal communication (2006-01-23)

Table 7.1: **Google search (2014)**

Phrase	Google results	compared to 2012
"Mondelēz"	1.590.000	
"Eckō"	106.000	╱
"Hōpital Erasme"	92.500	
"Estēe"	72.300	
"perlēge"	68.600	
"Phaic Tăn"	15.100	
"Xplōd"	14.900	╱╱
"innēov"	12.900	
"Cašmir"	12.700	╱╱
"nākd"	8.680	
"BlāK"	6.740	
"Jōvan"	6.270	╱
"Cašran"	5.010	╱
"snūzNlūz"	2.400	
"Nørdic Mist"	1.920	
"thē Corporation" Bederman	725	
"Cornē" Port-Royal	463	
"Pranarōm"	253	
"Pērēle"	164	
"Wĕbopēdia"	142	
"amǝna"	2	

╱ = decrease
╱╱ = rapid decrease

7.16 Conclusion

Overall, it is clear that there are different motivations for using diacritics as a style element:

- for ESTĒE/Estée, innēov/innéov, Pērēle/Pérèle, perlēge/Perlège, Pranarōm/Pranarôm, Hōpital/Hôpital, Sōrens/Sörens, and Sakė/Saké, the *alienation* is obvious (probably also true for Jōvan and aməna/amena)
- in the case of nākd, thē Corporation, snūzNlūz, Xplōd, Mondelēz and Eckō, there is a *direct phonetic constraint*
- in Wĕbopēdia/Webopedia, it is more the visual emphasis of the *dictionary character*
- in Nørdic Mist, Molvanîa/Phaic Tăn and Îthǻķǎ, diacritics mean *exoticism*
- in YŌURS Footwear, the macron function as allusion for to the *macron-shaped outlines* on the shoe's sole
- in Fïnlay, the trema points function as allusion for *bubbles*.

More difficult is the explanation for the brands Cašmir and Cašran, because it is not about length, shortening or vowel colourings, but actually a phonetically very different pronunciation (/ʃ/ vs. /s/), which implies in principle advanced language skills among consumers. This could be an indication of the increasing impact of globalization and Europeanization, which brings the advertising industry a greater supply of usable characters, but also has led to a general increase of inter-cultural competence among consumers. On the other hand, the use of "cryptic symbols" illustrates the intended exclusivity of the cosmetic products, as the correct pronunciation of these characters outside of their original linguistic context is only accessible to a circle of insiders.

Both the product lines of the brand Chopard (Cašmir, Cašran) and Jōvan belong to perfume manufacturer Coty/Lancaster. A targeted strategy of attracting attention by the use of diacritics can not be derived from it: all other brands of Coty/Lancaster do not use language foreign diacritics.[297]

In general, diacritics represent something new, innovative, unusual, that can be used by the manufacturer's or product logos to differentiate themselves from competitors and catch the eye of the customers and remain in their memory.

Under certain circumstances, the manufacturers of branded goods who employ diacritics, though only as a stylistic device, fulfil a vanguard role: due to the international proliferation of their products, they prepare the ground for the pan-European or global use of diacritics, as consumers—at least subconsciously—are getting used to the presence of diacritics. In addition, brand manufacturers are so far the only name owners who enforce the correct spelling of diacritics by legally sound manner (through distribution or sponsorship agreements).

---

297 List of the brands: http://www.coty.com/brands (2015-05-30)

Figure 7.16: **Brand names not researched:**

JĀSÖN

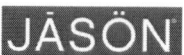

http://www.jasonnaturalcare.co.uk/ (2015-08-05)

Bēhance™

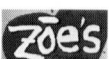

http://grrr.in/wp-content/uploads/2015/01/Behance1.jpg (2015-08-05)

Zoe's

http://www.amazon.com/Zoes-Granola-Almond-Cereal-11-Ounce/dp/B001E5E4G6 (2015-08-05)

PØP UP SABLON

https://www.facebook.com/popupsablon

VISIT

8 How people react to diacritics

8.1 Cartoons, sketches and jokes

- There seems to be a proper sub-genre: the *IKEA cartoon*, which draws a part of its funny effect from employing (written) Scandinavian diacritics. Examples: a tree that exclaims "Help, zømbies!" when he sees furniture escaping from a nearby IKEA shop on a moonlit night,[298] an old lady looking for her husband (who has fallen through an article named "høle"),[299] an IKEA employee in hell who exclaims "Fåck" when he realizes Satan is a tree,[300] a letter-box (company) named "tåx evasiön",[301] a vulture sitting on a cactus named "bårbed",[302] or simply fake IKEA user instructions, e.g.

---

298 http://ruthe.de/cartoon/2356/datum/asc/ (2014-12-14)
299 http://ruthe.de/cartoon/28/datum/asc/ (2014-12-14)
300 http://ruthe.de/cartoon/2738/datum/asc/ (2014-12-14)
301 https://www.facebook.com/extra3/photos/a.126985678917.103880.
 37621248917/10152543680318918/ (2014-12-31)
302 http://www.nichtlustig.de/toondb_iframe/f5f8590cd58a54e94377e6ae2eded4d9.
 html (2014-05-30)

how to build a PC named "elktåuer",³⁰³ a "hädrönn cjölidder"³⁰⁴ or a sex toy named "gäsm".³⁰⁵

- This was foreshadowed by the Muppet character Swedish Chef, e.g. the videos "Pöpcørn"³⁰⁶ (with hilarious captions) or "Cårven Der Pümpkîn".³⁰⁷
- In the parody of German TV series *Aktenzeichen XY... ungelöst* ("file reference XY... unsolved"), which features a Turkish investigator, the logo is changed to *ẌŸ... üngelöst*, a mocking of the frequent use of umlauts in Turkish language:³⁰⁸

- In one episode of *The Onion News Network*, a satirical US website, the video "Prague's Franz Kafka International Named World's Most Alienating Airport" features a row of diacritics (none of them Czech, though):³⁰⁹

---

303 http://www.heise.de/ct/schlagseite/2002/5/gross.jpg (2014-05-29)
304 http://www.collegehumor.com/post/6340023/if-ikea-made-instructions-for-everything (2014-05-30)
305 http://www.thelogoisbigenough.com/post/47263605346/ikea-produces-sex-toy-named-g-sm (2014-05-30)
306 https://www.youtube.com/watch?v=B7UmUX68KtE (2014-12-14)
307 https://www.youtube.com/watch?v=2Qj8PhxSnhg (2014-12-14)
308 http://www.zdf.de/ZDFmediathek/beitrag/video/2356698?fb_ref=Default#/beitrag/video/2356698/Uex-Uepsuelon-Uengeloest (2015-03-07, link no longer active)
309 https://www.youtube.com/watch?v=gEyFH-a-XoQ (2015-05-30)

- In German television show *Bullyparade*, the funny effect of the "Pavel & Bronko" sketches comes from the characters systematically enriching non-Czech words by adding Czech diacritics, especially č (Greenpeače, Greenič Villače, činema, Lopeč, pop-charč, syphilič, peničillin...).[310]

Pavel & Bronko (screen copy)

---

310 http://www.bullybase.de/gsa/search?SearchText=Pavel+%26+Bronko (2014-12-14).

- "[...] And we'll never be able to match the Lithuanian stockpiles of those little 'u' accent marks", O-tone STEPHEN COLBERT during a joke on the US vs. Lithuania (though those are actually v-shaped hačeks).[311]

The Colbert Report, January 11, 2011 (screen copy)

- On the HAZ Soccer fan pages:

»President Ilhan Aliyev recently spoke thus: "Az?rbaycan g?l?c?kd? çox z?ngin v? qüdr?tli ölk?y? h?cking çevril?c?kdir."—There also the fan who is not as savvy in foreign languages notes that the Azerbaijani language is full of question marks for our understanding... and typesetting system.«[312]

(Note: The typesetting system could not deliver the ə.)

---

311 http://thecolbertreport.cc.com/videos/oqami3/lithuania-perfume 0:53ff (2014-05-31)
312 http://www.das-fanmagazin.de/forum/hannover_96/pressebereich/34360-haz_roter_platz/ (2014-12-14)

SETTING SIGNS FOR EUROPE   125

- *The Big Bang Theory* character Amy uses diacritics in her made-up language:[313]

    Big Bang Theory: The Deception Verification (screen copy)

- *xkcd* web comic about the intricacies of Unicode:[314]

---

313 8:31ff
314 http://xkcd.com/1209/ (2014-05-30)

8.2 Decontextualized characters

I came across a Facebook user named BESI GÕNE WILD and asked him about the õ (Livonian diacritic). He said that it was just because Facebook did not allow "gone" in the name.
Unfortunately, there is neither a public list which expressions are prohibited by Facebook nor the possibility of searching for specific diacritics.

But apparently, this incident is part of a bigger picture, not just in user names. Communication designer SIRI POARANGAN:[315]

> This TEDx contribution is conceived as a favourite character-Best-Off, ideal for typographical remix. The freedom to access to the complete Unicode character inventory has led to an explosion of the typographic design freedom. Often characters are decontextualized and used to customize your text. Does Unicode fill the gap that is caused to digital text through the loss of individual handwriting? The variety of 'misappropriated' signs on the social web speaks for it. Let's see which are newly discovered next. I ♥ it.

---

315 http://tedxrheinhessen.de/siri-poarangan-decode-unicode/ (2011-12-30)

Figure 8.1: **Example of decontextualized characters** (screen shots from the TEDx talk)

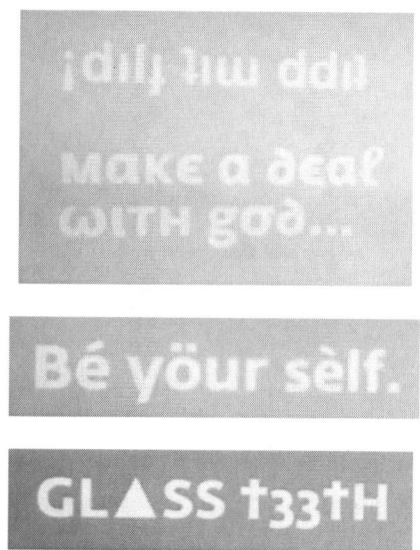

Figure 8.2: **Decontextualized characters with diacritics in various advertising campaigns** (own photo), followed by e.g. "le vöyäge seafãriüs"

Figure 8.3: Decontextualized character with diacritics in an advertising campaign (www.designbyhumans.com)

Figure 8.4: Decontextualized character with diacritics in a poster of the DJ Team Filtertÿpen (own photo)

Contrary to the *Sōrens* example in chapter 7.4 that employed the ō as trademark, the single Ÿ was apparently just used for one mix and T-shirts.[316]

Decontextualized diacritics in a book title[317] and (fake) URL.[318] As explanation, the author writes that she just created the book title from a "funky font".[319]

---

316 https://soundcloud.com/filtertypen/filtertypen-basstime-mix-jan-2010 (2015-08-05)
317 http://www.amazon.com/exec/obidos/tg/stores/detail/-/books/0452295637/reviews (2014-06-01)
318 http://www.darwinawards.com/i/darwin.logo.gif (2014-06-07)
319 http://www.darwinawards.com/misc/faq.html#logo (2014-06-07)

The EU used decontextualized characters in their logo for the 50th anniversary of the Treaty of Rome: [320]

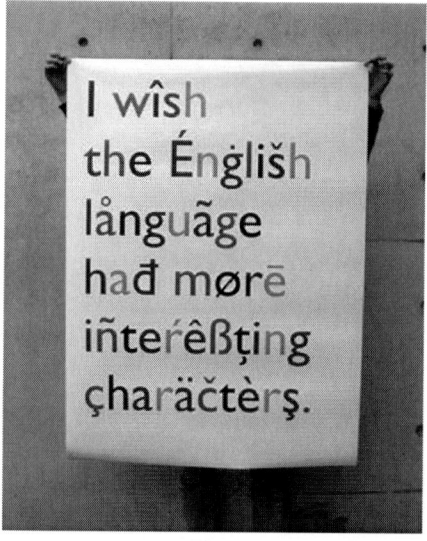

(Poster designed by MICHAEL CIANCIO)

---

320 http://ec.europa.eu/avservices/pdf/manuel_en.pdf (2014-12-14)

9 Legal basics of using diacritics in personal names

The issue of not being able to use diacritics in personal names is clearly a question of *discrimination* on grounds of language. Also, there is special protection of a person's own name by personality rights and by naming rights. These areas of law are covered both by international treaties as well as by Federal laws, which are presented below.

9.1 International agreements

9.1.1 Charter of the United Nations

The *United Nations Charter*[321] of 1945 commands respect for—and observance of—human rights, and prohibits discrimination on the basis of language (Article 1 section. 3, Article 13 b, Article 55 c).

---

321 http://www.unric.org/de/charta (2011-11-30)

9.1.2 Universal Declaration of Human Rights

The *Universal Declaration of Human Rights*,[322] which was proclaimed on 10 December 1948 by the General Assembly of the United Nations, is (as a declaration) not binding under international law. Nevertheless, it is generally regarded as part of United Nations law and as customary international law.[323] The Universal Declaration of Human Rights speaks of human dignity (preamble, Article 1) and equality (Article 7) and prohibits discrimination on the basis of language or national origin (Article 2, para. 1). Private and family life—which includes the right to use a name—are explicitly provided protection (Article 12).

9.1.3 European Convention on Human Rights

The Council of Europe *Convention for the Protection of Human Rights and Fundamental Freedoms* (non-official: ECHR)[324] of 4 November 1950 (as amended by Protocols No. 11, 12,[325] and 14) prohibits discrimination on grounds of language, national origin or membership of a national minority (Article 14). It also emphasizes the right that authorities have to respect private and family life (Article 8, para. 1 and 2), including the right to use the (full)

---

[322] http://www.ohchr.org/EN/UDHR/Pages/Language.aspx?LangID=eng (2014-12-14)
[323] http://de.wikipedia.org/wiki/Allgemeine_Erkl%C3%A4rung_der_Menschenrechte (2011-11-30)
[324] http://conventions.coe.int/treaty/en/treaties/html/005.htm (2014-12-14)
[325] "the enjoyment of any right set forth by law shall be secured without discrimination on any ground such as [...] language, [...] national or social origin, association with a national minority, [...] or other status", protocol No. 12 to the *Convention for the Protection of Human Rights and Fundamental Freedoms*, Council of Europe, opened for signature on 4 November 2000, ETS No. 177, Article 1(l).

family name. This view is also the one of the *European Court of Human Rights* (judgement Burghartz).[326]

All members of the Council of Europe have signed the ECHR. The EU itself has not yet signed but is bound to do so eventually according to Article 6, para. 2 of the EU Treaty.[327] But the *European Court of Justice* issued an opinion in December 2014 that identified a row of legal hurdles that have to be solved first.[328]

9.1.4 UN International Covenant on Civil and Political Rights

The *International Covenant of the United Nations on Civil and Political Rights* (ICCPR) of 19 December 1966 prohibits any discrimination on grounds of language (Article 26). This includes in principle the use of certain diacritics associated with a language. National minorities and their language are particularly protected (Article 27).[329]

9.1.5 Helsinki Final Act

In 1975 in Helsinki, 35 states from the two military blocs existing at that time signed the *Final Act of the Conference on Security and Cooperation in Europe* (CSCE, now OSCE).[330] The document evokes the respect for human rights

---

326 http://hudoc.echr.coe.int/sites/eng/pages/search.aspx?i=001-57865 (2014-12-15)
327 http://de.wikipedia.org/wiki/Europ%C3%A4ische_Menschenrechtskonvention (2014-12-14)
328 http://euobserver.com/justice/126993 (2014-12-31)
329 http://www.ohchr.org/en/professionalinterest/pages/ccpr.aspx (2014-12-14)
330 http://www1.umn.edu/humanrts/osce/basics/finact75.htm (2014-12-14)

and fundamental freedoms, particularly with regard to national minorities, and prohibits discrimination on the basis of language (chapter 1, section VII). It refers to the → *Charter of the United Nations* and the → *Universal Declaration of Human Rights*. The signatory States also commit to observe international law and the provisions of the *Final Act* itself in national law-making (chapter 1, section X). Other chapters emphasize the interest of international harmonization of technical standards and regulations (chapter 2, section 3) as well as cooperation in the fields of electronic data processing and communication (chapter 2, section 4). Among that falls definitely the use of an internationally applicable character set for data exchange.

9.1.6 Convention on the indication of surnames and forenames in civil status registers

The International Commission on Civil Status (ICCS)[331] Convention No. 14 of 13 September 1973 *on the indication of surnames and forenames in civil status registers* aims at ensuring that in all Contracting States surnames and forenames of a person, without regard to their nationality, are *uniformly* entered in the civil status registers. The Convention limits itself to prescribe how the names are entered. The regulations in each Contracting State for the acquisition, change and loss of name are not affected by the Convention.

---

331 French *Commission Internationale de l'Etat Civil* (CIEC)

It is valid for Austria, Belgium, Germany, Greece, Italy, Luxembourg, the Netherlands and Turkey.[332, 333]

In the case of foreign language certificates in which the names are written with the same *script* as in the language in which the entry in a civil status registers is to be made, the family name and given names must be reproduced *to the letter*—without *any* changes—from the foreign language certificate (Article 2). The literal reproduction also applies to the diacritical marks (dashes, dots, hooks, and others), even if the language in which the entry is made does not know them.

> For example, the letters "ä", "ö" and "ü" must be rendered with umlaut/diaeresis; they may not be broken up to "ae", "oe" and "ue".[334]

The German Federal Ministry of the Interior emphasized in his reports to the Council of Europe pursuant to Article 15, para. 1 of the *European Charter for Regional or Minority Languages* (see chapter 9.1.10):

> The specifics of the spelling of names of members of national minorities is taken into account in the »Instructions to the registrars and their

---

332 ICCS Secretariat: List of Conventions and of the signatories http://www.ciec1.org/SignatRatifConv.pdf (2011-10-27)

333 Although they are also ICCS Member States, France and Switzerland have not signed the agreement, as well as the later members Spain, Croatia, Hungary, Poland, Portugal and the UK.

334 Simader, August / Suppa, Rudolf *(Hrsgg.): Handakten für die standesamtliche Arbeit, Heft 15 / Leitfaden für die Standesbeamten, Folge 79: ISO-Transliterationsnormen für die Umwandlung ausländischer Schriften in lateinische Buchstaben*, Verlag für Standesamtswesen, Frankfurt am Main 1977

supervisors«,[335] i.e. diacritical marks (accents, hooks, etc.) contained in names or other words reproduced without change.[336, 337]

However, the Convention applies only to civil status registers, not to other documents from administration like certificates.

9.1.7 Document of the Copenhagen Meeting

The 1990 *Document of the Copenhagen Meeting of the Conference on the Human Dimension of the CSCE*[338] emphasizes the importance of respect for human rights and fundamental freedoms for peace in Europe (preamble, No. 1, 5, 5.7). It also contains a binding declaration on the rights (especially for linguistic identity), the protection and promotion of national minorities (No. 31, 32), referring to the → *UN International Covenant on Civil and Political Rights* and the → *Universal Declaration of Human Rights* (No. 24). Explicitly, any attempts of forced assimilation are denied (No. 32) and the right to use one's own language in public is stressed (No. 32.1). That must also include the use of one's name in the correct spelling through authorities (No. 5.5).

---

335 previously § 49 section 1, now A 1.1.2
http://www.personenstandsrecht.de/SharedDocs/Downloads/PERS/Themen/Rechtsquellen/allgvv.pdf?__blob=publicationFile (2014-12-15)
336 http://www.coe.int/t/dg4/education/minlang/Report/PeriodicalReports/GermanyPR1_en.pdf (2011-11-30)
337 http://www.coe.int/t/dg4/education/minlang/Report/PeriodicalReports/GermanyPR2_en.pdf (2011-11-30)
338 http://www.osce.org/odihr/elections/14304?download=true (2014-12-14)

9.1.8 Charter of Paris for a New Europe

The Heads of State and Government of the 34 CSCE States agreed on 19 November 1990 on their Paris summit in their *Charter of Paris for a New Europe*[339] that the division of Europe was ended. They committed themselves to democracy as the only form of government and ensured their peoples the guarantee of human rights and fundamental freedoms with reference to the → *Helsinki Final Act* and the → *Document of the Copenhagen Meeting*, including the protection of linguistic minorities and—this is new—migrant workers. Explicit reference is made to the protection and promotion of European cultural heritage, linguistic diversity being undoubtedly a part of it.

9.1.9 UN Declaration on Minority Rights

In more a general formulation, the 1992 *UN Declaration on Minority Rights* provides that "States shall protect the existence and the national or ethnic, cultural, religious and linguistic identity of minorities within their respective territories and shall encourage conditions for the promotion of that identity" (Article 1, para. 1). Furthermore, "[s]tates shall adopt appropriate legislative and other measures to achieve those ends" (Article 1, para. 2).[340]

---

339 http://www.osce.org/mc/39516?download=true (2014-12-14)
340 http://www.un.org/documents/ga/res/47/a47r135.htm (2015-03-29)

9.1.10 European Charter for Regional or Minority Languages

The *European Charter for Regional or Minority Languages* of the Council of Europe (1992)[341] provides for the protection and promotion of the *historical* regional and minority languages in Europe and emphasizes the cultural diversity as one of Europe's guiding principles. It refers to the → *UN International Covenant on Civil and Political Rights*, the Council of Europe → *Convention for the Protection of Human Rights*, the → *Helsinki Final Act*, and the → *Document of the Copenhagen Meeting*. The use of a regional or minority language in public life is seen as an inalienable right.

The Charter first lists the objectives and principles to which the Contracting Parties have to commit themselves for all regional and minority languages which are spoken on their territory: recognition as an expression of cultural wealth, need for promoting, facilitating its use and/or encouragement for their use in speech and writing in public life and the private sphere. Furthermore, the Charter sets out on a whole series of specific measures to promote the use of regional or minority languages in public life. These measures include, *inter alia*, education, law, administrative authorities, public services, and the media. Regarding the right to a name, particularly Article 10.5 is crucial: "The Parties commit themselves to allow the use or adoption of family names in the regional or minority languages, at the request of those concerned."

Each Contracting Party undertakes to apply a minimum of 35 paragraphs of this action plan, including a certain number of mandatory measures that are to select from a "core area" (Article 2.2). In addition, each Party shall

---

341 http://conventions.coe.int/Treaty/EN/Treaties/Html/148.htm (2014-12-15)

list in its instrument of ratification or declaration of acceptance all the regional or minority languages, common all throughout their territory or a part thereof, to which the selected paragraphs apply (Article 3.1).

Note that the obligations of the Charter do explicitly *not* refer to the languages of migrants (Article 1 a iii.), but only to the languages of "historically grown minorities".

The Charter has been ratified by 25 Council of Europe countries. Azerbaijan, France, Iceland, Italy, Macedonia, Malta, Moldova, and Russia have signed but not yet ratified.[342] France has signed but has been blocked from ratifying it by the Constitutional Council, as it would contradict the constitutional provision enshrining French as the language of the Republic.[343] Albania, Andorra, Belgium, Bulgaria, Estonia, Georgia, Greece, Ireland, Latvia, Lithuania, Monaco, Portugal, San Marino and Turkey have not signed (about minorities in Lithuania and Turkey see chapter 10).

In Germany, official minorities are the Danes, Frisians, Roma, Sinti and Sorbs (but not the Poles). But the Sorbian language, which cannot be represented adequately by the character set ISO 8859-1, should have been reason enough to switch the German administration to Unicode so that the requirements of Article 10 of the Charter are fulfilled.

The application of the Charter is controlled by a committee of experts which has the task of reviewing the reports submitted regularly by the States Parties. In its fifth national report (2013), they still see need for action in Germany:[344]

---

[342] http://de.wikipedia.org/wiki/Europ%C3%A4ische_Charta_der_Regional-_oder_Minderheitensprachen (2014-12-15)
[343] http://en.wikipedia.org/wiki/Languages_of_France (2014-12-15)
[344] http://www.coe.int/t/dg4/education/minlang/Report/EvaluationReports/GermanyECRML5_en.pdf (2014-12-15)

200. The Lower Sorbian speakers, however, informed the Committee of Experts that, according to an October 2012 statement of the Land Government, using Lower Sorbian in administration would be an unreasonable burden in technical and organisational terms. [...] In addition, it was stated that the correct use of Lower Sorbian in the electronic data processing system is very difficult, due to the lack of special characters. The Committee of Experts asks the authorities to comment on these allegations.

211. [...] there is no legal guarantee of the possibility to use the masculine and feminine forms of the names in Sorbian. In addition, problems relating to the correct spelling of family names in Lower Sorbian were reported (see paragraph 200).

212. The Committee of Experts asks the authorities to provide specific information in this respect in the next periodical report.

9.1.11 Framework Convention for the Protection of National Minorities

The *Framework Convention for the Protection of National Minorities*[345] of the Council of Europe (1995), in force since 1998, is the first legally binding multilateral European Convention on the protection of persons belonging to national minorities in general. It was ratified by 39 Council of Europe members (signed by 43). France (see chapter 9.1.10) and Turkey have not signed.[346]

In the preamble, emphasis is made on human rights, fundamental freedoms, and the enrichment by cultural diversity; the aforementioned international treaties are referenced.

---

345 http://conventions.coe.int/Treaty/EN/Treaties/Html/157.htm (2014-12-15)
346 http://en.wikipedia.org/wiki/Framework_Convention_for_the_Protection_of_National_Minorities (2014-12-15)

In this work, particularly Article 11.1 of the Convention is important: it admits the right to persons belonging to national minorities to lead their names in the minority language and explicitly the right to official recognition of that name. However, due to the very general reference to the "conditions of the legal systems of the Contracting Parties", the Contracting States retain a too large degree of discretion. For example, it is according to the Explanatory Report,[347] clause 68, allowed that states use the alphabet of their official language for a *phonetic* spelling of the names of members of a national minorities, i.e. v instead of w (Polish minority in Lithuania,[348] Kurdish minority in Turkey[349, 350]) or s, sh, sz, sch instead of š (Slovenian minority in Austria).[351]

In Article 5.2, the signatories also undertake it to protect persons belonging to national minorities against any measure aimed at assimilation. As such, one can view the subliminal or open pressure to change their name by waiving diacritics, which is often exercised by authorities. Article 5.1 requires Parties to promote the conditions necessary to ensure that persons

---

347 http://conventions.coe.int/Treaty/en/Reports/Html/157.htm (2011-11-30)
348 http://www.eurotopics.net/en/home/presseschau/archiv/results/archiv_article/ARTICLE113580-Poland-and-Lithuania-at-odds-over-bagatelles (2014-12-15)
349 http://web.archive.org/web/20070628171743/http://www.unhchr.ch/minorities/statements10/CLA3a.doc (2014-12-15)
350 Turkey Legalizes the Letters Q, W, and X. http://www.slate.com/blogs/lexicon_valley/2013/10/24/turkey_prime_minister_erdogan_s_democratizaton_package_legalizes_letters.html (2014-12-15)
351 *Bericht des Österreichischen Volksgruppenzentrums zur Durchführung des Europäischen Rahmenübereinkommens zum Schutz nationaler Minderheiten in der Republik Österreich* http://www.greekhelsinki.gr/bhr/english/articles/shadow_report_austria.doc (2011-11-30)

belonging to national minorities can preserve their linguistic identity. For authorities, this results in the need to switch to the Universal Character Set / Unicode, which also contains the diacritics of minority languages (Sorbian in the case of Germany).

The Parties are required to submit written state reports on the measures taken to comply with the obligations under the Framework Convention measures. The Committee of Ministers of the Council of Europe, which is advised by an committee of independent experts, monitors implementation of the Convention, that is, the fulfilment of the commitments under the Framework Convention by the States Parties, and gives them recommendations if necessary.[352]

However, the Framework Convention unfolds no *direct* domestic legal effects. Instead, it is to perform by "compliance laws" (formal laws or legal regulations, if an appropriate statutory authorization already exists). This means that the rules of the Framework Convention itself cannot be enforced by the administrative authorities or courts and that persons belonging to national minorities cannot derive subjective rights from the provisions of the Framework Convention at the national level.[353]

9.1.12 Oslo Recommendations Regarding the Linguistic Rights of National Minorities

The *Oslo Recommendations Regarding the Linguistic Rights of National Minorities*, adopted by the High Commissioner on National Minorities of the Organization for Security and Cooperation in Europe (OSCE), further explain:

---

352 http://conventions.coe.int/Treaty/EN/Treaties/Html/157.htm (2014-12-15)
353 http://www.greekhelsinki.gr/bhr/english/articles/shadow_report_austria.doc (2011-11-30)

Persons belonging to national minorities have the right to use their personal names in their own language according to their own traditions and linguistic systems. These shall be given official recognition and be used by the public authorities.[354]

9.1.13 Bilateral agreements

An in practice largely ignored international legal document is the *Treaty between the Federal Republic of Germany and the Republic of Poland on Good-neighbourliness and Friendly Cooperation* of 17 June 1991.[355] Although it is "only" a bilateral contract, the term "Europe" or "European" is very often used. Also the content of the Treaty is heavily influenced by the spirit of Europe: human rights, human dignity, fundamental freedoms and the protection of minorities (Articles 1, 2, 8) are invoked, as are mutual cultural enrichment and European cultural heritage (preamble). In addition, the *direct* application of the general rules of international law in domestic law is highlighted (Article 2). Also explicit reference is made on the above contract works such as the → *Helsinki Final Act* and the → *Charter of Paris for a New Europe* (Article 2). Explicit statements about the legally correct spelling of names is found in Article 20:

> (1) The members of the German minority in the Republic of Poland, that is, persons of Polish nationality who are of German descent or who profess the German language, culture or tradition, as well as persons of German nationality in the Federal Republic of Germany of Polish descent or who profess the Polish language, culture or tradition, have the right [...] to freely express,

---

354 http://www.osce.org/hcnm/67531?download=true (2015-03-29)
355 *Bulletin des Presse- und Informationsamtes der Bundesregierung,* 18 June 1991, No. 68, p. 541–546

> preserve and develop their linguistic identity; free from any attempts to be assimilated against their will. [...]
>
> (3) The Contracting Parties declare that the persons referred to in paragraph 1 shall in particular have the right [...]—to their first and last name in the form of the mother tongue [...]

Article 20 para. 1 clearly prohibits the application of pressure for the purpose of assimilating adaptation of Polish names in the German alphabet (in reality, however, see chapter 9.3.6). In Article 21 para. 1, both countries commit to protect and promote the linguistic identity of the respective minority. This used to be difficult to implement in administrative practice, as until recently both states used in their IT two different (and mutually incompatible) 8-bit character sets (ISO 8859-1 in Germany, ISO 8859-2 in Poland, now both Unicode).[356]

According to Article 18 para. 3, the Parties shall seek an extension, improvement and harmonization of the German-Polish communication links, taking into account the European and international standardization and development in technology, which is especially true for data connections. Article 18 may be considered as the basis for a transformation of the German and the Polish IT infrastructure for supporting the Universal Character Set / Unicode, both for interstate data exchange as well as (with regard to Article 20 section 1 and section 3, indent 1) at national level.

---

356 Maciej Szczygieł, Department of Teleinformatics, Ministry of the Interior, personal communication

On a general level,[357]

> [i]t is obvious, that bilateral agreements on reciprocal protection of national minorities can be more easily adapted to the particular needs of the Parties and the national minorities, residing in the territories of two neighboring States, and thus more effective. [...] For instance, at the time of the ratification of the Framework Convention Poland submitted a declaration reaffirming its readiness to implement the Convention by concluding bilateral agreements.[358] [...][359]
>
> [...] However, some of [the bilateral agreements] contain slightly different formulations that could be interpreted as more favorable to national minorities. For instance, the Treaty on Good-neighbourly Relations and Friendly Co-operation between the Republic of Hungary and Slovakia confirms the right of the Hungarian minority in Slovakia and Slovak minority in Hungary "to *register* and use their names and surnames in this [minority] language".[360] [The a]greement between Hungary and Croatia on the reciprocal protection of national minorities imposes the obligation on the Contracting Parties to ensure for the members of the minorities "the *free* use and

---

357 R. Satkauskas: Use of diacritics: towards a new standard of minority protection?
http://www.lvb.lt/primo_library/libweb/action/dlDisplay.do?vid=LDB&docId=TLITLIJ.04~2008~1367164906657&fromSitemap=1&afterPDS=true (2015-03-14)
358 "The Republic of Poland shall also implement the Framework Convention under Article 18 of the Convention by conclusion of international agreements mentioned in this Article, the aim of which is to protect national minorities in Poland and minorities or groups of Poles in other States." Text of the declaration from the Archives of the Treaty Office of the Council of Europe.
359 See for general approach Defeis E. F., 'Minority Protection and Bilateral Agreements: an Effective Mechanism', Hastings International and Comparative Law Review 22, 1999, p. 291–321
360 Treaty on Good-neighbourly Relations and Friendly Co-operation between the Republic of Hungary and the Slovak Republic of 19 March 1995, Article 15 (g), emphasis added.

registration of their *original* first names and surnames". ³⁶¹
None of the bilateral agreements contain provisions concerning the obligatory recognition of diacritics. [...]

The meaning of these provisions therefore can be found when looking at their implementation in the national legislation of the Parties. In Hungary, for instance, individuals belonging to a minority can "*register* their family names in line with the rules of *their* native language, and, within the framework defined in the legal regulations to have them appear in official documents". [...] ³⁶²

The overall impression after having examined the provisions of bilateral agreements concerning the use of minority names is that they tend to grant the rights to write the names according the grammar rules (by adding or omitting suffixes, endings, etc.) of minority languages but not the use of its [alphabet]. [...] However, [bilateral agreements] do not provide the definitive answer whether those principles encompass the right to use diacritics in official documents. [...]

Even though the majority of the State Parties to the Charter do not expressly prohibit the use of diacritics, only a few of them have indicated in their periodic reports as having already enacted domestic measures allowing the use of diacritics in their civil registers thus granting the members of national minorities the right to bear their names in the minority language, [...].
Probably the most protective system has been created in Slovenia where the languages of Italian and Hungarian national minorities have been granted

---

361 Convention between the Republic of Hungary and the Republic of Croatia on the protection of the Hungarian minority in the Republic of Croatia and the Croatian minority in the Republic of Hungary of 5 April 1995, Article 4, para. 1, emphasis added.
362 Report of Hungary under the Framework Convention, note 32 infra, emphasis added.

status of official languages.³⁶³ The Law on Personal Names of the Republic of Slovenia provides that the personal names of a member of the Italian or Hungarian national minority shall be entered in Italian or Hungarian [alphabet] and form [...].³⁶⁴ Bilingual documents are compulsory for the population on an ethnically mixed territory regardless of their national origin. In addition to the identity card (the form is trilingual: Slovene/Italian – Hungarian/English), passports (the passport is quadrilingual: Slovene/Italian – Hungarian/English/French) and passes for crossing the border in the border areas with Italy and Hungary, driving licences and certificates of registration, health insurance cards and weapons certificates are also bilingual.³⁶⁵ As stressed in the Initial Periodic Report by Slovenia under the Minority Languages Charter: "The provision that a record in the national community language must take into account the rules of writing of the Hungarian and Italian [alphabet], respectively, is *part of the inherent right of members of the national communities to use their mother tongue.*"³⁶⁶

Use of foreign diacritics is also officially recognised in Italy. Law No. 935 of 31 October 1966, amending the decree of 9 July 1939, established *inter alia*

---

363 Article 11 of the Constitution of the Republic of Slovenia reads: "The official language in Slovenia is Slovene. In those municipalities where Italian or Hungarian national communities reside, Italian or Hungarian shall also be official languages."

364 *Personal Name Act* (Uradni list RS, No. 2/87), Article 3: "The personal name of a member of the Italian or Hungarian nationality shall be recorded in the Italian or Hungarian script and form, unless otherwise decided by a member of this nationality." [...] See Initial Periodical Report by Slovenia under the Minority Languages Charter, note 32 supra.

365 The use of language by the national communities is also guaranteed in some main acts. See *Register of Births, Marriages and Deaths Act* (Uradni list RS, No. 2/87) Article 30, para. 2, *Personal Identity Card Act* (Uradni list RS No. 75/97, 5 December 1997) Article 6 and *Passports of Citizens of the Republic of Slovenia Act* (Uradni list RS, No. 65/2000) Article 13.

366 Report of Slovenia under the Framework Convention, note 32 supra, emphasis added.

that "foreign forenames given to children of Italian nationality must be written in the letters of the Italian alphabet, including the letters J, K, X, Y and W. In case of children belonging to the recognised linguistic minorities, the forenames may be written using the above-mentioned letters together with the diacritical signs of the alphabet of the language of the minority in question".

In Denmark, the names of members of the German minority, including the letters ü and ö are recognized in public and private relations.[367] [...]

Poland's new law on national minorities came into force on 1 May 2005 providing the right to the members of a minority to spell their names and surnames in passports and civil registers according to the orthographies of their own language. [...][368] Besides, Poland declares itself ready to issue identity documents using diacritics even before the adoption of the said Law.[369]

Others, without referring directly, changed their domestic legislation and allowed the use of diacritics after acceding to these Conventions.[370] [...]

Finally, the vast majority of State Parties to the Framework Convention and the Minority Languages Charter have not adopted this practice and, to be stressed, this was not considered a violation of the international norms. If the positive effect of the use of diacritics in preserving the identity of national minorities is obvious, then, what may be the reasons of those States in depriving them of this advantage?

---

367 Report of Denmark under the Framework Convention, note 32 supra
368 *Law on national and ethnical minorities and regional languages* [Ustawa o mniejszościach narodowych i etnicznych oraz o języku regionalnym] of 6 April 2005, Article 10, http://mniejszosci.narodowe.mac.gov.pl/download/86/16013/ustawaoMNiEijezreg-tekstujednolicony-9VII14.pdf, accessed 31 May 2015. See also Polish second report on implementation of Framework Convention, note 32 supra.
369 See for instance report of Slovenia, note 32 supra
370 See report of Germany, note 38 supra

The author then cites identity-integration conflict, i.e. the necessity to ensure the integration of national minorities into society, especially if there is only one official state language (France, Lithuania, etc.). That leads me to believe that bilateral agreements, though a noble cause, will not solve the problem. One has to think one level higher: *all* Latin languages—not only the minority languages—should be written with the appropriate diacritics, in any European country that uses the Latin script!

9.2 EU law

According to Article 6 para. 1 of the *Lisbon Treaty*, the Union is based, among other things, on the principles of respect for human rights. Under para. 2, the Union also respects the fundamental rights guaranteed by the → *European Convention on Human Rights*. Under Article 18 of the *Treaty on the Functioning of the European Union* (TFEU), any discrimination on grounds of nationality is prohibited. Thus the consistent spelling of personal names in accordance with national law of the name carrier must be met, even when the person is staying in another EU Member State. On the other hand, in the discriminations prohibited by Article 19.1 TFEU, language is not listed, only in the *Charter of Fundamental Rights of the European Union* (which is not legally binding in the UK and Poland): respect and protection of human dignity (Article 1), respect for private and family life (Article 7), equality before the law (Article 20), prohibition of discrimination on grounds of language or membership of a national minority (Article 21), respecting the diversity of cultures and languages by the Union (Article 22).[371]

---

371 http://bookshop.europa.eu/is-bin/INTERSHOP.enfinity/WFS/
EU-Bookshop-Site/en_EN/-/EUR/ViewPublication-Start?PublicationKey=
QC3209190 (2014-12-14)

A second starting point are trans-European networks, the construction and promotion of which is one of the activities of the Union according to Article 4.2 (h) TFEU. Priorities according to Article 170 TFEU are the telecommunications infrastructure (para. 1) and the interconnection and interoperability of national networks (para. 2). Pursuant to Article 171, section 1, the Union "shall implement any measures that may prove necessary to ensure the interoperability of the networks, in particular in the field of technical standardisation" to achieve these objectives. From this, one can derive the need for an EU-wide conversion of the interstate data exchange to the Universal Character Set / Unicode standard.

After lobbying the European Parliament, the European Commission, news agencies and national media, I got a first real "foot in the door" in CEN/TC 304 (scope: standardization in the field of information technology as applied to character sets).[372] They prepared a proposal in 2011 *("define the summary repertoire for use in name writing in European public registers, especially in the light of current and potential future legal requirements")* and tried to secure European Commission co-funding. The Federal administration of Germany, who meanwhile had warmed up to the topic of legal character set interoperability (after years of lobbying), would have been the co-sponsor (through the German national standardization body DIN).

The European Commission did unfortunately not fund the CEN proposal. Their argumentation was that there was already the overarching UCS/Unicode standard, not considering that it was highly impractical (113,000 characters and counting, including various non-European scripts that would have to

---

372 French *Comité Européen de Normalisation*, European Committee for Standardization

SETTING SIGNS FOR EUROPE 151

be covered with fonts), while there was still no legal guarantee for even an extended Latin subset (as it had been not defined).

The Federal administration of Germany went on with a national subset of foreign Latin characters (see chapter 9.3, with my participation),[373] as did e.g. Austria (see chapter 9.4), the Netherlands (see chapter 10.4), Sweden,[374] and probably some more countries.

9.3 German law

9.3.1 SAGA

For the initiative *Bund Online 2005*, a comprehensive standardization approach called SAGA *(Standards and Architectures for e-Government Applications)* was created. It holds all the technical norms, standards and architectures that apply to the e-government across the Federation. The Federal Ministry of the Interior is proposing these standards and architectures. The final proposal comes from the clues and comments from the public forum,[375] the assessment by the commission of experts, and the eventual formulation produced by the authors. The Ministry makes then sure to align with

---

373 https://books.google.be/books?id=3ZlB147dg1QC&pg=PA105&lpg=PA105&dq=Kappenberg-Listen+sein&source=bl&ots=3PCUzL0nE5&sig=78GGMNHYiWTTq0PWrWT-8xJ25HY&hl=de&sa=X&ei=bvqmVLekG8irU4fPgpgL&ved=0CC0Q6AEwAg#v=onepage&q=Kappenberg-Listen%20sein&f=false (2015-01-03)
374 http://sv.wikipedia.org/wiki/E-n%C3%A4mnden (2015-02-15)
375 http://de.wikipedia.org/wiki/Standards_und_Architekturen_f%C3%BCr_E-Government-Anwendungen (2014-12-15)

Federal government departments. SAGA is updated periodically and adjusted to the latest developments and findings.[376]

In SAGA version 2.1[377] under the heading "Character Sets", the use of ISO 10646-1:2000 / Unicode v3.0 UTF-8 was classified as "obligatory" for documents in HTML format[378] and for the exchange of data[379] in order to have available enough different characters for the worldwide existing letters, numbers and symbols. Under the next lower category "recommended", there was unfortunately still (due to their high distribution) the 8-bit character sets ISO 8859-1 and -15, which are inadequate for the processing all diacritics. These were however moved in SAGA 3.0 onto the "grey list", i.e. they enjoy still grandfathering but should no longer to be used in *new* projects, since the use offers no advantages over UTF-8.[380] SAGA 4.0 raised the bar to ISO 10646:2003 / Unicode v4.x UTF-8.[381]

Meanwhile SAGA 5.0 is adopted.[382] "Obligatory" is now at least version Unicode v2.1 (introduction of the € symbol).

---

[376] http://www.cio.bund.de/Web/DE/Architekturen-und-Standards/SAGA/saga_node.html (2014-12-15)

[377] http://www.cio.bund.de/SharedDocs/Publikationen/DE/Architekturen-und-Standards/SAGA/archiv_saga_2_1_download.pdf?__blob=publicationFile (2014-12-15)

[378] 8.5.1.4

[379] 8.4.2

[380] http://www.cio.bund.de/SharedDocs/Publikationen/DE/Architekturen-und-Standards/bestandsschutzliste_download.pdf?__blob=publicationFile (2011-11-04)

[381] http://www.cio.bund.de/SharedDocs/Publikationen/DE/Architekturen-und-Standards/SAGA/saga_4_0_englisch_download.pdf?__blob=publicationFile (2014-12-15)

[382] http://www.cio.bund.de/SharedDocs/Publikationen/DE/Architekturen-und-Standards/SAGA/saga_modul_tech_spez_de_bund_5_0_download.pdf?__blob=publicationFile (2014-12-15)

9.3.2 Civil Status Act

General Administrative Regulation on the Civil Status Act:[383]

> A 1.1.2
>
> After the Convention of 13 September 1973 on the indication of surnames and forenames in civil status registers [...], States Parties undertake to enter the names of individuals uniform without regard to their nationality.

At the time the Convention had been agreed, civil status documents were *written by hand*. But the new *Civil Status Act*[384] that came into force in 2009 made *electronic* civil status accounting mandatory (§ 3 para. 2).
Technical delays have, however, postponed the conversion:

> § 75 Transitional certification
> Registry offices which on 1 January 2009 do not yet have an outfit for the electronic management of the civil status register (§ 3 para. 2), enact the civil status events in a transitional period ending not later than on 31 December 2013, in a paper register. [...]

During the preparation of the new *Civil Status Act*, a commission was set up, comprising representatives of Federal and *Länder* level and the Federation of registry officers *(Bundesverband der Deutschen Standesbeamtinnen und Standesbeamten)*, to propose ordinances (implementing rules) for the structure of the electronic register, e.g. to set uniform national standards and benchmarks for the construction, on-screen representation, and communication (file formats, definition of interfaces, protocols) on the basis of § 73

---

383 *Allgemeine Verwaltungsvorschrift zum Personenstandsgesetz*
http://www.personenstandsrecht.de/SharedDocs/Downloads/PERS/Themen/Rechtsquellen/allgvv.pdf?__blob=publicationFile (2014-12-15)

384 *Personenstandsgesetz* http://www.gesetze-im-internet.de/pstg/ (2014-12-15)

No. 3 a) and 4 of the *Personenstandsrechtsreformgesetz*.[385] Federal and *Länder* level and communities should meanwhile develop common approaches with the aim of a far-reaching harmonization of IT use. It would largely depend on the proposals of that commission whether the topic "unchanged takeover of diacritics in civil status registers" would be sufficiently considered in the resulting uniform Federal implementing regulations.

For example, after the transitional period expired on 31 December 2013, the civil register is now only kept electronically. A registrar cannot insert diacritics by hand any more that are not present in the → *registration office software*. Strictly speaking, the new law was authoritative for the content of entries already with its coming into force. However, the possibility for manual insertion of diacritics would have been necessary in a non-Unicode-compatible electronic system to comply with the international ICCS Convention No. 14 / General Administrative Regulation on the Civil Status Act, A 1.1.2.

The only way to escape this dilemma was to issue a Federal ordinance—at the latest upon entry into force of the new *Civil Status Act*—to make the Universal Character Set / Unicode the mandatory character set in registry office software (and to give software developers time to adjust to it).

I have pointed this out to the person responsible in the Federal Ministry of the Interior[386] and it was taken into account:

---

385 *Personenstandsrechtsreformgesetz* http://www.bmi.bund.de/SharedDocs/Gesetzestexte/DE/PStRG.pdf?__blob=publicationFile (2014-12-15)
386 Rainer Bockstette, *Bundesministerium des Innern, Referat V 5a - Verwaltungsrecht und Verwaltungsverfahrensrecht, Personenstandswesen und Namensrecht*, personal communication (2005-12-19)

Regulation on the implementation of the Civil Status Act (Civil Status Ordinance, November 2008):[387]

> § 15 para. (3)
> The certification data shall be collected in the Latin alphabet; diacritics are reproduced without changes. The character set ISO/IEC 10646:2003 in the UTF-8 encoding is to use.

9.3.2.1 XPersonenstand—standardization of data interchange formats in civil status information

XPersonenstand is part of the *Online Services Computer Interface's* (OSCI) XML standards in public administration (XÖV, see chapter 9.3.3.1).[388] The project goal was to define data exchange formats, interfaces, and standards that allow in the field of civil status information a seamless electronic data exchange between registry offices on one side and citizens, other authorities (tax offices, pension institutions, youth services, etc.) or service providers (undertaker, collection agencies, etc.) on the other side.

Since it is an XML-based standard, Unicode (UTF-8 or -16) is in principle supported (Unicode 4.0 in XML 1.1). The data exchange formats in XPersonenstand should—as far as there defined—be built up on the results of the project → XMeld.

To avoid loss of information and data corruption, all diacritics according to *Civil Status Ordinance* § 15 must also be transmittable by XPersonenstand. Therefore, the Universal Character Set / Unicode must be defined as the character set for the corresponding elements.

---

387 *Personenstandsverordnung*
  http://www.gesetze-im-internet.de/pstv/BJNR226300008.html (2014-12-15)
388 http://www.xoev.de/sixcms/detail.php?gsid=bremen02.c.730.de (2011-12-30)

I have brought a proposal to the working group "XPersonenstand"[389] where it was taken into account:[390]

> **1.5 Technische Grundsätze des Aufbaus von XPersonenstand**
> [...] 4 As *character encoding* for XPersonenstand is set UTF-8.
> In the electronic message, only Latin characters within the meaning of § 15 paragraph 3 Civil Status [Ordinance][391] are allowed. This is technically assured by the use of XÖV data type String.Latin. Messages that contain Latin characters that are not included in the data type String.Latin are to be shipped conventionally.

9.3.2.2 Registration office software

The registration office software *AutiSta*, was developed by the *Verlag für Standesamtswesen* (VfSt). It has a monopoly since with the end of the year 2011 the company PROFI AG dropped further development and software maintenance of the competitor OpenElViS.[392] The first version of this program was introduced in 1985 and has since been constantly evolving, both professionally and technically. In the years 2006 to 2008, the program was completely redeveloped in Java (AutiSta 8, current version 10).[393] AutiSta can perform all tasks prescribed by the new → *Civil Status Act* and also takes into account all the different regulations of the *Länder*.[394] It also could cope with the transitional period until the final conversion to the electronic

---

389 Claudia Hertkens, work group XPersonenstand, personal communication (2005-12-16)
390 http://xpsw.domap.de/xpsw160/spezifikation.pdf (2014-12-15)
391 "Ordinance" is missing in the original
392 Torsten Reichmann, *Geschäftsbereich Öffentlicher Dienst* PROFI Engineering Systems AG, personal communication (2011-11-25)
393 https://www.vfst.de/autista/allgemeines/geschichte (2014-12-15)
394 https://www.vfst.de/autista/allgemeines/leistungsbeschreibung (2015-05-31)

media, and thus the coexistence of different technologies.[395] By acquisition of already entered data in other data fields, the program reduces a source of error in the spelling of names with diacritics. In an easy-to-use table with reminding function, all diacritics necessary for civil status registers are offered.[396]

9.3.3 Regulatory reporting

The *Regulatory reporting Framework Act*[397] makes no reference to diacritics, but it is stated where this might be the case: ordinances.

> § 20 Legal regulations for data transmissions
> (1) The Federal Government shall be authorized by issuing ordinances [...] to define the details concerning the method of transmission.
> (2) The Federal Ministry of the Interior is hereby authorized by issuing ordinances [...] to determine the form of the data and further details concerning the method of transmission.
> (3) On the form of data and method of delivery in accordance with para. 1 and 2, reference can be made to easily accessible notices from expert bodies [...]

---

395 https://www.vfst.de/produkt/site/10911-0?begriff=autista%20produktbeschreibung (2014-12-15)
396 https://www.vfst.de/autista/allgemeines/leistungsbeschreibung/komfortfunktionen (2014-12-15)
397 *Melderechtsrahmengesetz*
http://www.gesetze-im-internet.de/mrrg/BJNR014290980.html (2014-12-16)

Since May 2015, the Regulatory reporting Framework Act is overridden by the *Federal regulatory reporting Act*:[398]

> § 56 Authorization of ordinances
>
> (1) The Federal Ministry of the Interior is hereby authorized, by issuing ordinances [...] to define the form of the data to be transmitted and further details concerning the method of transmission [...]
>
> (2) As far as form and procedures of data transfers are to be determined in ordinances under this Act, reference can be made to easily accessible notices from expert bodies [...]

First Federal regulatory reporting data transmission ordinance:[399]

> § 2 Form and procedure for data transfers
>
> (3) When data transfers referred to in paragraph 1 are to be made, they shall be based on the record description OSCI XMeld [...]
>
> (5) The DSMeld as amended on 20 March 1994[!] shall determine the form and content of the transmitted data in automated or paper-based form.

Second Federal regulatory reporting data transmission ordinance:[400]

> § 7 Transmission on machine-readable data carriers
>
> (2) [...]. Data are to provide according to the specifications of the standard data set for reporting, using the character set ISO/IEC 10646:2003 for UTF-8 encoding in the Latin alphabet. [...]

---

398 *Bundesmeldegesetz*
http://www.mwalther.net/kompendien/210-7.pdf (2014-12-16)

399 *Erste Bundesmeldedatenübermittlungsverordnung*
http://www.gesetze-im-internet.de/bundesrecht/bmeldd_v_1_2005/gesamt.pdf (2014-12-16)

400 *Zweite Bundesmeldedatenübermittlungsverordnung*
http://www.gesetze-im-internet.de/bmeldd_v_2_1995/BJNR101100995.html (2015-01-02)

The new *First* and *Second Federal regulatory reporting data transmission ordinance* (that will override both old ordinances on 1 November 2015) state in § 3 that OSCI XMeld and DSMeld (1 May 2014) will be the standards of data transmission. [401, 402]

9.3.3.1 Standard dataset for reporting (DSMeld) and XMeld

Authoritative to entries in the reporting system is the standard dataset for reporting (DSMeld).[403] It determines for each data field presentation and content (a reproduction of the individual data sheets [only chapter 6] can be found in Appendix D of the specification of XMeld 1.3.0).[404] In chapter 3 "General preface for representing the data (notation and symbols) for automated data transmission", it is said in para. 1 that only the letters Aa to Zz plus Ää, Öö, Üü, ß are allowed. In para. 2, this is further specified: "[...] Accents [...] will not be considered." However, it continues: "This does not apply if the registration office and the data receiver agree on a process which would provide the processing of the special characters shown in Annex 4 [...]". This Annex 4 (identical to the character repertoire LA8 Passport of the *Bundesdruckerei* [Federal printing agency], see chapter 9.3.5.3) would allow about 180 more letters with diacritics (shown on pages 2 to 14 of the Annex).

---

401 http://www.bgbl.de/banzxaver/bgbl/start.xav?startbk=Bundesanzeiger_BGBl&jumpTo=bgbl114s1945.pdf (2015-01-02)
402 http://www.bgbl.de/banzxaver/bgbl/start.xav?startbk=Bundesanzeiger_BGBl&jumpTo=bgbl114s1950.pdf (2015-01-02)
403 *Datensatz für das Meldewesen – Einheitlicher Bundes-/Länderteil –* (DSMeld)
404 http://www.osci.de/xmeld130/xmeld-130.zip (2015-01-02)

The data shall then be submitted in UCS2 Unicode encoding.[405, 406]
This confusing statement means that, theoretically, that registration authorities should keep the entries in two spellings, to accommodate for both purposes, which will rarely be the case:

> 1. As basis is taken the list of valid characters in accordance with Section 3.1 of the DSMeld. We are ignoring the possibility of storing and transmitting according to the extended character set defined in Annex 4 of DSMeld, because—as we know—it is not comprehensively made use of this possibility.[407]

Note also that earlier versions of Annex 4 / LA8 Passport are missing e.g. the Romanian letters Ş/ş, Ţ/ţ (with comma instead of cedilla below).

When OSCI *(Online Services Computer Interface)* was established, there was also a part that should standardize messages of regulatory reporting. It was called XMeld and is based on DSMeld.[408] By means of XMeld, messages of regulatory reporting are defined in vendor-neutral and platform-neutral manner on the basis of XML schemata. Again, since it is an XML-based standard, Unicode (UTF-8 or -16) is supported (Unicode 4.0 in XML 1.1). The diacritic letters repertoire is called String.Latin (= DSMeld Annex 4 / LA8 Passport, plus additions)[409] and was back-ported into DSMeld.

---

405 Klaus M. Medert, Werner Süßmuth, Gaaz: *Melderecht des Bundes und der Länder, I. Bundesrecht, Ausgabe Niedersachsen, Anhang I F*, Deutscher Gemeindeverlag / W. Kohlhammer (1982)
406 Bundesvereinigung der Kommunalen Spitzenverbände (Hrsg.): *Datensatz für das Meldewesen – Einheitlicher Bundes-/Länderteil – (DS Meld), 6. Lieferung*, Deutscher Gemeindeverlag / W. Kohlhammer (October 2004)
407 http://www1.osci.de/sixcms/media.php/13/2009-10-09-konzept-anpassung-namensdarstellung.pdf (2015-01-04, copy link)
408 http://de.wikipedia.org/wiki/Online_Services_Computer_Interface (2015-01-02)
409 http://www.xoev.de/sixcms/detail.php?gsid=bremen83.c.4813.de (2015-01-02)

Thus, if a procedure stores names with diacritics (in which *internal* coding whatsoever), then these names can be transmitted by XMeld. The data will be brought in the procedure itself or by a XMeld codec in a (UTF-8 encoded) XML representation that corresponds to the current XMeld schemes. On the receiver side, the document is serialized back into the form and the encoding that the recipient needs (e.g. ISO 8859-1).

The current version is XMeld 1.8.1. From XMeld 1.7, all names, artist name, and place of death are coded as String.Latin (compulsory since 1 November 2012, previously limited by LA8 Passport). [410, 411, 412]

Meanwhile, all 8,000 German registration offices have been interconnected using the new authorities standard OSCI. [413]

9.3.3.2 Registration software

In the 5,412 registration authorities of the 16 German Federal states, about 20 registration programmes ('procedures') from different manufacturers were established within the framework of local self-government. In regard to the use of diacritics, the *diversity* of software systems was not so much a problem, but rather the use of 7- and 8-bit character sets (see table 9.1). The only solution was to switch to the Universal Character Set / Unicode or its Latin subset DSMeld Annex 4 / LA8 Passport (old) or String.Latin (new), respectively.

As it can be seen in figure 9.1, the conversion of registration software to support Unicode had already begun at some manufacturers own initiative

---

410 http://www.xoev.de/sixcms/detail.php?gsid=bremen83.c.11251.de (2015-01-02)
411 http://www1.osci.de/sixcms/detail.php?gsid=bremen76.c.2827.de (2015-01-02)
412 http://www1.osci.de/sixcms/detail.php?gsid=bremen76.c.4762.de (2015-01-02)
413 http://www.crn.de/markt/artikel-15876.html (2015-01-02)

(two-thirds of manufacturers would follow in the end). The last third followed only as there were legal requirements (the UCS/Unicode is mandatory for XMeld since 1 November 2012, see figure 9.2).[414]

9.3.4 Databases and Unicode

In addition to the diacritics-compatibility of the procedure itself, also the storage is a critical factor: many old storages of inhabitants records to which the procedures have access lie in relational databases on IBM mainframes, some still in the 7-bit format (ASCII or EBCDIC) or in capital letters (e.g. MOESSBAUER instead of Mößbauer), so that already the internal processing of lower case letters, umlauts and ß is a problem. Towards the outside, however, these characters are now generally used. Some manufacturers have the IBM DB2 database extended, as an interim solution on the way to conversion to Unicode, in that it also stores certain data fields in a second representation (with diacritics), but without to processing them.[415, 416]

All major databases and database management systems / platforms / interfaces support Unicode. Only the implementation varies from manufacturer to manufacturer: UCS-2 (= fixed length) at Microsoft,[417] UTF-8 (= variable length) at Unix, UTF-8 and UTF-16 at Oracle,[418] UTF-8 and UCS-2 at IBM.[419]

---

[414] Klaus Frank, mps, personal communication (2006-02-21)
[415] Mr Vassholz, DZBW, phone call (2006-03-16)
[416] Mr Schütz, KOB EDV-Systeme GmbH, phone call (2006-03-17)
[417] https://msdn.microsoft.com/en-us/library/ms186939.aspx (2015-03-24)
[418] http://www.oracle.com/technetwork/database/database-technologies/globalization/twp-appdev-unicode-10gr2-129234.pdf (2015-03-24)
[419] http://www-01.ibm.com/support/knowledgecenter/SSEPGG_8.2.0/com.ibm.db2.udb.doc/admin/c0004821.htm?lang=en (2015-03-24)

However, even if the associated database management system supports Unicode in principle, a database is created by default with the character set being used by the creating application, i.e. in most cases ASCII, EBCDIC, ISO 8859-1/-15 or Windows-1252. This setting can afterwards not be changed. If you want to convert an existing database to Unicode, you have to export the contained data and specifically generate a new database in Unicode format (by specifying the character set in the corresponding command). Subsequently, the data can be imported in this new database.[420, 421] In front of such an effort, those responsible are probably going first of all to shy away, because the database may not be accessible for several days during the conversion. However, this step is necessary to ensure the seamless Unicode compatibility of the German e-government. Otherwise, a remote enquiry with respect to a name with diacritics via OSCI XMeld would in fact wrongly produce the message "not found" when accessing an ASCII database. Oracle has introduced a new tool called *Database Migration Assistant for Unicode* (DMU) that facilitates the conversion.[422]

Conversely, there may be problems with the data medium exchange, e.g. with call-up list for military service or churches, if their software and database systems are not yet converted to Unicode. A temporary solution could be that certain data fields in the Unicode database are stored in a second representation in 7- or 8-bit format to be sent if necessary.

---

420 Bernd Jungbluth: MS SQL Server FAQ, section A1.1. *Zeichensatz nach Installation ändern* [change character set after installation]
http://www.berndjungbluth.de/sqlfaq/faqa1.htm (2015-03-24)
421 Rainer Makohl, Software AG, telephone conversation (2006-03-20)
422 http://www.dbi-services.com/index.php/blog/entry/oracle-database-12c-database-migration-assistant-for-unicode (2015-03-24)

Table 9.1: **Unicode ability of registration software (own survey 2006)**

Registration software (manufacturer)	Current character (sub-)set	Switch to Unicode?
MESO (HSH GmbH Berlin)	ISO 8859-1	possible
OK.EWO (Dataport / AKDB)	ISO 8859-1	long-term planning
UVN-EIWO (Zweckverband Kommunale Datenverarbeitung Oldenburg [KDO])	ASCII + German additional characters	possible
LEWIS-DB (Datenzentrale Baden-Württemberg [DZBW])	ASCII / EBCDIC + German additional characters	medium-term plan
CS.EIS (Schleupen AG)	LA8 Passport	done
mpsEM (MPS Software & Systems GmbH)	ISO 8859-1	only when legal regulations exist
KAI-EWOS (Kommunale Anwendergemeinschaft für Informations- und Kommunikationstechniken)	ISO 8859-1	in progress
Kommunalserie/400 Einwohnerwesen (INFOMA Software consulting GmbH)	EBCDIC	first considerations
GES KA Meldewesen (GES Systemhaus GmbH)	Unicode	done
EWO-PAMELA (ekom21)	ISO 8859-1	not planned
AKD-EWO (Institut für Informatik Duisburg [IfI])	ISO 8859-1	long-term planning
SASKIA.de-EWO (SASKIA Informationssysteme GmbH)	Unicode	done
AdKOMM EWO (KOB EDV-Systeme GmbH)	ASCII + German additional characters	long-term planning

Unicode ability of registration software
(own surveys: 2006 above, 2011-12 below)

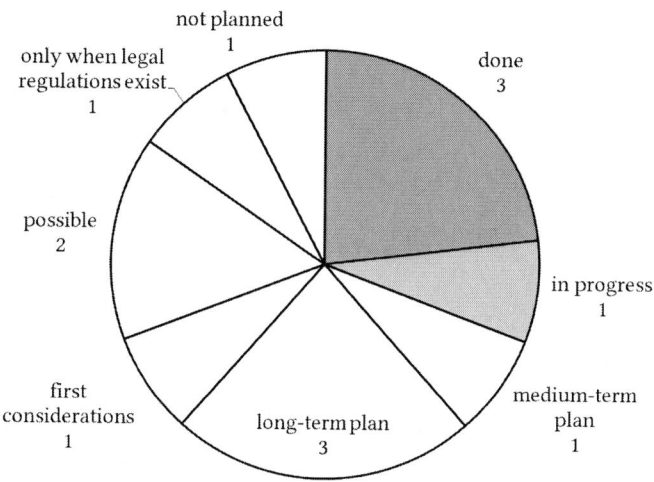

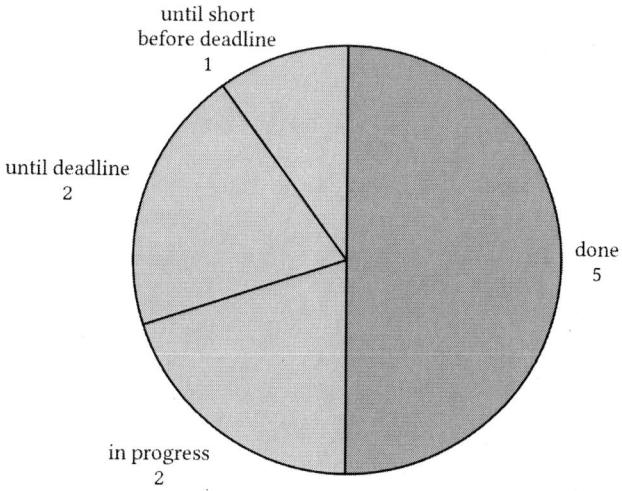

Table 9.2: **Unicode ability of registration software (own survey 2011/12)**

Registration software (manufacturer)	Current character set	Switch to Unicode?
MESO (HSH GmbH Berlin)	ISO 8859-1	done
OK.EWO (Dataport / AKDB)	ISO 8859-1	until deadline
LEWIS-DB (Datenzentrale Baden-Württemberg [DZBW])	ASCII / EBCDIC + German additional characters	until deadline (new software: KM-Ewo)
CS.EIS (Schleupen AG)	LA8 Passport	done
mpsEM (mps public solutions gmbh)	ISO 8859-1	work in progress
KAI-EWOS (Kommunale Anwendergemeinschaft für Informations- und Kommunikationstechniken)	ISO 8859-1	done
GES KA Meldewesen (GES Systemhaus GmbH)	Unicode	done
EWO-PAMELA (ekom21)	ISO 8859-1	work in progress
SASKIA.de-EWO (SASKIA Informationssysteme GmbH)	Unicode	done
AdKOMM EWO (KOB EDV-Systeme GmbH)	ASCII + German additional characters	only short before deadline

9.3.5 Passports and ID cards

Also passports and ID cards did get a legal makeover:

9.3.5.1 Passports

For the spelling of names in German passports are potentially to be considered: [423]

- The general administrative regulations (adopted according to § 27 Passport Act by the Federal Foreign Office, in consultation with the Federal Ministry of the Interior), [424]
- the regulation to determine the sample of passports of the Federal Republic of Germany, [425]
- the (non-binding) "guide for filling out an application for a passport". [426]

In the Passport Act itself, there is nothing about the spelling of names of persons, but in the general administrative regulations:

> 4.1.1.1 The family name and optionally the name at birth are generally to enter complete and unabridged. For the spelling [...] of names, entries in the civil registers are decisive; proof of this can be done by civil status records.

---

423 Klaus M. Medert / Werner Süßmuth: *Pass- und Personalausweisrecht, Band 2: Passrecht, Kommentar, Dritte überarbeitete Auflage 2001*, Kohlhammer-Verlag Stuttgart etc., 2001

424 *Allgemeine Verwaltungsvorschrift zur Durchführung des Passgesetzes (Passverwaltungsvorschrift)*
http://www.bmi.bund.de/SharedDocs/Downloads/DE/Themen/Sicherheit/PaesseAusweise/PassVwV.pdf;jsessionid=10FEB03868CA15ABEC4ADAAFBED2E087.2_cid373?__blob=publicationFile (2015-01-03)

425 *Passverordnung*
http://www.gesetze-im-internet.de/bundesrecht/passv_2007/gesamt.pdf (2015-01-03)

426 *Leitfaden zum Ausfüllen eines Antrages auf Ausstellung eines Reisepasses*

> 4.1.2.1 The first names are generally to enter complete and unabridged. [...] For the spelling [...] of first names, entries in the civil registers are decisive; proof of this can be done by civil status records.
>
> 21.4.3 When storing data, the dataset for reporting (Uniform Federal/*Länder* part) can be used.

That is to be interpreted in the case of names with diacritics in that way that "complete and unabridged entering" means no omission of the diacritics. This is supported by the notion that in cases of doubt about entries in the regulatory reporting, the civil status records are decisive ("normative reference"), because according to § 15 para. 3 *Civil Status Ordinance*, entries in the civil status registers have to be made under takeover of all diacritics. In this respect, names with diacritics have to be written in passports definitely *with* diacritics.

> [...] As experience shows that the entries in regulatory reporting are not always[!] right, the spelling [...] of names are generally to be proven by civil status records, unless that information has been already proven in the previous issue of a passport or identity card. [...][427]

As for the storage of data, the reference to the dataset for reporting (DSMeld) in general administrative regulation 21.4.3 was, however, a bit counterproductive: we already discussed in chapter 9.3.3.1 that in this data set, the basic character set was not fit to deal with diacritics. But since 1 November 2012, String.Latin is mandatory for DSMeld.

In the "guide for filling out an application for a passport" (chapter 3 "characters"), it said in para. 1 that again only the letters Aa to Zz plus Ää, Öö, Üü, ß are allowed. In para. 2, however, it went on that "for

---

427 *Erläuterung zu den allgemeinen Verwaltungsvorschriften, „Praxis der Gemeindeverwaltung / Niedersachsen"*

legally correct spelling of names", the use of "unauthorized" signs is inevitable (chapter 5.3 "fields with special provisions": family name, name at birth, and first name). Applications with diacritics were running at the *Bundesdruckerei* through a separate procedure to prevent them from being ignored ("must be ticked on the right side of the application form in the S/D field").[428] In the regulation to determine the sample of passports, there used to be nothing about the spelling of names of persons, but meanwhile the "guide for filling out an application for a passport" has been incorporated and modernized.[429] Especially Appendix 11 "Formal requirements for the entries in passports within the meaning of § 1 para. 2 the Passport Act, preliminary note" is interesting: String.Latin as repertoire and *UnicodeDoc* as font are to be used.

9.3.5.2 ID cards

For the spelling of names in German identity cards are potentially to be considered:

- *Act on Identity Cards and Electronic Identification,*[430]
- the execution laws, such as supplementary regulations of the *Länder,*
- *Identity Card Regulation* [431]

---

428 Gernot Schlebusch: *Praxis der Kommunalverwaltung, Landesausgabe Niedersachsen, Band K3 (Loseblattsammlung): Veterinärwesen, Melderecht, Wehrrecht, Personalausweis- und Passrecht, Ausländerrecht.* Kommunal- und Schulverlag Wiesbaden, 2000
429 http://dipbt.bundestag.de/dip21/brd/2010/0499-10.pdf (2015-01-03)
430 *Personalausweisgesetz*
http://www.gesetze-im-internet.de/englisch_pauswg/englisch_pauswg.html (2015-01-03)
431 *Personalausweisverordnung*
http://www.gesetze-im-internet.de/pauswv/ (2015-01-03)

- the "guide to filling out an application for issuance of identity cards" published by the *Bundesdruckerei*.[432]

The *Act on Identity Cards* and execution laws of the *Länder* makes no rules regarding the use of diacritics in identity cards. The "guide to filling out an application for issuance of identity cards" almost literally corresponds to the "guide for filling out an application for a passport". Accordingly, the comments made to the previous chapter shall apply *mutatis mutandis*.

See also the judgement of the Federal Administrative Court of 29 September 1992 with respect to the registration of names with umlauts in identity cards:[433]

> (21) The spelling of the family name is derived from the civil registry and issued based on the civil status records. The exchange of an umlaut by a vowel with attached "e" in the family name is, in legal terms, a name change within the meaning of § 3 para. 1 of the Act on the change of surnames and forenames of 5 January 1938 (RGBl I, p. 9), as last amended by Act of 12 September 1990 (BGBl. I, p. 2002) (see judgement of 1 October 1980 – BVerwG 7 C 21.78 – Buchholz 402.10 § 3 [Act on the change of surnames and forenames]; No. 40). The bearer of a surname written in the civil status registers with an umlaut may request that his surname is added unaltered to the ID card.

In the *Identity Card Regulation* used to be nothing about the spelling of names of persons, but meanwhile the "guide for filling out an application for issuance of identity cards" has been incorporated and modernized. In

---

432 Gernot Schlebusch: *Praxis der Kommunalverwaltung, Landesausgabe Niedersachsen, Band K3 (Loseblattsammlung): Veterinärwesen, Melderecht, Wehrrecht, Personalausweis- und Passrecht, Ausländerrecht.* Kommunal- und Schulverlag Wiesbaden, 2000

433 *Bundesverwaltungsgericht*, 1. Senate, judgement 29 September 1992, Buchholz 402.02 # 5, Az: 1 C 41/90, Juris-No. WBRE310554902, StAZ 1993, 118-120

Appendix 3 "Formal requirements for the entries in identity cards within the meaning of § 2 para. 1 of the Identity Card Act, preliminary note", String.Latin as repertoire and *UnicodeDoc* as font are to be used, like for passports.

However, even with the "new" digital identity card, it still comes sometimes to problems with diacritics:

> According to the registration offices, including the Berlin district of Charlottenburg-Wilmersdorf, there are problems in attempting to register the new ID cards digitally on the so-called change terminals. Especially names with diacritics are concerned. "Then the whole system crashes, and the real advantage of the new ID card, digital registration, is obsolete," said city council member JOACHIM KRÜGER.
> Citizens can pick up their ID cards, but would once again come to complete the digital registration. How long they have to wait still unclear.[434]
> The principle of federalism that is applied in Germany is not necessarily conductive to data processing. Federal, *Länder* and local governments use very different software for their administrative tasks. The new ID cards comes with a dozen front-ends which were written by the providers of local software. There are also different methods from *Land* to *Land* how the change terminals [...] communicate with the servers of the *Bundesdruckerei*.[435]

Only German umlauts and "ß" are sure to be properly supported (see chapter 9.1).[436]

In conclusion, therefore, is to say that persons whose names contain diacritics can, from a legal perspective, request and get easily passports and

---

434 http://www.fr-online.de/politik/gute-zeichen--schlechte-zeichen,1472596, 5199282.html (2011-11-30)
435 http://www.heise.de/newsticker/meldung/Verwirrung-um-diakritische-Zeichen-im-neuen-Personalausweis-Update-1168966.html (2011-11-30)
436 http://www.zdnet.de/magazin/41545014/innenminister-de-maizi-re-kann-neuen-personalausweis-nicht-nutzen.htm (30.11.2011)

identity cards in correct writing. BARTŁOMIEJ PAWEŁ J. informed me he had received a successfully a German identity card with Polish diacritics (procedure MESO, digital application procedure DIGANT, see chapter 9.3.5.4).

9.3.5.3 Bundesdruckerei

The *Bundesdruckerei* produces identity cards and passports in accordance with the information coming from the issuing authorities. It also can process and print diacritics. The *Bundesdruckerei* used internally an own standard called LA8 Passport (including those Latin diacritics from Universal Character Set / Unicode [UCS-2] prescribed by DSMeld, Annex 4). The font used was called LA8 Unicode. Most (Eastern) European and also Vietnamese diacritics could be printed. Since 1 November 2012, String.Latin is mandatory for DSMeld; the new font is *UnicodeDoc* (see figure 4.1)

However, the content of an application form determines the clerk in the issuing authorities. If the staff of an issuing authority claims (untruthfully) that the use of Polish or French diacritics in an identity card or a passport is not possible, and the citizen agrees by signature to the adjustments to the German alphabet, the *Bundesdruckerei* will have to print the document on an adulterated name, due to lack of control.[437]

9.3.5.4 Electronic data transfer to the Bundesdruckerei using DIGANT

The *Bundesdruckerei* offers already since the year 2000 the module DIGANT[438] (*digitales Antragsverfahren*, digital application procedure) for

---

437 Helpdesk team *Bundesdruckerei*, personal communication (2005-12-01)
438 DIGANT® / DIGANT® software modules BUDS, D-SAFE and KOMSYS / performance / status 01.08.2004, Bundesdruckerei (ed.)

municipal inhabitants procedures (see chapter 9.3.3.2, e.g. MESO,[439] LEWIS,[440] or OK.EWO).[441] The client module runs on Windows 7 (8 on some conditions) and some older versions. Through DIGANT, the application procedure for identity cards and passports is simplified (paperless), accelerated, and handled without "media breaks" (through direct electronic transmission of digitally encrypted data to the *Bundesdruckerei*). In addition, passport and identity register can be performed digitally (and in the future, digitally archived). Thus, multiple data capture (with the application procedure before the manufacturing process and during the subsequent archiving) is avoided. Possible sources of error in the spelling of names with diacritics are therefore consistently reduced.

For participation in the DIGANT process, a municipality must just demonstrate the DIGANT capability of their registration software (see above) and sign a participation agreement with the *Bundesdruckerei*. In January 2012, DIGANT was used by 6,500 German municipalities in combination with 10 different registration programmes.[442]

The module DIGANT allows the insertion of all diacritics from String.Latin (earlier LA8 Passport) via a menu, callable using the F4 key.[443] In the

---

http://www.kdzmainz.de/fileadmin/kdz/pdf/digant_leistungsbeschreibung_bundesdruckerei.pdf (2015-02-15)

439 HSH: products / MESO / system requirements http://www.hsh-berlin.com/modules.php?name=HSH_Content&cid=10&download=20 (2011-12-01)

440 http://www.tlrz.thueringen.de/imperia/md/content/tlrz/downloads/digant/v1_2_benutzerhandbuch_lewis_digant_lewis_digant_va.pdf (2015-05-31)

441 Dataport: *Digitale Ausweisanträge* DIGANT (2011-12-01)

442 Gerd Schlößmann, personal communication (2012-01-26)

443 direct 1/2005, Hannoversche Informationstechnologien http://www.hannit.de/cms/fileadmin/user_upload/PDF/Kundenzeitung_direkt/Direkt_01_2005.pdf p. 9 (2015-02-15)

control panel, first not the selected diacritic will appear, but the corresponding hexadecimal Unicode value (e.g. #011A instead of Ě). In the connected municipal inhabitants process, this coding method is then converted to the correct diacritic and displayed.

On the Unicode capability of the procedure itself, the combination with DIGANT has no effect. For example, although applications with diacritics could be created and transmitted to the *Bundesdruckerei* using DIGANT together with *Kommunalserie/400*, the diacritics were not stored in the register of residents.

9.3.6 Name Change Law

According to the *Introductory Act to the Civil Code*,[444] the name of a person is governed by the law of the country to which the person is a national (Art. 10 "Name" para. 1) and that if a person is bi- or multinational including German nationality, then that legal status shall prevail (Art. 5 "Personal statute", para. 1). This refers but only to the lawful acquisition of the name after the relevant statute of the individual. The *spelling* of the name remains untouched.[445]

A change in the *spelling* of a name is, according to decisions of the Federal Administrative Court[446] a public-legal name change under the *Act on the change of surnames and forenames* (NamÄndG) that requires a request from

---

444 *Einführungsgesetz zum Bürgerlichen Gesetzbuch*, EGBGB
http://www.gesetze-im-internet.de/englisch_bgbeg/index.html (2015-02-16)
445 Hinkel, Erich: *Personenordnungsrecht in der kommunalen Praxis*, Erich-Schmidt-Verlag, Berlin 1997, ISBN 3-503-04060-9, reference 1354, p. 242
446 Ruling of 29 September 1972, BVerwGE 40, 353; ruling of 1 October 1980, NJW 1981, 2713

the name's owner.[447] Details on the interpretation of NamÄndG regulate the *General regulations for the Act on the change of surnames and first names* (NamÄndVwV).[448]

According to § 1 NamÄndG, only family names of German citizens may be changed.[449] For foreign nationals, a name change by German authorities is completely excluded (No. 3 NamÄndVwV). According to § 3 para. 1 NamÄndG, there must also be an important reason for the change. The change has, moreover, only to be carried out on written application by the name carrier itself (§ 5 para. 1 NamÄndG, No. 6, para. 1 / No. 15, para. 1 NamÄndVwV), not arbitrarily from the administration or against the will of the person concerned.[450] For the decision about the change is the higher administrative authority responsible (§ 6 NamÄndG), not the lower administrative authority (registry office, registration office).

- Difficulties in legal dealings that are based on the incorrect reproduction of umlauts[!] in the family name by IT systems, printers and accounting machines, can justify a change of the name.[451]

However, data processing has since the 1980s, in which even German umlauts already constituted a serious technical problem and thus an

---

447 *Gesetz über die Änderung von Familiennamen und Vornamen*, NamÄndG
http://www.gesetze-im-internet.de/bundesrecht/nam_ndg/gesamt.pdf
(2015-02-16)
448 http://www.verwaltungsvorschriften-im-internet.de/bsvwvbund_11081980_VII31331317.htm (2011-11-22)
449 or of stateless persons who are resident or ordinarily resident in Germany
450 Brien Dorenz / Peter A. Ströll: *Namensrecht / Grundlage für einen namensrechtlichen Beitrag in „Professors Udolphs Buch der Namen"* (published 2005 by C. Bertelsmann), p. 12
http://www.nambos.de/download/veroeffentlichungen/personennamensrecht.pdf (2015-05-31)
451 Federal Administrative Court from 1 October 1980, StAZ 1981 p. 244

"important reason" for a name change under § 3, evolved considerably (Unicode, String.Latin) and can now basically the represent all Latin diacritics.

- A name change is usually further justified when difficulties in spelling or pronunciation of a surname lead to a "not insubstantial disability" of the applicant (No. 36 NamÄndVwV). However, from the mere fact that a name is of foreign origin or does not sound German, *no* "important reason" for a name change under § 3 can be derived in general (No. 37 para. 1 NamÄndVwV).

- Does the family name of a recently naturalized foreigner identify the foreign origin to a particular degree, and places the naturalized in the interest of his integration value to a more inconspicuous family name, this also justifies a change of name (No. 37 para. 2 NamÄndVwV). This provision, however, is very restrictive to apply: every person has, in principle, to guide the name established in accordance with the legal order at the time of the name acquisition.[452]

Especially the last two points assume here that stakeholders in general desire for a *change* of name, while in practice it is more often the desire is expressed to implement the names with their legally guaranteed notation (with diacritics). The application for a change of name, including the waiving of diacritics, however, is often the last, resigned reaction to a long, gruelling battle with the German bureaucracy for the correct spelling of their own name. The fatal consequence of the possibility of name change is a real pressure for Germanization that leads already to cultural impoverishment and a loss of identity, as these statements show:

---

452 Gerhard Stuber: *Die Beurkundung von Namen im Standesamt / Familiennamen – Ehenamen – Vornamen*, Richard-Boorberg-Verlag Stuttgart/München/Hannover/Berlin/Weimar/Dresden (2005), p. 109f., 113ff.

My uncle has decided to change his name after 30 years, because he was so stressed out that the Germans always write it wrong.[453]

In my family—to my knowledge—all have their spelling changed in that way, that they do not need any diacritics. Especially so there are no problems.[454]

When my parents moved to Germany, they found themselves in a situation resembling those of refugees—not only did we have to leave the whole household and all valuables behind, but also all important documents. The procedure to replace such basic documents, like birth certificates, was the creation of a so-called *Familienbuch* (literary 'family book'), an official recognized listing of our names, birth dates, parent's names etc. which could then be used when requesting all other official documents like ID cards, passports and so on.

The surprising part was that when my parents held the document in their hands, they found all our first names had been replaced by their German counterparts! The fact that this was done without consulting us, not to speak any active request from our side, leads me to the conclusion that the responsible public servants regularly took the freedom of Germanizing names of immigrants. My parents protested, and the family book was eventually corrected, but I fear that we were not the only case. Worse, most immigrants socialized in the totalitarian states of the back then Eastern Block were used to bow towards state authorities. In addition, it seems to me that many seemed to fear that their hopefully soon to be new home country would reject them for lack of gratitude if they protested. So my guess is that in almost all other cases, the persons concerned did not dare to demand a correction, so probably many of such cases of unlawful Germanizations of names occurred.[455]

---

453 Jana Pěnková, personal communication (2006-04-11)
454 Magdalena Janetzko, personal communication (2005-12-24)
455 Bartłomiej Paweł Jesionkiewicz, personal communication (2015-02-24)

It must be noted that the changing of the first names in the case above was indeed unlawful: according to Art 47 para. 1 point 5 of the *Introductory Act to the Civil Code*, the adoption of a German version of one's given or surname is possible, but requires a declaration of the person concerned, which clearly was never made in this case.

> To me it is known, however, that you can actually ignore during use the diacritics in the Polish language, and they are unfortunately omitted. People with unknown Polish first names are—or at least were—rechristened until a few years. For example, in one case, Leszek became *Georg*, Wojciech became *Adelbert* etc.[456]

9.3.6.1 Practical experience

Authentic examples of administrative practice, however, show that the legal requirements mentioned above are often not respected. Sometimes, the staff in the registration authorities fails already on letters that are included even in the simplest German character set (ISO-8859-1), as the following extracts from an Internet discussion forum of the computer magazine "Chip Online" (April 2005) show:[457]

> **megamazl**: [...] My second name is François. In my ID card, however, it is Francois. So far, I've always been satisfied with the terse statement of the officials "Errr, no, it's not possible!". But somehow I cannot believe that in a country where soon the biometric passport is mandatory it should not even be possible to include this umlaut. [...]
> **Ivanhoe**: Refer to the *Bundesdruckerei* and ask if that's possible. The officials at the registration office are stumped there. [...]

---

456 Monika Pawlica, personal communication (2005-12-18)
457 CHIP online / Forum „Smalltalk", *Thema: ausländische Umlaute im Perso* http://www.chip.de/c1_forum/thread.html?bwthreadid=827631 (2011-12-01)

tomexo30: [...] I cannot imagine that it causes problems to the registration office to insert accents like ë ï ç æ œ in a travel document I would just ask precisely; after all, there are also plenty of foreigners in Germany where the omission of diacritics totally distorts the name. [...]

Dark_Apollo: [...] Theoretically and practically it is, in my opinion, possible to print this letter. A fortiori to write. But unfortunately, German officials are too lazy to do that. This French "ç" can be represented and also printed employing the ASCII code. And I do hardly think the new ID cards are printed with a conventional typewriter where this letter is missing. If not, then corrected me.

Oh, one more thing ... laziness is everywhere. On my Norwegian Green Card they have unceremoniously made an ø of the ö in the first name. The ü in my home town, however, they have spelled correctly again. Crazy World... [...]

Colour: [...] But if I can understand that one would like to have his name spelled correctly especially in the identity card—I would insist on it, it is your prerogative! [...]

But the administration officials should generally be familiar with correct spelling, I think. They should be able to write such diacritics. It is but their job. [...]

Even if others see this as picky—a missing check mark on a letter is a missing check mark, and that has not to be missing.

systems: [...] In addition, ID cards are produced by the *Bundesdruckerei*, and not by the registration office. Maybe someone has a Win98 left for the *Bundesdruckerei*.

Colour: Especially the *Bundesdruckerei* should be able.

tomex030: Try pushing with your thumb on the Alt key [...] and enter with the other hand the number 0231. If you now release the Alt key, you have the ç. [...] This should be proficient also in the *Bundesdruckerei* in my opinion.

> Also I would insist that my name is spelled correctly in the personal documents. [...]
>
> **megamazl:** OK, then I will knock on the table properly there.
>
> But as I do know the officials, they will say my name is not written like this. Or I would have to prove first that it is not possible to write that name with a normal "c". [...]
>
> **megamazl:** Just called the *Bundesdruckerei*. They thought it would not be a problem. Now I have only to teach the officials at the registration office.

But even if the person who is making an application refers to the relevant legal provisions, the resistance at the registration authority is often large, as this report shows:[458]

> When [...] Anna Górecka applied for her new identity card and [...] toughly demanded the bar above the o, an official said that this was not so important, this little bar but could mean nothing. Then she said: » If your name was "Müller", you would also not like it to be written "Muller", or? « There the state servant accepted it! :-)

9.4 Austrian law

9.4.1 International agreements

Austria has, *inter alia*, signed the ICCS *Convention No. 14*,[459] the *European Charter for Regional or Minority Languages*,[460] and the *Framework Convention for the Protection of National Minorities*.[461] Austria declared at the ratification of the *Framework Convention* the caveat

---
458 Bartłomiej Paweł Jesionkiewicz, personal communication (2003-08-07)
459 BGBl. 1980/308
460 BGBl. III 2001/216
461 BGBl. III 1998/130

that it recognizes under the term "national minorities" only Austrian citizens resident in Austria that are covered by the scope of the *Minorities Act (Volksgruppengesetz)*,[462] with non-German mother tongue and their own folklore tradition (Croatian, Slovak, Slovenian, Czech, Hungarian, and the ethnic group of Roma). Thus it has excluded the Polish and possibly also other ethnic groups who live over several generations in Austria, but still are not recognized the *Minorities Act*.

9.4.2 Civil status law

On the question of compliance with the Law on Art. 11 para. 1 of the *Framework Convention*, the Austrian Federal Government notes that in § 5 para. 3 *Civil Status Ordinance*, personal names to be registered on the basis of a document submitted in Latin letters have to be reproduced with their original letters and characters. This means that also diacritics that are not used in the German language have to be taken over (similar to → German law).[463]

> **Civil Status Ordinance**
> **Ordinance of the Minister of the Interior of 14 November 1983, BGBl. No. 629/1983, implementing the Civil Status Act**
> § 5. [...] (3) Registrations on the basis of a certificate that contains person's or place names in Latin or the previously used Kurrent writing means the name must be reproduced to the letters and characters. [...][464]

---

462 BGBl. 1976/196
463 *Bericht der Republik Österreich gemäß Artikel 25 Abs. 1 des Rahmenübereinkommens zum Schutz nationaler Minderheiten* / Wien, 30 Juni 2000
www.austria.gv.at/2004/4/15/minderheiten_dt.pdf (2011-11-12)
464 Peter Reichstädter et al.: *Handbuch diakritische Zeichen / Grundlagen - Recht – Technik (1.2.0), erstellt im Auftrag des Österreichischen Bundesministeriums für Inneres*
http://www.ref.gv.at/AG-II-Architektur-DZ-1-0-dia.2489.0.html (2011-11-12)

The *Civil Status Ordinance* refers to the *Civil Status Act.* It states:

> **Civil Status Act**
> **Personal names** § 11. (1) Personal names are to take faithful to the letters and characters from the certificate used for registration. [...][465]

These standards also cover migrant workers and ethnic groups that do not fall within the scope of the *Minorities Act.*
We must not overlook the fact that the *Civil Status Act* does not cover e.g. the *Registration* Act, which is much more important in everyday life.

9.4.3 Registration Act and Central residents register

The Central residents register (ZMR) is the largest administrative register in Austria.[466] It was created in temporal association with the census (as at 15 May 2001). Since 1 March 2002, the new *Registration Act*[467] is in force; by this time, the Central residents register (legal basis: § 16 para 1 *Registration Act*) went into live operation. The ZMR is a central database with the possibility of Austria-wide overview of all residence notifications of a person. These notifications are constantly updated by 2,357 municipalities and cities in Austria in real time. It is accessible to all agencies and departments of the municipalities, the *Länder*, and the federal level. Even if the centralization of reported data stands in the foreground, the importance of the ZMR extends far beyond the area of registration authorities, also in other areas of administration (e.g. citizen card).[468]

---

465 http://www.ref.gv.at/AG-II-Architektur-DZ-1-0-dia.2489.0.html (2011-11-12)
466 http://www.bka.gv.at/DocView.axd?CobId=20024 (2011-11-13)
467 http://www.jusline.at/Meldegesetz_%28MeldeG%29.html (2011-11-13)
468 http://www.bmi.gv.at/cms/BMI_ZMR/buerger/ueberblick/start.aspx (2015-03-16)

Neither the *Registration Act* nor the *Regulation implementing the Registration Act*[469] contain provisions on the characters to be displayed or the character set to be used.

Nevertheless, the ZMR application developed by the Austrian Federal Ministry of the Interior (BMI) supported noteworthy from the beginning Unicode (UTF-8). The graphical user interface of the ZMR is based on HTML. As interfaces, generally SOAP and XML schemas are used.[470]

A request may be made without diacritics (also called wild-card search or phonetic search), but entries with diacritics are also found and transmitted.[471] Entering these characters is possible either directly or via copy/paste, e.g. from the Windows Character Map. For the most common characters, there are own buttons available in the application that insert this character at the current cursor position.[472]

9.4.4 E-Government Act

Only a year after the successful commissioning of the ZMR, efforts were made to provide a legal basis for the regulation of the character set issue. The *Association of Austrian Social Security Institutions* made the following

---

469 *Meldegesetz-Durchführungsverordnung* (MeldeV)
   https://www.jusline.at/Meldegesetz-Durchfuehrungsverordnung_%28MeldeV%29.html (2015-05-31)
470 https://joinup.ec.europa.eu/community/epractice/case/central-register-residence-austria (2015-05-31)
471 *Stabsstelle IKT-Strategie des Bundes, 20. IKT-Board-Sitzung 16.12.2003 - Protokoll-Auszug*, p. 2
   http://www.cio.gv.at/ikt-board/protokolle/2003_12_16_20.ikt-board-protokoll_oeffentlich.pdf (2007-05-05, link no longer active)
472 Mag. Alexander Roch, BMI, Support Unit ZMR, personal communication (2005-12-31)

comments in September 2003 on the draft *E-Government Act* by the Austrian Federal Government (July 2003):[473]

4. Identity characteristics and name spelling

[...] Identity designation requires also the **exact spelling of names**. There are many thousands of names in which diacritics are used. In typewritten paper documents, these characters could be added later manually. Umlauts and ß should now bring no more difficulties, even for mainframes. Latest word processing programs are also (depending on the version of the program, however, more or less easily) able to display characters as trema, tilde, accents, cedilla, hooks, ring, etc., ë, ñ, à, â, ç, r, Å, L, I, i, ì, ?, a, a, Đ Ø, K, L[474] (as diacritics). In mainframes, this is not always (yet) the case. Such characters are also possible in the names of Austrian citizens (not only for members of the ethnic groups). There will also be a number of cases in which data of foreign citizens will appear in processes of e-government. Technically (and probably [civil status] legally), a name with or without diacritics, however, are [two] different strings.

[...] Since as part of the e-government, name inventories from different agencies may be touched (e.g. when using a sector-specific personal identifier), it is necessary **to determine the regime which string the identity characteristics shall be based on**, whereas this regime would have to comply to the civil status and civil law requirements for valid name spellings (commitment to common international standards, code tables, transcription and transliteration systems).

---

473 Austrian Parliament: writing of the Association of Austrian Social Security Institutions to the Federal Chancellery (Constitutional Service) and the Bureau of National Council
http://www.parlinkom.gv.at/pls/portal/docs/page/PG/DE/XXII/ME/ME_00069_27/fname_000000.pdf (2011-11-12)

474 Ironically, on some of these examples—probably in the conversion to PDF—the diacritics were lost (ř, Ł, Ķ, etc.).

> [...] By regulation, a **default character set** should be defined which will be mandatory to use in the electronic data exchange between federal level, *Länder*, cities, municipalities, and all corporations under public law. This character set should include at least the diacritics of the national minority languages, but also the languages of neighbouring countries, and at least the most widespread international trade languages English, French and Spanish as well as some foreign languages (Turkish, Polish) more frequent in Austria.

The *E-Government Act*[475] came into force on 1 March 2004; it includes, however, contrary to the above-cited proposal *no* regulation on a standard character set or the treatment of diacritics. However, the hitherto independent civil status and registration registers were linked to each other (legalization of mutual data exchange) through an amendment as contained in Article 5 of the *Registration Act*. As a result, the same rigorous standards must now apply to the *Registration Act* as to the *Civil Status Act* (transfer of personal names faithful to the letters and characters), which translates to the use of Unicode.

The Austrian E-Government ABC (version January 2006) states under the keyword "diacritical marks":[476]

> The current legal situation[477] sees the use of diacritical marks mandatory in matters of civil status. Applications which derive from that (e.g. registration) must support diacritics in any case. All other applications should be switched quickly to avoid inconsistencies. New [software] developments

---

475 The Austrian E-Government Act / Federal Act on Provisions Facilitating Electronic Communications with Public Bodies
http://www.digitales.oesterreich.gv.at/DocView.axd?CobId=19380 (2011-11-13)
476 http://ict.satw.ch/SPIP/IMG/pdf/Oesterreich-Behoerden_im_Netz-mun200611.pdf (p. 78, link no longer active)
477 § 11 Civil Status Act *(Personenstandsgesetz)*, BGBl. No. 60/1983

should support Unicode in every case. A non-Unicode application shall accept Unicode in the Web interface and internally convert (transcribe).

[...] Currently, the Latin script has more than 700 of these characters; however, not used in all European languages. When restricting to European and neighbouring State's languages, 400 characters remain. This number is beyond the scope of the usual 1-byte ISO-8859-X encodings (e.g. Latin-1) by far. In order to use all these characters simultaneously, Unicode must be used.

[...] The technical support for Unicode is now very good. All major database systems, operating systems, and programming languages offer Unicode support. Also, host-based systems can handle Unicode after relevant updates. Only some PC-based database / 4GL Development Systems of the late 80s and early 90s have difficulties because their manufacturers are widely no longer in business.

9.4.5 Manual diacritics

As part of the Federal ICT Strategy, it was discussed since May 2002 how to deal with diacritics in personal names.[478] It was generally assumed that the legal situation would lead to diacritics having to be implemented in electronic data processing, i.e. that the correct name spelling is provided and facilitated.

The *Länder* addressed to the Federal Ministry of Interior (BMI) a request to develop a proposed solution and analyse the consequences. In December 2002, the BMI presented a comprehensive report about name spellings and diacritical marks, which should now form the basis of an implementation strategy.

---

478 http://www.cio.gv.at/ikt-board/beratungen/diacritic/discussion/ (2007-05-05, link no longer active)

Partly, huge technical problems were expected. As an example, a statement from the IT department of the *Land* government of Lower Austria (NÖ) to the BMI report:

> [...] While understanding the objective, it is to be noted that NÖ is not able to support diacritics in the medium term. In part, applications are on a technical basis where migration is not possible. The replacement of these applications will take years and can only be solved over the life cycle of the software, but not on the basis of the problem "diacritics". The conditions at the base software, however, will be created so that future new applications will support diacritics.
>
> Since in many cases, the data are being passed to a central register of the Federal government (reporting, commercial, driving license, gun registry, ...), changes must proceed in a coordinated way.
>
> It is suggested that the Federal side pushes the national, but also EU-wide cooperation, so that resource-efficient solutions can be found.
>
> If there is still the need for a list of problems associated with diacritical characters, here is our incomplete, quickly compiled list: *[followed by twelve points]*

Finally, on behalf of the BMI, the working group "communication architecture" created a comprehensive and detailed "manual diacritics" that should assist authorities and their service providers in implementing applications with diacritics. The version 1.0.0 from 13 July 2005 received a negative opinion of Styria.[479] The revised version 1.1.0 of 21 June 2006 was raised to a recommendation.[480]

---

479 Naber, Larissa / Duscher, Silvia: *Handbuch diakritische Zeichen / Grundlagen – Recht – Technik* (13 July 2005), created on behalf of the BMI http://www.ref.gv.at/Handbuch_diakr__Zeichen_-_Vers.655.0.html (2007-05-05)

480 Naber, Larissa / Danner, Peter: *Handbuch diakritische Zeichen / Grundlagen – Recht – Technik* (21 Juni 2006), created on behalf of the BMI

An update (1.2.0) was submitted on 27 September 2010, supplemented by a publication "diacritic characters":[481]

(3) Encoding

For electronic data exchange between applications, generally UTF-8 is to use or to expect, respectively, and to accept. [...] Web applications must support for user input at least the encodings UTF-8 and ISO Latin-1, since both encodings are often used by browsers in the transmission of web forms. The more encodings can be received (and internally processed or transformed), the better. To send, UTF-8 should be used wherever possible.

(4) Transcription

Transcription referred to in this document means the mapping of Latin characters with diacritics and special characters to the 26 characters of the modern Latin alphabet.

Applications should offer the following variants for the purpose of exchanging data: [...]

- Partial transcription: all letters except for Ö, Ü, Ä, ö, ü, ä and ß are transcribed according to the table annexed
- Original spelling without transcription.

[...]

(6) Search

Applications should support three types of searches:

- Exact search: expects exact match of the name
- Approximately search: search for/with the above-mentioned transcription types (full, partial, and original)
- Phonetic search according to the BMI-ZMR algorithm ("formalize") [...]

---

http://reference.e-government.gv.at/Handbuch_diakr__Zeichen_-_Vers.927.0.html (2007-05-05)

481 Markus Triska et al.: *Diakritische Zeichen*
http://www.ref.gv.at/uploads/media/DZ-1-0_24092010.pdf (2011-11-13)

By the way, Kumaran and Haritsa propose a special format for multilingual data fields, Cuniform (Compressed Unicode Format). Experiments show that the processing of (diacritics-free) data only takes ≈ 20 % longer (compared to ASCII), although the data occupy twice as much memory.[482] The manual diacritics continues:

1.2.1 Unicode

In contrast to previous approaches, which allow the simultaneous display of only a few languages in the same text (examples are Latin-1, Latin-2, ...), with Unicode, all supported languages can be written simultaneously.

2.2 Legal framework

Relevant legal source for the spelling of names of persons in matters of civil status is the Civil Status Act (PStG). § 11 para. 1 PStG contributes to the liability that Austria has taken over from the ratification of the Convention on the Indication of Surnames and Forenames in Civil Status Registers, BGBl. No. 308/1980. On the resulting obligation under this Convention, reference is also made to in § 5 para. 3 to 5 of the Civil Status Ordinance (PStV).

Extract from the Convention on the indication of surnames and forenames in civil status registers (Reference: BGBl. No. 308/1980)

"Article 2 Where a record is to be made in a civil status register by an authority of a Contracting State and there is produced for that purpose a copy of or extract from a civil status record or some other document that shows the surnames and forenames in the same characters as those used in the language in which the record is to be made, those surnames and forenames shall be reproduced literally without alteration or translation. Any diacritic marks forming part of such surnames and forenames shall also be reproduced, even if such marks do not exist in the language in which the record is to be made."

---

482 http://www.vldb.org/archives/website/2003/prog_orderProceedings.html (2011-12-01)

The obligation to reproduction faithful to characters according to § 5 para. 3 PStV refers to reproduction of diacritical characters that are added to the usual Latin characters. [...]

Following the Civil Status Act, in principle all Latin characters are to support.

3.1.3 Recommendation: Unicode

There is the need to support the Unicode code points from the separate convention "diacritic characters" (DZ), in the latest version of the codes listed in the convention.

3.1.4 Recommendation: Governmental and private sector management

Applications which are derived from matters of civil status (e.g. matters of citizenship [naturalizations, ...]) must be converted to Unicode as soon as possible. Other applications should be changed as soon as possible (for example, in the course of the next major releases) to avoid inconsistencies. Applications of private sector management can thereby be given lower priority. [...]

3.1.8 Recommendation: Latin Extended B

New desktop developments for official use should, in accordance with the possibilities, already support the relevant characters from Latin Extended B (range U+0180 to U+024F).

3.2.1 Formats for data exchange

SOAP web services [...] **services without diacritics obligation** If there is no legal obligation, newly created or redesigned services should still support diacritics, in order to achieve homogenization as quickly as possible. [...]

3.2.5 Web interface

Problems and procedure

When using diacritical marks in Web forms, care must be taken that the characters are passed in UTF-8 encoding. Several steps are required:

- The page that contains the form must already be UTF-8 encoded (if necessary, install a diacritic in a comment to outwit the ASCII compatibility). <meta http-equiv="content-type" content="text/html; charset=UTF-8">
- XHTML documents should have additionally a XML prologue with specification of the encoding <?xml version="1.0" encoding="UTF-8" ?>
- The form must contain UTF-8 as only allowed encoding variant <form action="out.php" method="GET" accept-charset="UTF-8">
- It may be necessary to indicate in the <form> element additionally enctype="multipart/form-data" to persuade older browsers to cooperate.
- The Web server must not be instructed to override the encoding of web pages (e.g. Apache directive AddDefaultCharset), or he must be instructed to set the encoding to UTF-8.

3.2.6 Recommendation: Continuous application

Especially with web applications, UTF-8 should be used **throughout** to suppress implied transcoding between pages with different encoding.

3.4.4 Best Practices

Dual data fields

To simplify the search, indexed fields with diacritics should be performed twice: once with special characters and once without, if such a functionality is not provided by the database itself. [...] [483]

No negative opinion was received to the with the letter of 27 September 2010, VSt-1712/427, submitted documents *"Diakritische Zeichen V.1.0"* [diacritic characters] and *"Handbuch diakritische Zeichen Grundlagen – Recht – Technik diakrit 1.2.0."* [manual diacritics], so these documents were raised to recommendations.

---

483 http://www.ref.gv.at/AG-II-Architektur-DZ-1-0-dia.2489.0.html (2011-11-12)

9.4.6 Name Law Amendment Act

By the *Name Law Amendment Act*,[484] there was a large measure of liberalization introduced into the *Name Change Act*.[485] It is now easier for a person to change the name. This gives members of a linguistic minority who already have a (forcibly) Germanized name the option to revert to the original name in the minority language (cf. § 2 para. 5). The change is free of charge in this case.[486]

9.5 Swiss law

Switzerland did not sign the ICCS Convention No. 14 (paradoxically signed in Berne). Approved for official use, therefore, are only those diacritics that are also present in at least one of the four Swiss national languages (German, French, Italian, and Romansh).

The "Guidelines and instructions concerning the definition and spelling of the names of foreign nationals" of the Federal Department of Justice and Police (EJPD) of 1 December 1995 state:[487]

> **3.1.4 Diacritics**—special characters (diacritics) are to be copied unchanged from the identity cards insofar as they are part of a Swiss official language. Other characters are converted according to the list in Annex 2. Umlauts are

---

[484] BGBl. No. 25/1995
[485] BGBl. No. 195/1988
[486] Report of the Republic of Austria under Article 25 para. 1 of the Framework Convention for the Protection of National Minorities / Vienna, 30 June 2000 www.austria.gv.at/2004/4/15/minderheiten_dt.pdf (2011-11-12)
[487] http://www.bfm.admin.ch/fileadmin/user_upload/Themen_deutsch/ Rechtsgrundlagen/Rechtsquellen/Weisungen_Kreisschreiben_Asyl/20-2_d.pdf (2006-11-10, link no longer active)

recognized according to the entry in the passport and taking into account uppercase and lowercase.

This policy applies to all employees of federal, cantonal and municipal authorities who are responsible for the detection and recording of names of foreign nationals.

Civil status data are stored in an all-Swiss, purely electronic civil register called *Infostar*, based on the ISO-8859-1 character set. Any additional diacritics can only be placed in additional free-text fields:[488]

> On closer inspection, it is clear that the fully-computerized register no longer permits customizations "by hand". What is not intended in the system cannot be subsequently inserted or "corrected" in sole discretion. For example, the number of possible characters is final and cannot be amended at the request of persons involved by inserting additional diacritics. Where this appears to be necessary, however, fields are provided with so-called free-text that enable the individual input of necessary, legally permissible data (e.g. clarification of foreign locations).

The annotated *Civil Registry Ordinance* (ZStV) of the Swiss Federal Council of 28 April 2004 continues:[489]

> **Art. 80 Character set**—the data is captured according to the Western European character set standard of the International Organization for Standardization ISO 8859-1.

---

[488] Martin Jäger, Head of the Federal Office for Civil Status: from family records over the idea of a "StaR" to the system INFOSTAR / conditions and individual impact of the transition to a computerized, all-Swiss civil registry / information meeting on the introduction of electronic civil registry / Brunnen, 7/8 November 2001
https://www.bj.admin.ch/dam/data/bj/gesellschaft/zivilstand/dokumentation/referate/ref20011107-familienregister-d.pdf (2015-03-22)

[489] http://www.bfm.admin.ch/content/dam/data/gesellschaft/eazw/weisungen/kreisschreiben_97/20040428-beilage3-d.pdf (2011-11-11, link no longer active)

> *"Infostar" cannot establish its own new standard for characters. Crucial is an optimum compatibility at the interfaces (printers and other systems). That is why the Western European character set standard of the International Organization for Standardization (ISO 8859-1) shall be applicable. Some diacritics (especially in Eastern and South-eastern European names) may not be reproduced. If these change the sound and thus at most the meaning of the word, they are not to be omitted, but to be transferred to the Western European character set according to accepted principles of transcription. Legally, this solution is based on Article 40 of the Federal Law on the Private International Law (IPRG, SR 291).*

Behind the euphemism "accepted principles of transcription" stands the simple omission of diacritics, as a look at the guidelines shows:[490]

> The Lithuanian diacritics are recognized as follows: ą = a / č = c / ė = e / ę = e / į = i / š = s / ū = u / ų = u / ž = z (cf. Appendix 2).

With the commitment to the Western European character set ISO-8859-1, Switzerland has sacrificed in a short-sighted way the future viability and European compatibility of its electronic civil registry in favour of the "sacred cow" of backward compatibility.

It remains to be seen if one day the successful claim by a Swiss citizen from Eastern Europe to the European Court of Human Rights in Strasbourg will cause Switzerland to convert their electronic civil register to Unicode support, in order to handle all Latin characters. Reason to hope this is the judgement *Burghartz vs. Switzerland* of the ECHR (49/1992/394/472), after which Switzerland was already compelled to change a legally relevant

---

490 EJPD: Policies and Guidelines about the spelling of names of foreign nationals, states leaflet Lithuania
http://bfm.mit.ch/fileadmin/user_upload/Themen_deutsch/Rechtsgrundlagen/Rechtsquellen/Weisungen_Kreisschreiben_Asyl/Litauen_d.pdf (2006-11-10, link no longer active)

article to naming of the *Civil Registry Ordinance* because of (gender) discrimination.[491]

On 4 June 2010, the civil status regulation was changed slightly when ISO standard 8859-1 (Latin-1) was replaced by -15 (Latin-9):[492]

> *Art. 80* Character Set
> The data is captured according to the deposited default character set (ISO 8859-15). [...]

The problem of a non-Unicode-compatible standard, however, remains.

Also for **companies**, the legal spelling of persons depends in principle of the rules on the Swiss civil status register:[493]

> **2.6.3 Foreign proper names**
> *Foreign proper names must be written in Latin letters, with the notation according to the rules of the Swiss civil register.*
> If a language written in Latin characters uses diacritics (such as š, ñ, ø), corresponding foreign persons names are entered with these characters in the commercial register, *provided they can be recorded technically.*

Swiss television has revised the editorial own interpretation of German spelling. Effective immediately for foreign-language surnames is the phonetic notation. It follows the phonetic rules, but dispenses fully of diacritical marks.[494]

---

491 Parliamentary Initiative / family names and citizenship of the spouse and children / Report of the Legal Committee of the National Council on 31 August 1998 (94.434), p. 4942
http://www.admin.ch/opc/de/federal-gazette/1999/4940.pdf (2015-03-22)
492 http://www.admin.ch/ch/d/as/2010/3061.pdf (2011-11-11)
493 http://www.decisions.ch/weisung_firmenrecht.html (2011-11-11)
494 Netscout: new spelling for foreign-language surnames
http://www.facebook.com/permalink.php?story_fbid=10150154017123659&id=62662673658 (2011-03-12)

Only the database *Ordipro* (for diplomatic personnel) already used Unicode.[495] But since November 2014, the database of the *Central Migration Information System* (ZEMIS) also uses Unicode (UTF-8).[496] This means, like in the case of Turkey, that only foreigners will have their names written correctly.

In regulatory reporting, there will be a XML scheme set up (eCH-0011), with Unicode as character set.[497] We can only hope that in the course of stronger interoperability, Infostar will soon follow.

9.6 United Kingdom law

9.6.1 Birth certificates

United Kingdom birth certificates can be filled electronically or by hand, so adding diacritics is no problem.[498] However, the United Kingdom is not a member of the ICCS, so diacritics in foreign birth certificates could potentially become a problem.

---

495 https://www.bfm.admin.ch/content/dam/data/bfm/rechtsgrundlagen/weisungen/auslaender/aufenthalt/20120101-weis-namen-anh2-f.pdf (2015-03-09)

496 Maryse Bonguardo, support service, Federal Department of Justice and Police (EJPD), 2015-03-11

497 http://www.ech.ch/vechweb/page?p=dossier&documentNumber=eCH-0011&documentVersion=8.1 (2015-03-09)

498 http://www.argyll-bute.gov.uk/council-and-government/births-questions-and-answers (2015-03-01)

9.6.2 "Disallowed characters" cannot be used in passports and ID cards

The *United Kingdom Passport Agency* (UKPA) accepts only the letters Aa to Zz. Any attempt of a clerk to enter an accentuated letter would be answered by an error message from the used computer system.[499]

> **Numbers, Symbols and Punctuation Marks (Diacritical characters and accent characters)**
>
> The computer system used to produce British passports does not allow the use of numbers, symbols or punctuation marks other than hyphens or apostrophes in the names fields. It is therefore not possible to include these or any diacritical marks such as accents on a passport. Our specifications meet those that have been agreed internationally through the International Civil Aviation Organisation (ICAO), which sets standards for passports and other identity documents used for international travel [...] Diacritical characters and accent marks cannot be included on British passports, but in most languages there are alternative spellings of names to take this into account, known as transliterations. An acceptable list of transliterations as agreed by the ICAO is shown below: [...]
>
> Where an applicant's name includes a diacritical character not listed here, then evidence of the alternative spelling will be required. The applicant can provide the evidence themselves (an official document showing the correct transliteration or a letter from the relevant foreign authorities) or their case can be referred to HQ Policy so that the relevant Embassy may be contacted on their behalf, however there is no guarantee how long this may take and

---

499 https://www.whatdotheyknow.com/request/disallowed_characters_in_names_o?unfold=1 (2015-01-31)

they must be advised that if they choose this option it could considerably impact the time their application takes to be resolved. [...] [500]

First, there is to say that the ICAO specification (cf. ICAO Document 9303) refers only to the *machine readable zone* of identity documents, nothing more. So British passports as such could in principle well be issued with diacritics. It looks to me more like a legacy software problem.

Also, the "transliterations" should in fact be called "mappings" (Latin → Latin), as you can only transliterate a word into *another* script, e.g. from Cyrillic into Latin.

9.7 European electronic registration information

A prime example of the application of e-government is the European electronic registration information: project RISER *(Registry Information Service on European Residents)* is a Java application based on the platform PSI*inquiry* (based on XML and Java, and supports Unicode)[501] and open-source products. RISER stores data using SQL and communicates with the local and national electronic registers using, *inter alia*, the protocols OSCI-XMeld, XML/SOAP,

---

500 https://www.gov.uk/government/uploads/system/uploads/attachment_data/file/118564/Names-changes-of-name.pdf p. 12ff (2015-01-31)
501 Rolf Sedlmayr, PSI Information Management GmbH, personal communication (2005-12-15)

WebServices and SFTP/HTTPS,[502, 503] i.e. it supports Unicode (UTF-8). The front-end application allows the customer to directly enter Latin diacritics. Moreover, there is the possibility for the customer to upload inquiries with Latin characters in text files in any coding.[504]

RISER holds itself no reporting data and will also build no European register, but instead forwards requests to the local electronic registers, which are managed in almost all EU Member States by local authorities. September 2004 marked the launch, with the pilot operation between Germany, Austria, and Ireland. Meanwhile it is extended to Slovenia, Finland, Estonia, Lithuania, Sweden, Switzerland, Hungary, Italy, and the UK.

The RISER project has been funded by the European Commission under the eTEN work program *Deploying services for at Information Society for All.*[505]

---

502 Bernhard Krabina, Hendrik Tamm: RISER: Challenges of a Trans-European access to resident registers
http://caf-zentrum.at/de/riser-challenges-trans-european-access-resident-registers (2015-03-23)

503 PSI: RISER: European registration information—across borders
http://194.204.38.16/publications/RISER-Flyer_German.pdf (2006-02-06, link no longer active)

504 Yorck Rabenstein, Projekt RISER, PSI Information Management GmbH (phone call, 2005-12-09)

505 *Unabhängiges Landeszentrum für Datenschutz Schleswig-Holstein:* projekt "RISER" / Registry Information Service on European Residents
http://www.datenschutzzentrum.de/riser/projekt.htm (2012-02-02)

10 Landmark court decisions

Good letters, bad letters.

– Newspaper *Frankfurter Rundschau*

10.1 International law and European law

So far neither the *Human Rights Commission of the United Nations* (UNHRC) nor the *European Ombudsman* have had a dispute submitted about the spelling of person or place names with (missing) diacritics.

The *European Court of Human Rights* (ECHR)[506] and the *European Court of Justice* (ECJ)[507] each had one case. Both were decided negatively, however, because the claimants (Turkish Kurds in *Taşkin and others vs. Turkey*, an ethnic Pole from Lithuania in *Runevič-Vardyn and Wardyn vs. Vilnius City Municipality and others*) sued their own state which did not allow letters used in the alphabet of a national minority, but absent in the alphabet of the language of the majority (for the admission of "w" and "x" or "w", respectively).

---

[506] http://hudoc.echr.coe.int/sites/eng/pages/search.aspx?i=001-97088 (2015-05-31)
[507] http://curia.europa.eu/juris/recherche.jsf?language=de&jur=C,T,F&td=ALL&text=diakritische (2015-01-04)

- As Turkey has ratified the → *Convention on the indication of surnames and forenames in civil status registers*, this lead to the strange effect that foreigners could use these letters, but Turkish Kurds could not (in 2013, Turkey "legalized" the use of q, w, and x).[508]
- Lithuania's official spelling of the names of ethnic Poles—a recognized minority—uses phonetical transcriptions in the Lithuanian alphabet,[509] a practice made possible by the infamous Explanatory Report to the → *Framework Convention for the Protection of National Minorities*, clause 68.[510]
  - Article 14 of the *Treaty on Friendly Relations and Good-Neighbourly Cooperation between Lithuania and Poland* provides that names and surnames must be used "as it is pronounced in the language of the national minority".[511]

Even in cases where the ECJ had to deal with "limping" family names,[512] the omission of diacritical marks was not an issue, as no diacritics were involved.[513]

In this context it should be noted that all the documents in the databases of the ECJ and ECHR (both web pages and plain text files) reproduce the names

---

[508] Turkey Legalizes the Letters Q, W, and X.
http://www.slate.com/blogs/lexicon_valley/2013/10/24/turkey_prime_minister_erdogan_s_democratizaton_package_legalizes_letters.html (2014-12-15)

[509] http://www.eurotopics.net/de/home/presseschau/archiv/article/ARTICLE165300-Q-W-und-X-in-litauischen-Paessen-erlauben (2015-06-26)
Original: http://www.lrytas.lt/komentarai/seimas-tilta-i-lenkija-gali-nutiesti-is-keliu-raidziu-bet-bijo.htm?p=2

[510] http://conventions.coe.int/Treaty/en/Reports/Html/157.htm (2011-11-30)

[511] http://www.lfpr.lt/uploads/File/2008-21/Satkauskas_ENG.pdf (2015-03-03)

[512] "limping" = the official family name is a different one in a Member State than in another, e.g. Garcia Avello vs. Garcia-Weber

[513] e.g. EuGH, case law C-148/02 (Garcia-Avello), collection 2003, I-11613

and terms in the respective national language in correct spelling, with the necessary diacritics.

Since no guideline was set by these courts on pan-European level, the legal situation on national level is characterized by a patchwork of inconsistent and often contradictory national court decisions. Therefore, a "Diacritics Directive" on EU/EEA level should be seriously considered. Also, these national court decisions are like the proverbial "tip of the iceberg"—we do not know the number of *potential* cases that did not make it to court, for various reasons.

10.2 Germany

10.2.1 German given name must not have a foreign letter

Two German citizens, one of Norwegian descent, wanted to name their child "Bjørn". The registrar did not want to enter that spelling into the civil status documents, because—in his opinion—according to § 49 para. 1 *Standing Instructions for Registrars and Their Supervisory Authorities* "ø is clearly not a […] Latin [sic!] letter".

The parents then requested a court decision. The District Court Hamburg ruled that no legal action against this would objectively be justified. The court corrected the obviously incorrect part of the argumentation where it said that ø was not a Latin letter, but at the same time argued that ø and ö were identical in sound, so the child could be named "Björn" instead. In addition, according to the court, the Norwegian spelling would cause the child problems in daily life and in legal relations [sic!].[514]

This was a difficult case to win for the parents in 1970. First, the → *Convention on the indication of surnames and forenames in civil status registers*, which the parents maybe could have referred to, came into force almost 7 years later.[515] Also, similar to the ECHR and the ECJ case described above, this was a non-transnational case, whereas the *Convention* deals only with transnational cases. The parents could not even claim minority status, as Norwegians are not recognized as a minority in Germany.

In 2015—45 years later—the case would be ruled maybe differently, with all that European case law strengthening the freedom of movement for EU citizens (Art. 21 TFEU) and the *Free Movement of Citizens* Directive 2004/38/EC, which includes also Norway (not an EU member). To sum up the case law, a Diacritics Directive would be a good idea in my opinion.

10.2.2 Czechoslovakian birth name is to be entered with diacritical marks

A Czechoslovak citizen married a German and moved to Germany with him. When starting a civil status entry on the occasion of the birth of a daughter, the registrar was unsure if he would have to convert the mother's maiden name (with the female suffix –ová) into the male form, and asked the

---

514 *Der Standesbeamte ist nicht verpflichtet, einen nach deutschem Recht beigelegten Vornamen mit einem einer fremden Sprache eigentümlichen Schriftzeichen in das Geburtenbuch einzutragen*, District court Hamburg, decision of 29 June 1970, reference No. 60 III 100/1970, StAZ No. 10/70, p. 286
515 signed 13 September 1973, ratified 17 January 1977, entry into force 16 February 1977
http://www.ciec1.org/SignatRatifConv.pdf (2015-02-22)

District Office Deggendorf as the supervisory authority for information. According to § 57 para. 6 of the *Standing Instructions for Registrars*, the male form of foreign family name is to be used if German law is to be applied for name management. Mrs. G. was, however, still a Czechoslovak citizen. After referring to the Local Court Deggendorf and the District Court Deggendorf, the Bavarian Supreme Court issued the following resolution on the 25 November 1977:

> 53 b) The birth name of the party to 1) remained unaffected by the circumstances of marriage. Since the Czechoslovakian personal status coming into consideration at the time of birth of the child was unchanged, as set out above to II 4b, c (cf. § 57 para. 6 sentence 1 Instructions; Article 2, paragraph 1 of the ICCS Convention No. 14 of 13 September 1973), her maiden name would have to be registered in the child's birth certificate according to § 9 Civil Status Ordinance, as it is shown in the Czechoslovak marriage certificate, namely including the diacritic over the last letter, and thus as "V.[-ová]" (cf. Higher Regional Court of Berlin StAZ 1968, 351).[516]

There is nothing to say on this ruling; everything went correct. It must be remembered that according to the *Introductory Act to the Civil Code*, the name of a person is governed by the law of the country to which the person is a national; the spelling of the name remains untouched (cf. chapter 9.3.6).

10.2.3 Registration of Czechoslovak name in civil status registers

A Czechoslovakian couple was naturalized in 1978 in the Federal Republic of Germany, but kept the Czechoslovak citizenship. When creating a

---

516 *Namenswahl, tschechoslowakischer und deutscher Staatsangehöriger.*
Bavarian Supreme Court, 1st Civil Senate, decision of 25 November 1977, case No. BReg 1 Z 94/77, StAZ 1978, p. 100–103

family book[517] in 1989, the spouses applied for entering the surname with −nik (without tone marks and feminine suffix) instead of −ník and −níková. The registry office supervision submitted the case to the District Court Oldenburg. This referred to the international → *Convention on the recording of surnames and forenames in civil status registers* that had entered into force in 1977 and ruled:

> As it is clear from the birth certificate of the involved husband and the marriage certificate that the surname of the involved husband has been written with an accent mark over the "á" and "í ", these characters are to accept in the entry of the family book to be created in the Federal Republic of Germany [...] Since the extension "−ová" has by Czechoslovak naming rights thus become a legally binding part of the name of the family name of the involved wife, this ending is to be entered in the newly created family book in terms of the family name of the involved wife.[518]

Here, we have an issue of attempted Germanization. The problem is that the applicants chose the wrong procedure: they should have applied for an official change of name after the *Name Change Law* (see chapter 9.3.6). But also the timing is odd: the couple was naturalized in 1978, but only in 1989—11 years later—they decided to "de-diacritizise" their names. That sounds more like frustration than free will.

---

517 The family book was in Germany a kind of register (until 2008), issued by the registrar who performed the marriage, or on request for marriages that were contracted before.

518 *Zur Eintragung tschechoslowakischer Namen in Personenstandsbücher – Betonungszeichen – Endung „ova"*, District Court Oldenburg, 5th Civil Chamber, decision of 20 March 1990, case No. 5 T 940/89, StAZ No. 7/1990, p. 196–197

10.2.4 Diacritical characters cannot be removed by approximation statement

A woman of Turkish origin applied after her naturalization in 2002 by a statement of name leadership (approximation statement) for the civil registry change of her surname Selçuk into Selcuk, i.e. the diacritic cedilla (‚) under the letter c should be deleted.

The technical committee engaged rejected the approximation statement as invalid, on the ground that the condition for the approximation statement is that the home state does not know first and last name, but only so-called proper names. However, since the Turkish law recognizes first and last name, an approximation was excluded. A diacritical character contained in the family name could only be removed by an official change of name after the *Name Change Law* (see chapter 9.3.6).[519]

Here, we have another issue of attempted Germanization, with a different but equally wrong procedure chosen.

On the other hand, we can see that at least when it concerns "established" diacritics *acute* (see case before) and *cedilla*, the German administration quite consistently adheres to the original spelling.

10.2.5 Vietnamese names have to be spelled including diacritics

A registrar entered the names "Tr.-thành-thị-Diệp-Hòng", "Tr.-thành-Kiêm", and "Ng.-thị-Sen" in the family book without the diacritics.

---

519 *Können mittels einer Angleichungserklärung diakritische Zeichen entfallen?* Fachausschuss-Nr. 3654, StAZ No. 6/2003, p. 179f.

The supervisory authority requested a correction. The District Court Bonn ruled that this request was substantially to correspond to.[520]

10.2.6 Birth registration without the diacritic belonging to it has to be corrected in civil status registers

In 1992, the parents of a Turkish child and the competent registrar requested at the District Office the rectification of the birth entry "Oguz Han" in "Oğuzhan". The inspectors submitted the request for correction to the District Court Rottweil for decision. The District Court rejected the modification of the separate spelling, since both spellings are possible under Turkish name laws, but assessed a correction of the accent over the "g" in accordance with § 47 Civil Status Act to be admissible:

> According to the Turkish name law that is relevant here, there is no spelling of the given names "Oguz Han". The spelling of the first given name is rather correct "Oğuz". The notation without the accent markings is not possible under Turkish name law. Accordingly, to that extent the civil registry entry was to be corrected.[521]

Now we are leaving the established diacritics and turning to the more exotic, Vietnamese and Turkish ones. But also with this, the German courts had no problem in prescribing the original spelling.

---

520 *Zur Wiedergabe vietnamesischer Namen in den Personenstandsbüchern*, District Court Bonn, decision of 23 December 1985, reference No. 36 III 126/85, StAZ No. 9/1986
521 *Entspricht der im Geburtseintrag eines türkischen Kindes eingetragene Vorname nicht der türkischen Schreibweise, so ist der Eintrag von Anfang an unrichtig und ist deshalb zu berichtigen*. District Court Rottweil, decision of 25 September 1992, case No. GR I-37/92, StAZ No. 6/1993

10.2.7 The Turkish first name Yılmaz is to be reproduced with dotless i

In the notification sent to the registrar's office about the birth of a son in 1985, the parents specified the given name as "Yılmaz David" (first given name with dotless i, second given name with dotted i). However, the registry office also equipped the first given name with a dotted i. The parents then requested from the Local Court Stuttgart the rectification of the birth record. The request was rejected, and the parents appealed for complaint. The District Court submitted the complaint to the Regional Court Stuttgart, which treated it as well founded. The entry with i instead of ı had been wrong from the beginning and is to be corrected according to § 47 Civil Status Law. The spelling "Yılmaz" corresponds to the name's spelling in its country of origin (Turkey) and is therefore to be entered into German civil status registers (§ 49 para. 2 *Standing Instructions for Registrars and Their Supervisory Authorities*) in its original form. The Regional Court continues:

> Since the Turkish language uses as the German [language] Latin characters, it also requires no transmission according to sound rules or phonetic rules of German spelling into the local area Latin characters. The name can be rather taken literally. [...] The notation with the dotless i is a peculiarity of the Turkish language, which in this respect has priority over the spelling in the German legislation. Both of § 49 para. 2 sentence 1 Standing Instructions for Registrars and Their Supervisory Authorities as well as from Art. 2 of the Convention on the recording of surnames and forenames in civil status registers (ICCS) follows the general principle that names from other language areas should be transferred as possible without any alteration because of the attachment of those names with the right to privacy. Therefore, according to both provisions cited, names of foreign origin are to be provided with the characters peculiar to the foreign language, even if the German language

does not know such signs. This is true not only for accents and hooks, but in the same way also for the peculiarity of spelling of the letter I existing in the Turkish-speaking countries. The—also in the opinion of the registry office and the legal supervisory authority's—faulty entry with dotted i is therefore to be corrected as prescribed.
(Regional Court Stuttgart, decision of 13 February 1986 – 2 T 1040/85). [522]

10.2.8 Turkish letters ı and İ have to be transferred to the civil status registers

The Higher Regional Court of Berlin had to deal in 2003 with a case in which a civil status office had refused to adopt the Latin character ı (dotless i) from a Turkish document to the German civil status register. The Court of Appeal took into account § 2 para. 1 [Civil Status Ordinance] "The civil status registers are kept in German language" and § 49 para 1 sentence 3 of the *Standing Instructions for Registrars and Their Supervisory Authorities* "The civil status registers must be kept in German language with Kurrent or Latin fonts." However, it summoned § 2 para 1 of the → *Convention on the recording of surnames and forenames in civil status registers* and § 49 para 1 sentence 3 of the *Standing Instructions* and ruled as follows:

> 1. If an entry of family and given names is to make according to Art. 2 Convention on the recording of surnames and forenames in civil status registers in a civil status register on the basis of a foreign certificate which also reflects the names in the Latin alphabet, peculiarities present in the foreign language have, in any case, to be taken over if the variation plays only a diacritical function. This is also the case when the peculiarity of the foreign language does not consist in the addition of an extra character not used in

---

522 *Der türkische Vorname Yılmaz ist auch in deutschen Personenstandsbüchern ohne i-Punkt wiederzugeben*. StAZ No. 6/1986, p. 168f.

the German alphabet, but in the omission of a character component which only changes the letters diacritically.

2. According to this principle, the Turkish characters "I/ı" and "İ/i" are both to be entered unaltered according to the notation in the Turkish name. (Case No. 1 W 34-38/03)[523]

The *Convention*, as it turns out, has an undefined area: what if something is not *added* to a letter, but *taken* away? Still, German courts prescribed the original spelling of ı, because the rest of the name was written in Latin alphabet.

10.2.9 The Icelandic letter ð is not eligible for registration

In 1998, a mother wanted to register the Icelandic male name Sigurður as her son's middle name. The registrar refused this name as ineligible, as letters that were not from the Latin alphabet were not registrable. At the request of the mother, the District Court instructed the registrar to perform the registration in accordance with § 49 para. 1 sentence 3 of the *Standing Instructions for Registrars*. Against this decision, the county as the supervisory authority immediately appealed and affirmed the view that "ð" did not constitute a Latin letter. The District Court dismissed the instant complaint: the differing writing of a letter was comparable with diacritics, generally deemed admissible. That was targeted by another immediate appeal of the district government. The Higher Regional Court Celle upheld this complaint: as diacritics according to the → *Convention on the recording of*

---

523 Summary: http://www.rechtscentrum.de/search.php?q_all=t%FCrkischen+Schriftzeichen&q_any=&q_exact=&q_not=&q_fref=&q_tframe=&q_date=&q_law=&db=zivilrecht&mode=Erweiterte+Suche (2011-12-01)

surnames and forenames in civil status registers, only additions to letters of the German alphabet are permitted, according to the Court, such as accents, hooks or points above or below a letter. It is not permissible, however, to replace a letter of the German alphabet because of the changed pronunciation of a foreign name by a letter that is foreign to the German alphabet. The Icelandic letter "ð", however, is foreign to the German alphabet and is not a mere diacritical change in the German "d". It describes not only a separate sound not found in the German alphabet, but also cannot be assigned from its notation unambiguously to the "d" contained in the Latin alphabet. Hence the entry of this letter is not possible.[524]

The *Convention*, as it turns out, has another undefined area: what to do with *additional* letters? Following the Higher Regional Court Celle, also the Icelandic letter þ would not be eligible for registration, as well as the Sami letters ŋ, ʒ and ǯ, and the Azerbaijani ə (þ was taken from the runic alphabet to the Latin alphabet, ŋ, ʒ, and ə come originally from the *International Phonetic Alphabet*).[525] To correct the defect that at least three European languages cannot fully be represented in a German registry office, although based on the Latin alphabet, one can proceed as follows: either you extend on ICCS level the term "Latin script" on the characters that appear in modified Latin alphabets, or you can explicitly add ð, þ, ŋ, ʒ/ǯ, ə—and the German sharp ß. Again, in the hypothetical EU Diacritics Directive, this should be spelled out to leave no room for guesswork (a precedent would be an Italian law for minorities, see p. 148).

---

524 *Der isländische Buchstabe »ð« ist nicht eintragungsfähig, weil er dem deutschen Alphabet fremd ist und nicht bloß eine diakritische Veränderung des deutschen »d« beinhaltet.* StAZ No. 6/1998, p. 176f., juris No. KORE583199800

525 When defining the mapping on Latin base character A–Z, the common mapping is ð = d, þ = th, ŋ = n, ʒ = z (not y!).
http://xoev.de/latinchars/1_1/supplement/identverfahren.pdf (2015-01-07)

In Unicode, the names of the relevant letter read, by the way, always LATIN [sic!] CAPITAL/SMALL LETTER. Icelandic sources[526] and following them also the *European Committee for Standardization*[527] indeed consider the letter þ as basic character of the Latin alphabet and ð as modified d. In addition, the letters Ð/ð and Þ/þ are in the repertoires DSMeld Annex 4 / LA8 Passport and String.Latin. The ICCS itself does also assume that in the case of Iceland, Article 2 of the → *Convention on the recording of surnames and forenames in civil status registers* (unchanged takeover) applies, since the Icelandic and German language make use of the same script.[528] So not only from a linguistic point of view, the decision of the Higher Regional Court Celle is therefore questionable.

The Higher Regional Court of Berlin argued later in a justification to another naming rights verdict:

> It can be left open whether Art. 2, para. 1 Convention on the recording of surnames and forenames in civil status registers is to be understood as meaning that "same characters" already exist when the language in which the name is given in the document and the language in which to make the entry use the same script, and it is not necessary that all the characters with which the name is set out in the certificate will be also found in the registration language. In favour, so the Court believes, speaks the purpose of the Convention, which shall ensure a uniform indication of name in the civil registers of the individual States, according to its preamble (see *Bundestag*

---

526 Ágústa Þorbergsdóttir [sic!], Icelandic language Institute, personal communication (2006-02-24)

527 Michael Everson, Evertype / Baldur Sigurðsson, Íslensk Málstöð: ON THE STATUS OF THE LATIN LETTER ÞORN AND OF ITS SORTING ORDER, Report to CEN/TC304. Presented in Reykjavík 1994-06-07
http://www.evertype.com/standards/wynnyogh/thorn.html (2011-12-01)

528 Chantal NAST, Administrative Director ICCS, personal communication (2006-02-26)

document 7/5203, p. 9; Federal Court StAZ, 1994, 42, 44). This goal can only be achieved if additional signs or single letters of the document language that the entry language does not know are accepted at the entry of the name. Languages that operate the same script—here Latin—may have specifics regarding individual characters; e.g. the character of the German language "ß" is alien to other languages that use the Latin alphabet; the Turkish language does also not know the letters of the German alphabet "q", "w" and "x". Should such individual characters be transliterated according to Art. 3 Convention on the recording of surnames and forenames in civil status registers, this would lead to (partly) different and—in the absence of relevant transliteration norms—inconsistent civil status registers. Also the German legislator has assumed an abstract understanding of the term "same characters" in Art. 2, para. 1 and "other characters" in Art. 3, para. 1 Convention on the recording of surnames and forenames in civil status registers, and the acquisition of each existing peculiarities of the foreign language in the civil status entry (see *Bundestag* document, supra, character "ß").[529]

Figure 10.1: **Use of ð in a German book store** (own photo)

---

529 Higher Regional Court of Berlin, 1. Civil Division, decision of 23 September 2003, case numbers 1 W 34/03, 1 W 35/03, 1 W 36/03, 1 W 37/03, 1 W 38/03, juris No. KORE439212003

Use of ð in an English newspaper:

> *Jóhanna Sigurðardóttir The world's first openly gay head of government, 69, is a former flight attendant and trade unionist who became Iceland's Prime Minister in 2009 after the collapse of her country's banking sector. She has been in a civil union since 2002.*[530]

Sadly, the District Court Berlin-Schöneberg did not heed the argument of the Higher Regional Court of Berlin when he ruled that the Icelandic letters ð and þ were not letters with diacritical characters and therefore not part of the Latin alphabet. Instead of taking transcripts of Icelandic civil status records, he reverted to passports (where those letters were mapped in the *machine*[!]-readable zone as d and th) and conveniently found that this notation was to take in the German civil status records.[531]

—The machine-readable zone is *only* thought for machine-reading, as it complies only to the ICAO Document 9303 (cf. chapter 9.6.2, see also judgement of the Federal Administrative Court of 29 September 1992 with respect to the registration of names with umlauts in identity cards, cf. chapter 9.3.5.2):

> The representation of an umlaut by the appropriate vowels, following the rules for typewriting, is appropriate and necessary to accelerate the identity control in international border traffic. The spelling with "ue" was foreseen in recommendations by the international standard organization for ID cards and machine-readable passports as well as the International Civil Aviation Organization.

However, for civil status registers, the *Convention* applies, i.e. the District Court Berlin-Schöneberg's ruling was unlawful. The original spelling with

---

530 http://www.independent.co.uk/news/world/europe/gay-socialist-and-born-in-a-squatters-camp--meet-the-new-pm-of-belgium-6273193.html (2011-12-08)
531 District Court Berlin-Schöneberg, 18 November 2011, 70 III 282-283/11, StaZ 8/2012, p. 245

ð and þ, respectively, would have to be taken over. Also, none of the courts bothered to ask the ICCS for a statement.

10.2.10 ! is not a letter

According to a ruling of the District Court Münster, it is not possible to accept click sounds (ʘ | ! ǂ ǁ) of African Bushmen (e.g. in the name Xam!ua), despite the fact that their languages are otherwise written in Latin script.[532] That case seems very difficult at first, as it opens up the whole new subject of *African* Latin letters (ɓ ɗ ɛ ɨ ɔ etc.),[533] which I otherwise specifically excluded from this book. On the other hand, Latin letters are Latin letters, so in principle, the name Xam!ua should be eligible for registration (nowhere is written that you should know how to *pronounce* it).[534]

10.2.11 Conclusion for Germany

Since the → *Convention on the indication of surnames and forenames in civil status registers* came into force, diacritics—even exotic ones—are consistently ordered to be written in the original spelling by German courts. Where the *Convention* really has holes is in how to deal with additional letters. The rulings in the cases with ð, þ, ! contradict the *purpose* of the Convention, which is to ensure a uniform indication of all names written in Latin script. This purpose can only be achieved if single Latin letters of the document that the entry language does not know are also accepted (the

---

532 District Court Münster, StAZ 1984, p. 129
533 http://en.wikipedia.org/wiki/African_reference_alphabet (2015-02-22)
534 see Russell Peters and his problems to pronounce the name !xobile
　　https://www.youtube.com/watch?v=Yj-1kp777NM (2015-02-28)

Higher Regional Court of Berlin cited q, w, x and ß, and the ICCS cited ð, þ, so ! is just the logical extrapolation).

In an Annex to the hypothetical EU Diacritics Directive, this should be spelled out, best with examples.

10.3 Austria

10.3.1 In the spelling of a surname, diacritics are also to be taken into account

In 1958, the Innsbruck District Court confirmed the adoption agreement completed between Anton Černy as adoptive father and Antonia Anna A. as adopted child, with the remark that subject to this contract, Antonia Anna A. would from now on have to lead the name A.-Cerny [sic]. Against such a modified spelling, the Office of the Provincial Government of Tyrol as the supervisory authority of the civil registry office appealed, but unsuccessfully.

The Appeal Court (District Court Innsbruck) stated that nothing[!] was changed to the form (pronunciation, spelling) of the name by the agreement and the confirmation of the court. Only if the court had departed from the spelling of the name in the adoption agreement, it would have been a writing mistake (which could at any time be corrected by the court of first instance itself upon request or on its own motion). But when the spelling in the court decision and the spelling in the agreement were the same, the court decision was correct and could not be corrected. If the registrar's office or its supervisory authority was of the opinion that the name in the adoption agreement was not right—may it be either be a real inner error or only a formal incorrectness (different from the spelling in the birth register)—so this should be dealt with by the administrative procedure provided therefor. The court would go beyond its jurisdiction if it wanted to impose on the parties a form of the name other than the one rendered by them in the contract.

Against this judgement, the supervisory authority of the civil registry office raised extraordinary appeal (successfully) on the Supreme Court. The Supreme Court reversed the decisions of both lower courts and charged the Court of first instance with a new decision following supplementary proceedings. The citation reads:

While it is true that there is no need for an explicit agreement and therefore also no explicit pronouncement of the confirming court, because of the name acquisition through the adopted person will enter into effect already by operation of law, the court has yet to determine whether the family name of the adoptive father, mentioned under § 182 sentence 2 Austrian Civil Code in the adoption agreement [...], to lead by the adopted child in connection with his former family name, matches his real family name, also from the spelling. The opposite view of the Appeal Court that the choice of name should be left to the parties, contradicts the clear, explicit provision of § 182 sentence 2 Austrian Civil Code, after the (real) name of the adoptive father must be part of the double name, and is therefore obviously illegal. Since, according to the applicant's appeal, lodged against the Court of First Instance's decision, the surname of the adoptive father is not C., but Č.—also diacritics have to be taken into account in the spelling of a surname—the Court of First Instance will have to consider whether this claim is true. If so, the parties are to be guided to improve their input as well as the affiliated adoption agreement (2 § 2 para. point 8. Non-dispute law). (Supreme Court of Justice, business number 6Ob184/58)[535]

---

535 http://www.ris.bka.gv.at/jus/ *(Under "Geschäftszahl" enter business number 6Ob184/58 and click on "Suche starten".)*

Here, we have presumably an issue of attempted Germanization. But like in the two German cases, the applicants chose the wrong procedure: they should have applied for an official name change after the *Name Change Law* (see chapter 9.4.6). Interesting also the Appeal Court's statement that "nothing was changed to the form (pronunciation, spelling) of the name", which is clearly wrong (pronunciation Ce = [tse], but Če = [tʃe]).

10.3.2 Suppression of diacritical characters is a violation of the right to a name

In 1998, a member of the Slovenian minority argued at the Austrian Ombudsman Board that he attached great importance to the correct spelling of his surname and considered it particularly discriminatory that authorities refused to comply to the duty to reproduce his own name to the letter and character, and had even asked him to change the spelling[!], which the complainant rejects as well as the "computer-compatible" toleration the wrong spelling of his name in certifications or transcripts (cf. chapter 10.4.1). The Ombudsman Board stressed that the proper name is an essential part of the identity of the legal subject, and reiterated:

> The authorities are obliged to accurately reproduce the family name to the letter and character. Although diacritics (marks, check mark, etc. over, under or in a letter that are mainly important for the pronunciation) are commonly referred to as non-computer-compatible, this does not change the fact that the naming right is an absolutely protected right, and these proper names or their spelling, respectively, may not be changed arbitrarily. Although computers are used in many areas, there is actually hardly a computerized system whose printer has a character set that contains diacritical marks. This does not change the fact that correct spelling of proper names would be

technically manageable also in the context of computing, if one developed appropriate applications that would also meet the requirement raised justifiably by the complainant (spelling Č/č).

So found the Ombudsman Board in the course of an investigation procedure that also the Federal Police Department Klagenfurt could not meet the demands made by the complainant when issuing licenses, passports, etc. due to lack of diacritical marks in the automation-assisted application. The problem is known to the Federal data centre which has taken over the system's support, and it is also working on a solution. The ombudsman notes about this:

> However, the fact remains that all applicants have a right that their names continue to be written as they have been handed down, since § 11 para. 3 and 4 Civil Status Act, Federal Law Gazette No. 60/1983, as amended, would only allow a certification of a different spelling that deviates from the legal name at the request of the person concerned. But this also may not result in the need for citizens to justify themselves why they insist on a proper registration of their personal name, or constantly be confronted with statements like "We don't have that" or "Why you get upset because of such pettiness". If and as long as a computerized technical implementation of this problem awaits a solution, all authorities shall perform handwritten or typewritten entries without comment. (Ombudsman Board 135-V/98)[536]

Fast forward 40 years, the situation has reversed: while in the context of an emancipation movement in the 1970s (see chapter 11), the Slovenian minority is more confident in demanding its naming rights, the authorities hide behind sentences like "our computer cannot do that" (note: that is five years

---

[536] Eighteenth and Nineteenth Report of the Ombudsman Board to the Regional Assembly of Carinthia (1998–1999), German
http://volksanwaltschaft.gv.at/downloads/fftvn/K%C3%A4rnten%20Bericht%201998%201999.pdf (2011-11-12)

after the introduction of the Unicode standard), and had even asked the applicant to change the spelling (not the other way round), which is a clear violation of chapter 5.1 and 5.2 of the → *Framework Convention for the Protection of National Minorities*.

Luckily, the Austrian Ombudsman Board are sympathetic to the Slovenian minority's complaints.

10.3.3 Handwritten or typewritten complement of diacritics is permitted

In the same year, a citizen asked at the Federal Police Department in Klagenfurt for the issuance of a duplicate driver's license. When he came to pick it up, he noticed that in the driver's license the diacritics were not entered in his name. His related complaints were unsuccessful, and it was being communicated to him that these diacritics were not present in the computer. Since the driver's license was therefore not issued by the Federal Police Department Klagenfurt with the correct spelling of his name, he brought a complaint about it with the Ombudsman Board.

The Ombudsman Board initiated an investigation and also informed the Federal Minister for Science and Transport of the complaint submissions. Because of this intervention of the Ombudsman Board, the Federal Ministry of Science and Transport has pointed out to the Federal Police Department Klagenfurt that there are no specific rules regarding the method of registration in driver's license forms. Thus a handwritten or typed entry is also permitted. Then a new driver's license with handwritten complement was issued free of charge to the complainant by the Federal Police Department Klagenfurt. (Ombudsman Board 135-V/98) [537]

10.3.4 Diacritics in driver's licenses are to complement by hand if required

In 2003, Mrs. S. applied to the Ombudsman Board for assistance, since a diacritic in her given name did not appear in her driving licence (issued in 2003), because it could not be reproduced in electronic data processing. The Ombudsman Board commented as follows:

> The Ombudsman Board had already shown in the 22nd Report to the National Council and the Federal Council that authorities are obliged to reproduce surnames accurately in terms of both letters and characters, whereby the fact that diacritics (e.g. diaeresis, cedilla) are generally held to be unsuitable in electronic data processing does not alter the circumstance that the name right is an immutably protected one and that authorities may not arbitrarily alter proper names and/or their orthography. In light of private and family names constitutionally protected in Art. 8 of the European Convention on Human Rights, which indubitably protects the right to bear one's (full) name, (cf. Constitutional collection 13.661/1994 [538] and 15.031/1997 [539]

---

537 22. Report on the activities of the Ombudsman Board in 1998 to the National Council and the Federal Council, German
http://www.eoi.at/d/EOI%20-%20Jahresberichte/Austria/Wien/Volksanwalt-Berichte-Parlament-Bundesrat/PB-22-1998.pdf (2015-01-10)
538 Excerpt: *"The regulation of name leadership is not exhausted in the regulation of private living conditions, but beyond this unfolds an regulatory function serving important public interests."*
539 In both judgements on family and naming right, the Constitutional Court referred to Article 8 of the ECHR. Cf. http://www.ris.bka.gv.at/vfgh/ *(Under* "Sammlungsnummer" *enter business number and click on* "Suche starten".*)*

and the decision of the ECHR in the case Burghartz[540, 541] from 22 February 1994, published in *Österreichische Juristen-Zeitung* 1994, 559), every applicant for the issuance of a driving licence has the right to have their given and surnames always written the way they actually are. Therefore, if a character cannot be reproduced in electronic data processing, the entry must be made by hand or in typewritten characters. (VA BD/244-V/03)[542]

Thanks to the intervention of the Ombudsman Board, the competent Federal Ministry instructed the transport authorities to enter diacritics in driver's licenses by hand if and as need be.

Already in another case, the Ombudsman Board ruled:

> The Ombudsman Board is of the opinion that the name of a person is an expression of identity and individuality, and the right to use the family name falls into the scope of Article 8 of the ECHR (see to that from the recent literature exemplified in detail WIEDERIN, Art. 8 of the Convention, in KORINEK/HOLOUBEK (ed.), Constitutional law (5th issue 2002) marginal notes 33 and 39, who while citing further decisions of the ECHR points to the "now unanimous opinion that the name of a person as a means for the expression of personal identity concerns his/her private life", as well as Constitutional

---

540 Judgement *Burghartz vs. Switzerland*: impossibility for the husband to let the name of his wife, chosen as family name, preceded his own name violates Article 8 in conjunction with Article 14 of the Convention. Excerpt from the document: *"As a means of personal identification and for binding to a family, the name of a person relates to their private and family life, although Article 8 of the ECHR contains no express provision in this regard."*

541 Swiss Federal Chancellery: Administrative practice of the Federal http://vpb.admin.ch/deutsch/doc/58/58.121.html (2011-11-12)

542 27th Report on the activities of the Ombudsman Board in 2003 to the National Council and the Federal Council, German http://volksanwaltschaft.gv.at/downloads/7etrn/pb27.pdf (2011-11-12) English http://volksanwaltschaft.gv.at/downloads/9j6cp/Annual%20Report%20-%20Summary%202003.pdf (2015-01-11)

collection 13.661/1994 and 15.031/1997 and the decision of the ECHR in the case Burghartz [...]. (Ombudsman Board BD/11-AA/03)[543]

The next two cases were about diacritics in driver's licenses. The Ombudsman Board contacted the Federal Ministry of Science and Transport, who pointed out that a handwritten or typed entry is also permitted if "the computer cannot do it".

10.3.5 Correct spelling of the family name is constitutionally required

In 2006, Dr. M. turned to the Ombudsman Board because his last name was written often inaccurately by authorities (the diacritical mark over the corresponding letter of the family name was missing). During the investigation procedure, the Ombudsman Board had to discover that last names are often incorrectly written that way by authorities. The Ombudsman Board commented as follows:

> Art. 8 ECHR contains a constitutionally guaranteed right to respect for private and family life. In view of the relevant legal practice of the Constitutional Court as well as of the European Court of Human Rights (in that sense also the judgements in the cases *Stjerna* and *Guillot* of 25 November 1994 and 24 October 1996), there can be no doubt that the right to respect for private life also includes a constitutionally guaranteed right to respect for one's own name.
>
> From the aspect of constitutional law, one must therefore ask whether the range of protection of the right to respect for one's own name also includes

---

543 27th Report on the activities of the Ombudsman Board in 2003 to the National Council and the Federal Council, German
http://volksanwaltschaft.gv.at/downloads/7etrn/pb27.pdf (2011-11-12)

the right that first and last names must be reproduced in correct characters by authorities.

This is supported, in the opinion of the Ombudsman Board, by some very strong arguments:

First of all, it already appears obvious that the respect of the name is expressed in its correct spelling. If this were not so, the administration would be allowed to change names through arbitrary spellings or the mere consideration of an arbitrarily defined number of letters (e.g. the first five of the family name), or replace a first name by another by means of consistently held writing "errors" in all official documents. It is methodologically not clear to what extent the deduction of the right to correct spelling of names out of the right to respect of the name may be a bigger step than the deduction of the right to respect of the name out of the right to respect for private life.

With respect to the counterfactual situation representing the complaint, the objection could possibly be raised that legally, the omission of a diacritical mark is to be assessed differently than for example the shortening of the family name or the deliberate alteration of the given name as a result of conscious misspelling. To such an argument has to be replied, of course, that also the omission of a diacritical mark equals to the above-mentioned examples that the name is not displayed in the correct spelling. It cannot matter, out of general basic doctrinal considerations, on the intentionality of the regulatory action, but only on their actual repercussions—in this case, the incorrect name spelling.

Also systematic considerations to the constitution speak for this interpretation of the result:

In determining the normative content of constitutional norms, not only the interpreted norm itself, but also its normative environment and ultimately even the entire constitutional legal system are to be used. Such a constitution-systematic interpretation is also required in the representational context, because the ECHR is in force as Federal constitutional law in Austria, and its decisive normative content for Austria completely opens up only by taking into account other normative requirements of the Austrian Federal constitutional law.

It can therefore not be regarded as irrelevant that the Federal constitutional legislator himself has felt compelled in form of Art. 7, para. 3 Federal Constitutional Law to state specifically that official names, titles, degrees and job titles may be used in the form that expresses the gender of the incumbent. All authorities have to respect the relevant decision and also issue the official documents in accordance with the relevant statutory simple design rules.

It is true now of course that an official name, a title, a degree, or a job title is different from the pre- or surname of a person. Nevertheless, the disputed constitutional norm is representationally of great relevance, because it is not thinkable of the Federal constitutional legislator, in the opinion of the Ombudsman Board, to have created a constitutional rights situation that protects the correct naming of official names, titles, degrees, and job titles at constitutional level but leaves the correct spelling of the given and family name of a person to the discretion of the administration, although diacritical marks that are attached to other characters (usually letters) alter their meaning, emphasis, or pronunciation. This may even go so far that a combination of letter and diacritical character is in one language an independent character with its own sound, while this only indicates the emphasis in other languages.

In the given context, it may eventually not be overlooked that the non-character-true spelling of the family name is especially for members of linguistic minorities particularly offensive, because of the discursive perception and recognition of the minority and its identity by the majority population and the state are especially performed by diacritics in the written language. Diacritics have full orthographic importance. They serve, as their name indicates, as distinctive marks in connection with otherwise identical-looking letters. The—only a few years before in Art. 8, para. 2 Federal Constitutional

Law anchored in the Constitution—commitment of the Republic of Austria to its traditional linguistic and cultural diversity, which is reflected in the autochthonous ethnic groups, involves a value judgement of the Constitutional legislator, that puts it at least close that only one correct spelling of the family name of members of minority groups cannot be regarded as a violation of the constitutional sphere.

The Ombudsman Board therefore considers summarized that at least from the cohesion of the constitutional provisions of Art. 8 ECHR, in conjunction with Art. 7, para. 3 and Art. 8, para. 2 Federal Constitutional Law, it is deduced that also the correct spelling of the name constitutionally enjoys protection. The Ombudsman Board also assumes that this interpretation seems necessary in order to allow the value judgements of the Constitutional legislator, expressed in fundamental rights and state objectives, to be effective in practice in the reality of life. Only such an understanding sufficiently addresses the dynamic case law of the ECHR (see detail in GRABENWARTER, *Europäische Menschenrechtskonvention* [2005] 39 recital 12 f with numerous case law references).

In the given context, finally the following comments should be made:
In accordance with the in Article 18, paragraph 1 Federal Constitutional Law enshrined principle of legality, the entire state administration must be exercised only on the basis of law. This central constitutional principle is in the particular case yet clarified and reaffirmed by Art. 8, para. 2 ECHR, by arranging that any interference within the scope of protection constitutionally guaranteed by Art. 8, para. 1 ECHR must be provided by law.

In the current legal situation, diacritical marks are mandatory in matters of civil status. Applications which derive from that (e.g. regulatory reporting) must support diacritics in any case. All other applications should be switched quickly to avoid inconsistencies. In the examination procedure of the Ombudsman Board, no statutory regulation has come to light that would authorize the administration—for whatever reason—to make an incorrect representation of names. In particular, neither could the constitutional service—according to its statement, "to justify an intervention [in guaranteed legal positions by Article 8, Section 1 of the ECHR] [would] fall at the lack of legal basis"—nor the Federal Ministry of Finance refer to such provisions. This is also in so far as no surprise, as it was not disputed before the introduction of the software primarily triggering the problem, that the authority—if necessary by handwritten additions—had to make a correct spelling of the name. A statutory scheme according to which it is allowed in the course of using new software—possibly also for economic reasons—not to require the correct spelling of the name does not exist.

From the above, it follows therefore that a lawless and therefore unconstitutional status is caused as the result of the improper storage and representation of diacritics by the software and hardware of the [Federal Computing Centre]. The compliance with the Federal constitutional law requirements, flowing from the principle of legality, is vital to the disposition and therefore can be placed under no circumstances to the discretion of the—whatever organizationally set up—electronic government.

In December 2007, the members of the Ombudsman Board therefore unanimously agreed that a failure to take suitable measures to save and present diacritic characters correctly with the software and hardware used by the Federal Computing Centre must be qualified as **maladministration**. To eliminate this instance of **maladministration**, the **recommendation** was addressed to the Chancellor and Vice-Chancellor to take steps which by reference to the—in the context of e-government between the Federal, state and local agreed—"manual diacritics" *(Handbuch diakritische Zeichen – diakrit-1.1.0)* [are] required to adjust the storage and representation of diacritics of the software and hardware used in the [Federal Computing Centre] and thus to ensure the correct spelling of people's names (gradually).

In response to this **recommendation**, it was admitted by the Federal Chancellery that the entire scope of UTF-8-displayable characters (8-bit Unicode

Transformation Format) can not currently be reported in the electronic record. However, the electronic record is to be modified in such a way that in the future, diacritics can be stored, represented, and transferred to the care of business. In addition, the representational subject matter will be brought on the agenda to the next meeting of the platform "Digital Austria".

By the Vice-Chancellor and Federal Minister for Finance, the Ombudsman Board was promised that in the context of the currently-starting project "e-Tax", all IT processes of financial management will be set up step by step diacritical-fit. (VA BD/25-BKA/06, BKA-184.490/0010-I/8/2008) [544, 545]

Here, the Ombudsman Board goes to great depths explaining why Art. 8 ECHR, mentioned already in the previous chapter, and supported by growing case law, has also direct implications for the Austrian Constitution, and why the failure to set up an electronic government fit to deal with Unicode qualifies as maladministration.

10.3.6 Correct spelling of surnames with diacritic characters is a requirement of the Federal Constitution

The report 2013(!) of the Ombudsman Board still states (after reminding the government since 2007):

---

[544] Report on the activities of the Ombudsman Board in 2007 to the National Council and the Federal Council, German
http://volksanwaltschaft.gv.at/downloads/cfhu7/Parlamentsbericht%202007.pdf (2011-11-13)

[545] Report on the activities of the Ombudsman Board in 2008 to the National Council and the Federal Council, English
http://volksanwaltschaft.gv.at/downloads/8j2c9/Annual%20Report%20-%20Summary%202008.pdf (2015-01-11)

For years, the Austrian Ombudsman Board has been lobbying for a change to the software and hardware used by administration to save and display diacritic characters, so as to allow surnames to be spelled correctly.

Right to respect for own name: Article 8 of the European Convention on Human Rights (ECHR) contains a right by order of the Federal Constitution to respect private and family life. In light of the relevant legislation by the Constitutional Court and European Court of Human Rights (see Collection of decisions of the Austrian Constitutional Court 13.661/1994 and 15.031/1997 as well as the rulings by the European Court of Human Rights in the case "Burghartz" dated 22 February 1994 and the cases "Stjerna" and "Guillot" dated 25 November 1994 and 24 October 1996), there can be no doubt that the right to respect for private life also comprises the right to respect for one's name by order of the Federal Constitution.

This then raises the question under the Federal Constitution whether the scope of protection of the right to respect for one's own name also includes the right for first and surnames to be spelled correctly by the authorities.

Ombudsman Board demands correct spelling of names: As the Ombudsman Board reported in detail in its Annual Report of 2007 [German version, p. 424ff], substantial arguments can be presented in favour of answering this question in the affirmative. In December 2007, the members of the Ombudsman Board therefore unanimously agreed that a failure to take suitable measures to save and present diacritic characters correctly with the software and hardware used by the Federal Computing Centre must be qualified as a deficit in administration. A letter was sent to the Federal Chancellery to rectify this deficit, recommending that the software and hardware used by the Federal Computing Centre should be adjusted to allow diacritic characters to be saved and displayed and surnames to be spelled correctly (in steps).

Need for action across federal administration: The Federal Chancellery responded to this recommendation by stating that all characters of the format UTF-8 (8-bit Unicode Transformation Format) cannot currently be displayed in the Federal Electronic Records Management System. However, the Federal Electronic Records Management System is to be modified so that diacritic characters can be saved, displayed and used in notifications in the future. In addition, the current problem was discussed repeatedly at information and communication technology meetings [IKT-BUND] where the individual federal ministries also presented specific implementation plans [e.g. the land register, the company register, and the central commercial register].

Unfortunately, it is still unclear when the Ombudsman Board's recommendations will be implemented in full. However, in the meantime the understanding that a uniform handling of diacritic characters would be desirable for interoperability and/or cost reduction reasons alone has spread across nearly all areas of administration. But the need to adapt a number of Austrian e-government applications to deal with diacritic characters is nevertheless an extensive project.

Substantial progress can be seen: The Federal Ministry of Finance is now able to reproduce names to the letter. IT processes applied by the Federal Ministry of Finance must support the input, processing, and output of Unicode to handle diacritic characters in the names of individuals, addresses and the names of legal entities, based on the convention on "diacritic characters [DZ-1.0]" [This convention supplemented and concretized the existing convention "manual diacritics" *(Handbuch diakritische Zeichen_diakrit-1.1.0)*. It notes which characters are supported in any case in names, how they are each transcribed, coded and transmitted in the Latin alphabet, and how to search for words with diacritics.] If individual software is developed, the software library "diacritic characters" must be used. The Federal Ministry of Finance has obtained a federal license for this library [based on the central residents register "ZMR"]. The software library "diacritic characters" comprises the transformation, verification, presentation and input of diacritic characters (in an input screen).

> The SAP process at the Federal Ministry of Finance (federal budget and personnel management) has already been converted to Unicode, and can therefore process diacritic characters. Tax and customs applications are currently being converted for use with diacritic characters, as part of the program E-Finance Tax and Customs. April 2014 has been set as the planned completion date for this IT process.
> Individual case: VA-BD-BKA/0026-A/1/2009.[546]

Fast forward six years, the Ombudsman Board still sees need for action across federal administration regarding the human right to respect names, but acknowledges that also substantial progress can be seen, both in theory—the stronger desire for interoperability—and in practice: the "manual diacritics", existing already in 2007, has meanwhile been transferred to the software library "diacritic characters" that new software has to use. Still, it is unclear when the Ombudsman Board's recommendations will be implemented in full.

10.3.7 Correct spelling of names on the health insurance card

In 2005, the use of inappropriate or incompatible character sets as part of the introduction of the electronic health card (e-card) caused resentment among those affected, especially in the ethnic group of the Slovenes. In August 2005, Vladimir Smrtnik, chairman of the Unity List / *Enotna lista* (EL, national association of the Slovenian city council fractions), demanded the "consistent and equitable consideration of Slovenian characters" in the spelling of names of the new e-cards. According to Smrtnik, they sent a

---

546 http://volksanwaltschaft.gv.at/downloads/144k2/Austria_AOB_Annual%20Report_2013_EN.pdf (2015-01-13)

note in writing on this problem to the *Association of Austrian Social Security Institutions* and the competent Federal Ministry. "The failure to include the correct name spellings would be a clear violation of the principles of the European Convention on Human Rights and should therefore be avoided," stated the EL chairman.[547]

On 10 August 2005, the news channel ORF reported on its web site: "No problem with Slovenian characters." The Director of the Carinthian Health Insurance, ALFRED WURZER, promised that the demand of the Carinthian Slovenes for "consistent and equitable consideration of the Slovenian characters" in the spelling of names of the new e-cards had already been implemented. "The new e-card can do that all, and we will take the spellings of all known and to-be-announced names into account," Wurzer told the news agency APA.[548]

Indeed, the document "Certification Practice Statement for e-Card SV-signature", shared by the smart card operating company on 24 March 2005, states: "The official name can contain umlauts and diacritics (UTF8 Unicode)."[549]

In the *benefits and coverage plan* of the Lower Austrian Health Insurance in October 2005, however, it says:

> At the request of the user, the spelling of titles and letters (diacritical marks) are to be rectified in the context of the possibility of the character set used in each case for the e-card and the EHIC. Here, the user has to denote the

---

[547] http://volksgruppen.orf.at/slowenen/aktuell/stories/36236/ (2011-11-13, link no longer active)
[548] http://ktnv1.orf.at/stories/50774 (2011-11-13)
[549] http://www.sozialversicherung.at/mediaDB/102803.PDF (2007-05-05, link no longer active)

> diacritic in the respective code table or submit civil status documents which establish the correct spelling.[550]

This suggests that at least a part of the issued e-cards at this time still used an 8-bit character set (that were not able to represent Slovene characters) instead of Unicode. This is also indicated through the reply to a Parliamentary inquiry (No. 3973 J on the cost of the e-card project), which took place on 12 April 2006 by the Federal Ministry for Social Security, Generations and Consumer Protection, that quotes for the financial year 2004 (note: two years after commissioning of the Unicode-compatible central residents register) following cost point:[551]

> Extended character set on the smart card (correct representation of minority languages and the languages of the new EU members) | € 20.000

In addition to the open discrimination of persons with diacritics in the name—they must apply specially for the correct spelling and officially prove it—it is remarkable that the *benefits and coverage plan* demands obviously a higher technological knowledge from the name owner than from the competent authorities (dealing with a code table).

On 9 December 2005, the Unity List / *Enotna lista* felt compelled to issue a press release titled "Still problems with e-card":

> With the 56th General Social Security Act amendment from the Association of Austrian Social Security Institutions, a social security chip card (e-card) was created as a basis for an electronic management system of social security.

---

550 http://www.noegkk.at/mediaDB/103083.PDF p. 33 (2007-05-03, link no longer active)
551 http://www.parlament.gv.at/PAKT/VHG/XXII/AB/AB_03912/fnameorig_061167.html (2011-11-13)

In this context, EL Chair Vladimir Smrtnik called already in August for the consistent and equitable consideration of the diacritical characters Šš, Čč, Ćć, Žž in the spelling of names on the e-card.

Although the Carinthian Health Insurance has assured that there would be no discrimination for people with diacritical characters, it must be noted four months after this commitment that there are still disadvantages, criticized EL Chair Smrtnik.

Specifically, it's about two problems:

1. People with diacritical characters in their names usually need to specially request an e-card with the correct spelling of their name separately, which is associated with additional effort. [...]

2. In several medical offices, e-cards with diacritical characters are still not accepted by the IT systems of doctors, which can lead to very problematic situations.

The EL calls on the Carinthian Health Insurance and political leaders in state and federal government to repair immediately these disadvantages faced by people with diacritical characters in their names, and finally to ensure that equality is not only announced full-bodied, but that it is also implemented in practice, concludes EL Chair Smrtnik.

Also the Austrian Ombudsman Board in its 2005 report gave strong support for taking into account the correct spelling:

> Several complaints during the reporting period also related to the successive introduction of the e-card in the social health insurance. So it could be achieved in the examination procedure VA BD/841-SV/05 that in the representation of the name of the insured, an accent was taken into account. From the perspective of the Ombudsman Board, the correct rendering of the spelling of a name plays a particularly important role, because the naming rights is an absolutely protected right, and proper names or their spelling, respectively, must not be changed arbitrarily by authorities. The Ombudsman

Board has therefore pointed out towards the Main Association of Austrian Social Security Institutions that when issuing an e-card, the corresponding consideration of the respective names spelling of the insured is imperative in order not to violate constitutionally protected spheres. [552]

The "manual diacritics" mentioned above states:

3.3.4 Transferring data from citizen cards

Basics

Data are stored in citizen card info boxes in UTF-8 encoding. The citizen card supports in principle the entire Unicode character range [...]. But in practice, there are limits to that range of characters [...] in accordance with the recommendations in this document, it refers to Latin characters, more precisely, letters from the Unicode blocks Basic Latin, Latin-1 Supplement, Latin Extended A, Latin Extended B, and Latin Extended Additional. Characters are in normalization form C.

e-Card

The e-Card supports all character of the WGL/4 set supported by the Main Association of Austrian Social Security Institutions, [...] both in the [digital] certificate as well as in print [...]. [553]

Likewise, the website of the smart card operating company now (since 2007) specifies: "First and last name are stored with and without diacritics." [554] Thus, the legally correct spelling in accordance with the naming rights would be satisfied, at the same time the backward compatibility with legacy

---

552 http://volksanwaltschaft.gv.at/downloads/9f5sn/pb292005.pdf (2011-11-13)
553 Peter Reichstädter *et al.*: *Handbuch diakritische Zeichen / Grundlagen – Recht – Technik* (1.2.0)
    http://www.ref.gv.at/AG-II-Architektur-DZ-1-0-dia.2489.0.html (2011-11-12)
554 http://www.chipkarte.at/portal27/portal/ecardportal/content/contentWindow?contentid=10007.678597&action=2 (2015-01-25)

computer systems would remain guaranteed. As I heard no other complaints, I close this investigation.

10.3.8 Conclusion for Austria

I have found no complaints regarding the → *Convention on the indication of surnames and forenames in civil status registers* (trans-national cases). In Austria, it is especially the Slovenian minority (i.e. national cases) who suffers from the legacy computer systems' limit in characters, e.g. in driver's licenses and official letters. The Ombudsman Board continuously lobbies for Unicode-compatible e-government applications, with some success.

10.4 Netherlands

Since 1 January 1993 in the Netherlands, the "Decision standard notation personal data" *(besluit standaardschrijfwijze persoonsgegevens)* of the Ministry of Interior of 1 September 1992 [555] is in force. [556] Therein, the use of two by the Dutch Standards Institute (NEN) developed standards is mandatory for government agencies (NEN 1888 for general personal data, NEN 5825 for addresses). A corresponding system in the field of social security was still in preparation at the time (case 1999/434).

---

555 government gazette 176
556 http://wetten.overheid.nl/BWBR0005634/geldigheidsdatum_02-02-2015

10.4.1 Cases of the national ombudsman

In the Netherlands, nine persons appealed to the national ombudsman[557] between 1993 and 2007 because their names were written by authorities or companies continuously without diacritics.[558]

Already in the first case 1993/033, the national ombudsman had noted:

> 1. Regarding the spelling of the names of citizens
>
> From government agencies, it can be required to write (in the salutation in their correspondence with citizens and in their collections of personal data) the name of the citizen concerned in the correct manner. This requirement also applies to the names that contain characters with diacritical marks. While such signs may not occur often in names of Dutch-speaking origin, the situation is certainly different with names from a number of other language regions. Such names are found increasingly in the Netherlands, as a result of the development of our country towards a multicultural society. The representation of a diacritic is one of the preconditions for the correct spelling of the name in which the character appears. The state should not ignore this fact with respect to the correct spelling of the names of registered persons, with a view to the future, when it comes to the creation of automated systems. In doing so, however, it behoves some understanding of the fact that any necessary adaptation of existing systems in this respect is not always to be implemented in the short term, due to financial consequences [...]

The Ministry of Transport was therefore recommended to ensure

> that the Road Traffic Authority develops a proposal for adjustment of the license registration system in terms of use diacritical characters, and gives an

---
557 www.nationaleombudsman.nl
558 reports of the national ombudsman, cases 1993/033, 1996/023, 1997/223, 1997/224, 1997/518, 1998/325, 2003/195, 2007/161, 2007/288

indication on the date on which the adjustment can be seen, both technically and financially, implemented.

Likewise, the national ombudsman recommended in the case 1996/023 to the Ministry of Justice,

> concerning the Foreigners Management System (VAS), in collaboration with the Ministry of Interior, to ensure that all measures are taken in time that are necessary to meet the requirements which are needed to fulfil the requirements as a result of the decision standard notation personal data, that from 1 January 1997 in the issuing of residence documents, diacritical marks can be used.

The legally defined transition period for the "Decision standard notation personal data" ended on 1 January 1997. Nevertheless, seven complaints fall in the period after the end of the transition period. This makes it clear which problems are caused by the neglection of timely and consistent adaptation of corporate data processing to current developments in technology, standardization, and regulation. Some agencies, as it turned out, maintained their registers still in uppercase letters in the 7-bit ASCII character set. In the case 2003/195, a diacritics-compatible system had already been purchased, but this was coupled with older systems and thus the advanced skills were left unused for reasons of backward compatibility. In a number of cases, the ombudsman notes:

> Administrative organs may be generally expected to set up their management in such a way that personal data are recorded correctly in their automated information systems, and that these data will be used in their correspondence with those affected in a correct manner.

In practice, this looks different. In 2007, there was an action regarding an "ü". The RDW (Dutch regulatory authority for vehicles) said it was technically not possible to reproduce the name with an umlaut. It was probably a gap in the software of their system. The ombudsman recalled that the "Decision standard notation personal data" actually should allow the generation of diacritical characters since 1997 (10 years!). Sometime later, the RDW announced that due to a system adaptation, diacritics in form letters were now possible, which the Ombudsman benevolently took note of.

At the same time, the ombudsman asked the Minister of the Interior to verify compliance with the Regulation on the "Decision standard notation personal data" in all government departments to which the regulation was applicable.[559]

Also in 2007, there was a lawsuit during the investigation of which it turned out that the municipal personal records database (*gemeentelijke basisadministratie*, GBA) in the town of Dordrecht worked with the TELETEX character set (based on the outdated CCITT standard T.61). The Ombudsman instructed the municipality to adaptation work, in order to ensure that the Dutch digraph "IJ" would be possible as first letter in names.[560]

> The administration is there for the citizens, and service to the citizens has therefore always to come first. It is not acceptable that a complaint about a service is dismissed with a reference to the limitations of "the computer", because that is thought only a means to improve service.

10.4.2 Conclusion for the Netherlands

Again, I have found no complaints regarding the → *Convention on the indication of surnames and forenames in civil status registers* (trans-national cases). In the Netherlands national cases, already Latin-1 diacritics seemed

---

559 https://www.nationaleombudsman.nl/rapporten/2007/161#samenvatting (2015-01-31)
560 https://www.nationaleombudsman.nl/rapporten/2007/288#samenvatting (2015-01-31)

to be a problem (mainly the ü). This is probably due to the fact that the Netherlands were the fastest (1993) to introduce a national standard corresponding to the *Convention*. The last case before the national ombudsman was in 2007, which makes 14 years from standard introduction to successful implementation.

10.5 Switzerland

Even for persons with "recognized" diacritics in the name, there can be problems, as the following case shows:

10.5.1 Margit Széchényi against Department of the Interior of the Canton of Zurich

Margit Széchényi arrived in 1956 in Switzerland as a Hungarian refugee. In an order dated 9 May 1984, she received the Canton of Zurich civil rights and Swiss citizenship from the Department of the Interior of the Canton of Zurich, and the start of the citizenship in the city of Zurich, which took place on 5 October 1983, was confirmed. The applicant was registered as a result with the family name "Szechenyi" in the family register of Zurich, while the original spelling was "Széchényi".

With inputs of 14 and 15 May 1984 to the Department of the Interior of the Canton of Zurich, Margit Széchényi demanded that her name would be registered with the notation "Széchényi" in the family register of Zurich. The cantonal authorities took the inputs as a complaint and rejected these as of 24 May 1984 (partly because they did not want to create a precedent for the general adoption of diacritics [and probably even less diacritics from the then hostile "Eastern bloc"]). Margit Széchényi submitted against this an

Administrative Court complaint. On 15 November 1984, the II. Civil Division of the Swiss Federal Court ruled:

> Foreign-language surnames are to enter with the accents in the family register if the accents *also appear in the typeface* of Swiss official languages.[561]

In the recitals to the judgement, which I want to reflect in detail because of their linguistic details here, it says:

> 3. The contested decision is based on the aforementioned Art. 9 para. 1 and Art. 43 para. 1 Civil Registry Regulation and is based on a long-standing practice of the Zurich authorities that exotic names, which cannot be assigned to any [Swiss] national language, are for registration in the civil register matched to the typeface of the German language. As far as accents for names of French or Italian origin (or possibly also originating in other Romance languages) are used, the Department of the Interior of the Canton of Zurich states in their consultation that the relevant rules of language are taken into account. But the lower instance does not believe to be able to ask civil status officials to take into account also the accentuation of the languages that are of non-Latin origin—as in this case, the Hungarian language, which is attributable to the Finno-Ugric language group.
>
> Regarding the Hungarian family name "Széchényi" in particular, the Department of the Interior admits that the accent here appears with the same image as "accent aigu" in the French language. Unlike in the French language, where the "accent aigu" indicates a close-pronounced "e", the accent marks in the Hungarian language a long-pronounced vowel, according to the statements of the lower court. Therefore, the complainant could not infer from

---

561 PolyReg: collection of the decisions of the Swiss Federal Tribunal, reference No. BGE 110 II 324
http://www.polyreg.ch/bgepub/Band_110_1984/BGE_110_II_324.html (2015-01-25)

this that the typeface marked in her original Hungarian name with an accent "e" is the same as is known by the French language.

4. This approach, however, is not convincing. If the registrars of the German-speaking cantons may add accents of other national languages and other languages of Latin origin without the question of transcription being raised, there is no reason why accents of non-Romance languages, yet having exactly the same typeface as those, should be ignored. An accent with a specific typeface—so the from the lower left to the upper right corner running [accent], as it is known by the French and the Spanish language, or the from the top left to bottom right running [accent] of the French and Italian language—has not consistently the same function within the Romance languages. It usually is a dynamic or pressure accent with which in different ways the reinforcement of the vocal sound or a change in the vocal progression is expressed, but sometimes also a grammatical accent that lifts out words and parts of words for meaning and significance (for example, participle constructions and word distinctions in the French language, such as "ou" and "où"—cf. *Der Grosse Brockhaus*, keyword "*Akzent*"); occasionally, an accent has both a dynamic and a grammatical function (e.g. Italian "é" and "è"). The argument of the lower court that the erroneous impression could arise, the accents in the name of "Széchényi", which can be easily recognized as coming from an Eastern European language, pointed to a closed "e" as in the French language, therefore cannot be upheld.

However, since the word image with the accent from bottom left to top right on the "e" in the French language already exists and therefore this accent already exists on the typewriters of all registrars, public offices, and private offices in Switzerland, it cannot be seen why confusion and difficulties might arise. Other cantons of German Switzerland—as the complainant outlines and which is not denied by the lower court—have admitted the accent on the two "e" of the Hungarian family name "Széchényi" for register entry; and other authorities have issued identity cards in the name of "Széchényi".

The lower court can also deduce nothing from BGE 106 II 103 ff. that would support its position. That case concerned the modification of a surname, depending on male or female name carriers, unknown to the Swiss naming right. Here, however, is only the question to decide whether an accent that is used in the Hungarian language and appears with the same typeface in a Swiss official language should be entered by the registrars in civil status matters.

Contrary to the fears of the lower court that also characters that do not occur as a typeface in the Swiss official languages should be permitted if the entry of the name "Széchényi" would be granted, such a conclusion from the present decision can hence not be drawn. The question, which rules registrars have to observe for the registration of names with Eastern European origin, or even only of Hungarian origin, will and can not generally be answered here.

As follows from the above that no serious work-related difficulties conflict with the legitimate desire of the complainant, her name should be registered with the letters "Széchényi" in the family register, and the impact that these spelling should be used in official communications, the desire of the complainant is upheld.

10.5.2 Conclusion for Switzerland

The situation in Switzerland is insofar different, as it has not signed the → *Convention on the indication of surnames and forenames in civil status registers.* Switzerland has however signed the European Convention on Human Rights, but apparently not made the same conclusions from its Article 8 as Austrian Ombudsman Board regarding respect for private and family life.[562] E-government applications still use the outdated character set ISO 8859-15 (Latin-9), e.g. the civil register *Infostar*. On the other hand, the database of the *Central Migration Information System* (ZEMIS) switched recently to Unicode, and in regulatory reporting there will be a XML scheme set up with Unicode as character set. We can only hope that in the course of stronger interoperability, *Infostar* will soon follow.

10.6 Outlook

Country	Netherlands	Austria	Germany	Switzerland
Convention No 14 in force?	yes	yes	yes	no
trans-national cases	–	–	10 (2 negative)	1
corresponding national standard	1993	2007	2012	(to come)
transition period over	1997	2014?	2015	(to come)
national cases	9	5	1 (negative)	–
last case/report	2007	2013	2011	–
Σ (years)	14	7	3	?

The Netherlands were the fastest to introduce a national standard corresponding to *Convention No 14* (NEN 1888, 1993), followed by Austria ("manual diacritics", 2007), Germany (String.Latin, 2012) and Switzerland (eCH-0011,

---

562 http://www.admin.ch/opc/de/classified-compilation/19500267/index.html (2015-03-08)

to come). When we measure the time between the introduction of the national standard and the time either the transition period was over or for the last case/report, 14 years (Netherlands) is apparently the worst case. Austria managed to do it in 7 years, provided that the Ombudsman Board report 2014 will be "clean". Germany seemed to manage to do it in 3 years, though 2015 is not yet over. So for Switzerland, the time span should be short.

Again, a European approach, with a common European Norm of Latin diacritics, prepared by the *European Committee for Standardization* (CEN), together with a EU/EEA Diacritics Directive and thus with a uniform legal basis, would be the better solution.

> With respect to the increasing mobility of citizens as well as the increasing cases with an migrant background, I am sure that we continue to deal with trend-setting decisions of the higher courts that IT specialists will find a hard nut to crack when it comes to timely to electronic implementation of these decisions. Also, the continuous integration of Europe will probably cause the one or other decision of the European Court of Justice.
>
> – Reinhold Vogt [563]

---

[563] http://www.standesbeamte-bayern.de/downloads/vogt_namensfuhrung_in_der_ehe.pdf (2015-01-11)

11 Diacritics as political symbolism

Smouldering for decades in one part of the Austrian province of Carinthia is the so-called "road sign dispute" *(Ortstafelstreit)*, a controversy surrounding bilingual topographical signs (German/Slovenian) on signposts and direction signs. The place name signs in question are constitutionally guaranteed to the Slovenian minority, in accordance with Article 7, para. 2 and 3 of the Austrian State Treaty of 1955,[564] but until today—50 years after the signing of the State Treaty!—are still circumvented by right-wing groups such as the Carinthian 'defence fighter alliance' *(Abwehrkämpferbund)* and local politicians such as the infamous right-wing Carinthian governor JÖRG HAIDER (now deceased).[565]

> **Article 7 (Right of the Slovene and Croat minorities)**
> 3. In the administrative and judicial districts of Carinthia, Burgenland and Styria, Slovenian, Croat or mixed populations, the Slovene or Croat language is additionally admitted to German as an official language. In such districts, terminology and inscriptions of topographical nature are both written in the Slovene or Croat language as in German.

---

564 Federal Law Gazette 152/1955, 59/1964
565 http://de.wikipedia.org/wiki/Ortstafelstreit (2011-12-02)

The road sign dispute has its origins in the 1970s, as young Carinthian Slovenes—in the context of an emancipation movement—championed for their still unfulfilled rights. With so-called 'inscription actions'—adding Slovene place names on the German name signs—they brought the conflict to public awareness.[566] In response, the National Council decided—against the votes of conservatives (ÖVP) and right-wing populists (FPÖ)—on July 6, 1972, the *"Federal Law with which the provisions are made relating to the attachment of bilingual topographical signs and designations in the areas of Carinthia with Slovene or mixed population"*. In the autumn of 1972, Chancellor BRUNO KREISKY had erected 205 bilingual signs. In consequence of this action, the so-called 'road sign storm' *(Ortstafelsturm)* took place: throughout Southern Carinthia, bilingual signs were removed or destroyed by pan-Germanists, in some cases on camera or in presence of the police.[567]

In July 1976, the National Council adopted the *National Minorities Act* (this time supported by all parties). This provided for the establishment of bilingual topographical signs only for those municipalities or districts in which at least 25 % (a quarter) of the population profess of belonging to the Slovene-speaking minority. In a 1977 adopted regulation (the so-called *Topography Ordinance for Carinthia*), the *National Minorities Act* was elaborated and the municipalities/districts where bilingual topographical signs had to be attached were delineated. In another regulation *(Regulation on Slovene place names)*, the Slovenian names of towns were officially established. Simultaneously with the *National Minorities Act*, an amendment was passed to

---

566 Daniela Schopf: *Artikel 7 – Unser Recht (Filmbeschreibung)*, Freier Rundfunk Oberösterreich, 03 May 2005
http://www.fro.at/frozine/show.php?news_id=678 (2006-01-22, link no longer active)

567 http://de.wikipedia.org/wiki/Ortstafelstreit (2011-12-02)

the census law which created the prerequisites for the secret collection of native language. The corresponding regional census, on 14 November 1976, was boycotted by many Carinthian Slovenes, but the overall turnout was about 87 %. As a result, only in ten communities bilingual signs would have to be installed. But from the 91 affected signposts, only 77 were actually placed between 1977 and 2005.[568]

In 2001, movement came back in the village sign dispute: the Carinthian Slovenes representative RUDOLF VOUK drove his car intentionally too fast through the village of St. Kanzian/Škocijan, whose road sign was not—as required by the Regulation—bilingual. He reported himself to the police and subsequently appealed against the penalty mandate he received: the local area was not named correctly, therefore the speed limit of 50 km/h did not apply. The process went up to the Constitutional Court.[569] The Constitutional Court quashed the *National Minorities Act*[570, 571] and ordered bilingual signs already from a Slovenian-speaking population of about 10 %.[572] The details he left to the legislator.[573] However, the Federal government

---

[568] http://de.wikipedia.org/wiki/Ortstafelstreit (2011-12-02)
[569] *Die Presse: Chronologie: Der Ortstafelstreit*
http://www.diepresse.at/diashow/artikel.aspx?channel=p&id=489872&bild=4 (2006-01-22, link no longer active)
[570] Constitutional Court decision 2001/12/13 B 2075/99
[571] see http://www.vfgh.gv.at/cms/vfgh-site/attachments/9/8/8/CH0006/CMS1108400716489/g213-01ua.pdf (2011-12-02)
[572] *Die Presse: Chronologie: Der Ortstafelstreit*
http://www.diepresse.at/diashow/artikel.aspx?channel=p&id=489872&bild=5 (2006-01-29, link no longer active)
[573] Peter Filzmaier: *Was macht die Politik mit dem Recht? Zum Verhältnis von Legislative, Exekutive und Judikative in Kärnten und anderswo* / Abstract to the presentation held 6 April 2005
http://www.sodalitas.at/index.php/events/vortraege_more/160/ (2011-12-02)

did nothing to implement the judgement of the highest court, despite legal obligation.

In spring 2002, the Klagenfurt cultural initiative *Unikum* was starting a gluing initiative under the slogan *"Haček (k)lebt – Háček živi"* ("Haček sticks—Haček lives"): hačeks should be glued to German-language inscriptions in order to demonstrate for the introduction of bilingual signs.[574]

Interesting is the processing of the initiative from media technology: in the reporting of the *Kärntner Tageszeitung* of 05 February 2002, diacritics on č, š and ž were reproduced correctly in the description of modified words *(Šaal, Anwendungšbeišpiel, Ergänžung, einšprachigen Ortštafeln, Aufščhriften)* and in the slogan.[575] The *Kleine Zeitung* used diacritics on č, ř and š in its issue dated 26 April 2002 *(Klagenfuřt, Bürgerservice, Freiheitliche, Šachbeschädigung, Haček)*.[576] Overall, it sticks out that *Háček* is inconsistently spelled: the *Kärntner Tageszeitung* used the correct Czech spelling with acute over the a, which the *Kleine Zeitung* and even the authors of the initiative itself apparently had forgotten. The tabloid *Kärntner Krone* from 16 April 2002 on the other hand completely renounced the use of diacritics, and simply wrote *hacek*.[577] In Slovenian, the correct name for the diacritic is incidentally not *háček* but *strešica* or *kljukica*.[578]

---

574 http://www.unikum.ac.at/hacki_FI/Hacek_karte.jpg (2011-12-02)
575 *Háček über Maria „Schal"*, KTZ 05 Februrary 2002, p. 19
  http://www.unikum.ac.at/hacki_FI/KTZ050202.html (2015-02-01)
576 *Die Haček-Maler gehen um, Kleine Zeitung* 26 April 2002
  http://www.unikum.ac.at/hacki_FI/kleine260402.html (2015-02-01)
577 *Eine Schande, Kärntner Krone* 16 April 2002
  http://www.unikum.ac.at/hacki_FI/noricus160302.html (2015-02-01)
578 „*Akcija s slovenskimi strešicami*" [Action with Slovenian small hooks], in: *Nežen pozdrav normalnosti, Slovenski Vestnik* 18 February 2002
  http://www.unikum.ac.at/hacki_FI/VESTNIK180202.html (2015-02-01)

SETTING SIGNS FOR EUROPE 251

Figure 11.1: **Sticker of the initiative "Haček sticks/lives"**

Figure 11.2: **Diacritical mark as a means of political expression**

A "consensus conference" appointed by Chancellor WOLFGANG SCHÜSSEL in the fall of 2002 (instead of an implementation of the Constitutional Court judgement) remained without result,[579] so did three further consensus conferences. In April 2005, SCHÜSSEL announced an interim result of the now fifth consensus conference: the 20 road signs missing since 1977 should be put in place until 26 October 2005.[580] In the village Schwabegg/Žvabek, there was a mishap that is symptomatic for dealing with diacritics in German-speaking countries: the company which had supplied the signs forgot the diacritic in the Slovenian place name Žvabek.[581]

Figure 11.3: **Missing Slovenian *strešica* on the road sign of Žvabek**

---

579 Peter Filzmaier: *Was macht die Politik mit dem Recht? Zum Verhältnis von Legislative, Exekutive und Judikative in Kärnten und anderswo* / Abstract to the presentation held 6 April 2005 http://www.sodalitas.at/index.php/events/vortraege_more/160/ (2011-12-02)

580 *Die Presse: Chronologie: Der Ortstafelstreit* http://www.diepresse.at/diashow/artikel.aspx?channel=p&id=489872&bild=5 (2006-01-29, link no longer active)

581 *Wiener Nachrichten Online* http://www.wno.org/images/k050512a.jpg (2011-12-01, link no longer active)

The resulting notation "Zvabek" was thus explained by the municipality that the documents had been downloaded from the Legal Information System (RIS) of the Federal Chancellery, and there "Žvabek" had been written without diacritic.[582] Its absence was noticed shortly before the arrival of the guests of honour. A community worker quickly cut out the missing characters from black film and taped it temporarily on the signs—an irony of history, because legally, it was the same kind of damage to property that the performers of the action "Haček sticks/lives" had been accused.[583] Apparently, yet in the late afternoon, the diacritics were removed again in one of the four panels on both the front and back by unknown culprits—another act of political expression.[584, 585]

In response to the mishap, representatives of Carinthian Slovenes suggested jokingly to compensate for the missing diacritic in the Slovenian name by writing the German name in Slovenian transliteration (with diacritic).[586]

---

582 Oberösterreich.com: *Ortstafel-Schlamperei*
http://www.rundschau.co.at/artikel/00/03/24/art32490.html (2006-01-29, link no longer active)
583 *Die Haček-Maler gehen um, Kleine Zeitung* 26 April 2002
http://www.unikum.ac.at/hacki_FI/kleine260402.html (2015-02-01)
584 *Wiener Nachrichten Online*, 13 May 2005
http://www.wno.org/newpages/eth06.html (2011-12-01, link no longer active)
585 *Slowenisch: Hacek müsste Stresica sein, KomInform* 13 May 2005
http://www.kominform.at/article.php?story=20050513174424617 (2011-12-01)
586 Festival Oktet-Suha
http://www.oktet-suha.at/images/novice/000062.jpg (2011-12-01)

Figure 11.4: Satiric Slovenian compromise proposal with *strešica* in the German name

In ruling V 64/05 of 12 December 2005,[587] the Constitutional Court asked to erect bilingual place name signs in 2006 the town of Bleiburg/Pliberk, not later than 30 June. He therefore uphold a complaint of Vouk, and explained that the currently only-German place names were inadmissible. With the Constitutional Court are pending 20 other complaints to 14 additional villages.[588]

In a discussion in Carinthian radio ORF, however, Governor Jörg Haider announced to refuse the bilingual signs in Bleiburg demanded by the Constitutional Court, and instead—citing the Highway Code—to have rebuild the German signposts shifted by a few meters *(Ortstafelverrückung)*.[589]

---

[587] *Ortstafel von Bleiburg aufgehoben!*
http://dielinke.at/artikel/innenpolitik/innenpolitik-ortstafel-von-bleiburg-aufgehoben/
(2015-06-04)

[588] *Die Presse: Chronologie: Der Ortstafelstreit*
http://www.diepresse.at/diashow/artikel.aspx?channel=p&id=489872&bild=7
(2006-01-29, link no longer active)

[589] *Die Presse: Chronologie: Der Ortstafelstreit*
http://www.diepresse.at/diashow/artikel.aspx?channel=p&id=489872&bild=8
(2006-01-29, link no longer active)

Social Secretary SIGISBERT DOLINSCHEK even declared that the Constitutional Court ruling was "in practical absurdity not be beat" and "wrong".[590] For HAIDER is the Austrian State Treaty, on which the Constitutional Court does rely upon in support of the road sign dispute question, anyway lost in "historical insignificance".[591] Instead, he had already called in May 2005 to first carry out in the affected communities a new survey of the native language prior to the implementation of the Constitutional Court judgement, according to the results of which the change in the number of signposts should be based.[592] After he failed in this endeavour, he launched a local survey[593] and called for a referendum in Carinthia on the subject for or against bilingual signs.[594] Federal President HEINZ FISCHER explained, however, in the *Kärntner Tageszeitung*: "I believe that on a decision of the Constitutional Court, you cannot make a public opinion poll or a referendum." The majority could not vote on minority rights.[595]

---

[590] *Höchstgericht ruft Fischer zu Hilfe*, Salzburger Nachrichten 19 January 2006 http://www.salzburg.com/sn/06/01/19/artikel/1929567.html (2006-02-01, link no longer active)

[591] *Ortstafelstreit: VfGH sieht Grenze überschritten*, Wiener Zeitung 19 January 2006 http://www.wienerzeitung.at/themen_channel/wirtschaftsservice/job/124318_Ortstafelstreit-VfGH-sieht-Grenze-ueberschritten.html (2015-06-04)

[592] *Die Presse: Chronologie: Der Ortstafelstreit* http://www.diepresse.at/diashow/artikel.aspx?channel=p&id=489872&bild=6 (2006-01-29, link no longer active)

[593] *Wende im Streit um Ortstafeln: Jörg Haider startete Umfrage in betroffenen Gemeinden* http://www.news.at/a/wende-streit-ortstafeln-joerg-haider-umfrage-gemeinden-129978 (2015-06-04)

[594] *Ortstafel-Streit – Haider will kärntenweite Volksbefragung*, ORF http://kaernten.orf.at/stories/86196/ (2011-12-01)

[595] *Fischer gegen Volksbefragung*, Der Standard http://derstandard.at/2305213 (2011-12-01)

To prosecute the bodies responsible for the ongoing denial of justice of the instructions and mockery of the Federal Constitutional Court under Article 142 of the Austrian Federal Constitution (indictment for failure to follow instructions from the Federal level)[596] is not even a consideration.[597] In this, President FISCHER could now have even (hypothetically) the Austrian army march towards Carinthia to establish the missing bilingual place signs: if an arrangement of the Constitutional Court is stubbornly not followed, the Chairman may ask the Federal President for help under Article 146 of the Federal Constitution.[598] He can instruct "in his discretion" relevant subsidiary bodies, "including the Austrian Armed Forces", to enforce the court decision.[599] However, it was highly unlikely that it actually happened. As a last resort, the deputy chairman of the Council of the Carinthian Slovenes, KAREL SMOLLE, therefore considered in the meantime an action before the European Court of Justice (ECJ) in accordance with Article 7 of the Treaty on European Union because of constant breach of its own legal principles by Austria.[600]

The "road sign dispute" was at the latest since the beginning of Austria's EU Presidency on 1 January 2006 anyway no regional or local incident any more, but a European basic question of dealing with minorities. Since the Republic of Austria, who has worked so hard to ensure the interests of the

---

596 http://www.jusline.at/142._B-VG.html (2015-02-05)
597 *Peter Warta: Staatsvertrag? Was ist das? Standard* 12 January 2006
   http://derstandard.at/2302821 (2011-12-01)
598 http://www.jusline.at/146_B-VG.html (2015-02-05)
599 *Im Land der Taferl-Klassler / Der Kärntner Ortstafel-Streit ist Politik der erbärmlichsten Art. profil* 08/06
   http://manschindler.twoday.net/stories/1378094/comment (2015-06-03)
600 *Ortstafelstreit / Rat der Slowenen erwägt Klage beim EuGH*, ORF 18 January 2006
   http://kaernten.orf.at/stories/83510/ (2011-12-01)

German minority in Italian South Tyrol, must respect its own and EU-wide principles of law and international law in return. She must not allow in any case that fundamental rights of minorities are systematically violated and judgements of the Austrian Constitutional Court are disregarded. Otherwise, her credibility and the protection of minorities suffer damage throughout Europe.[601] Federal Chancellor WOLFGANG SCHÜSSEL was even followed by the "road sign dispute" to Strasbourg, where he completed his performance as EU President in the European Parliament. There, MEP HANNES SWOBODA (SPÖ) had asked how SCHÜSSEL could call for minority rights in the EU, when he could not even defend this against his own coalition partner in his own country.[602]

As of 25 August 2006, there was a new development in the "road sign dispute": HAIDER started—with great media attention—to turn all bilingual signs in Carinthia again into monolingual ones. The *National Minorities Act* should be fulfilled by additional panels in Slovenian—of much smaller size—that are hung under the actual road sign.[603] However, the writing on these additional tables was smaller than on the official name signs, who are in accordance with road traffic regulations (Highway Code), and they do not have the usual layout of a road sign, since they lack the blue border. As reason for this "compromise", HAIDER mentioned that the Highway

---

601 *Grüne Fraktion im Südtiroler Landtag: Kärntner Ortstafelstreit: keine innerösterreichische, sondern eine europäische Frage des Minderheitenschutzes*, 20 January 2006
http://www.landtag-bz.org/la/banches-dac-abinedes/frazions.asp?aktuelles_action=4&aktuelles_article_id=126854 (2015-06-03)

602 *Höchstgericht ruft Fischer zu Hilfe, Salzburger Nachrichten*, 19 January 2006
http://www.salzburg.com/sn/06/01/19/artikel/1929567.html (2006-01-29, link no longer active)

603 http://diepresse.com/images/uploads/2/b/8/524984/ortstafel_bleiburg20091129100158.jpg (2015-02-07)

Code will not tolerate "confusing and crowded designations" to road signs. Yet in December 2006, the Constitutional Court declared the measure of the additional panels to be unconstitutional: it would still be a matter of monolingual signs, since the additional panelling was not part of the above sign.

Figure 11.5: **No**.

Later HAIDER announced to dismount in these localities the road signs completely and to replace them by 50 km/h speed limit signs. Various constitutional lawyers declared such an approach to be illegal, as road signs govern not only speed limits.

Also the representatives of the Slovene minority sharply criticized the actions of HAIDER. They asked the prosecutor to investigate HAIDER and the road building officers GERHARD DÖRFLER on suspicion of abuse of office. In early February 2007, the prosecutor of Klagenfurt did a preliminary investigation against HAIDER and DÖRFLER. The case against DÖRFLER was set in July 2009 (with constitutionally questionable grounds); the case against HAIDER was becoming invalid due to his death.

On 22 February 2007, the place name signs in Bleiburg and Eberdorf were redesigned again: the small additional signs with the Slovenian name of the places were mounted over on the sign itself, in its lower half, inside the blue border.[604]

Figure 11.6: **Also no.**

On 9 July 2010, the Constitutional Court explained in a recent finding that also the "mounted-over" signs in Bleiburg/Pliberk were unconstitutional. From the new Governor Dörfler, the verdict was implemented "surprisingly" quick; already on 13 July 2010, panels in the same font size (German on the top, Slovenian at the bottom) were set up.[605]

Figure 11.7: **Yes.**

604 http://diepresse.com/images/uploads//3/9/e/467870/u_Ortstafelstreit_in_Kaernten.jpg (2015-02-07)
605 http://imgl.krone.at/Bilder/2011/04/26/Chronologie_des_Kaerntner_Ortstafel-Streits-Etliche_Anlaeufe-Story-254300_476x268px_20_npBHcODfRHnPw.jpg (2015-06-03)

In early 2011, an agreement was reached that was accepted by both the Federal Government and the State Government of Carinthia. On 1 April, Secretary of State Josef Ostermayer and Governor Dörfler announced one had agreed on the establishment of bilingual signs in all locations with at least 17.5% of Slovene population (based on the census of 2001). Valentin Inzko as negotiator of the Slovenian associations approved the agreement in part, and subject to present the result to the bodies of the organizations for decision-making. They had to be renegotiated due to the partial rejection of the last negotiation results by one Slovenian association.

In the meantime, President Fischer and Slovenian President Danilo Türk met. Both were of the opinion that not percentages of the population should be the basis for the bilingual topographical signs, but that the places should be anchored by name in the law. On 26 April 2011, all parties agreed at a recent round of negotiations to a memorandum, in which 164 places are enshrined in 24 municipalities. Another point of the memorandum relates to a waiver of any minority finding. In those places where bilingual signs are to be installed, Slovenian shall also be recognized as a second official language. In July 2011, the National Minorities Act, drafted to implement the memorandum, was decided in constitutional status in the National and Federal Council, and signed by President Fischer.[606]

---

606 http://de.wikipedia.org/wiki/Ortstafelstreit (2011-11-20)

12 Summary and discussion

The main goal of this book was to raise data on the state of "diacritic integration", especially on the German-speaking countries' example, and to identify the specific technical and legal basis under which conversion of authorities and media on national level to a common "Europeanized notation" could be enforced (if possible, compulsory). Besides that, more interesting things came to light: diacritics in brand and product names, diacritics in cartoons, sketches and jokes, decontextualized diacritics, and diacritics as political symbolism in connection to minorities.

12.1 Technical aspects

For a long time, the commonly voiced regard about the technical impossibility of setting diacritics in computer applications could not be denied, as there *was* indeed no alternative to the extremely limited 8-bit character sets. But with the introduction of the Universal Character Set / Unicode early in the 1990s, the *Unicode Consortium* and the *International Standards Organisation* (ISO) have created optimal conditions for the correct representation and processing of diacritics in administration, the IT industry, and the media. That is, the use of a pan-Latin character set, including diacritics, for foreign personal names, place names, and terms.

The IT industry in the form of market leaders Apple, HP, IBM, Microsoft, Oracle, etc. responded first: in many common technical standards such as HTTP, SOAP, HTML, XML, Java, JavaScript, PDF, etc., Unicode has long been integrated.[607] Most modern operating systems and computer programs support Unicode, though often not automatic, but only after the user actively modifies the system settings. Therefore in the future, Unicode should always the factory setting (default).

In addition, institutions offering computer courses should especially point out the software settings that make computer programs and the files created with them "Europe-competent".

A further step is the provision of assistance for character input, for each computer novice knows only the characters that are available on the physical keyboard in front of him. Therefore, I developed *Šibboleth* (see chapter 14) as an important step. A broad public notice and use of this aid, however, is still pending.

The other parts of industry responded more hesitantly. Except for the occasional use of diacritics as a stylistic means in brand or product names, or as decontextualized diacritics, as well as some smaller service companies which write the name of the Yugoslav or Turkish owner with the correct diacritics in advertisements, no cases of successful diacritical integration are known to me.

In the area of print and online media, the situation is very heterogeneous: some progressive media (FAZ, *Die Zeit*, *Spiegel*, Guardian) already use consistently an extended Latin character set, while others (*Die Welt*, *Süddeutsche Zeitung*, HAZ, FTD, tagesschau.de, *Deutsche Welle*) block as tenaciously

---

607 Barry Trute: The Unicode Imperative
  http://www.oracle.com/technology/pub/columns/trute_unicode.html
  (2006-02-07, link no longer active)

(*Deutsche Welle* and *Süddeutsche Zeitung* only very recently joined the progressive media).

One must however not ignore the fact that the problem usually starts already at the level of news agencies that must orient themselves on the customers with the lowest standard, i.e. Latin-1.[608] But with the XML format *NewsML*™-*G2*, the news agencies are not the bottleneck any more. Regarding the individual newspapers, the solution could be a central or local file to look up foreign personal names in correct spelling.

The HAZ as conversion opponent invokes on the one hand economic arguments (high financial cost for conversion to Universal Character Set / Unicode, acquisition of licensed fonts against a small proportion of diacritics on the text as a whole), on the other hand—a little narrow-minded—they claim that the average reader does not understand these diacritics anyway. To that argument is to say that the use of the correct diacritics represents in each case a qualitative improvement of the editorial work, and even the acquisition of an educational function. Who still does not know how to read a diacritic can simply ignore it.

A dangerously large normative influence is the electronic mail services (e-mail) as the predominant means of communication of the Internet age. Since its genesis is historically based on the (7-bit) standard US-ASCII, every character not in US-ASCII is always a potential victim of data corruption in data transmission. Within Western Europe, the situation looks a bit better through the predominant use of the (8-bit) standards Latin-1/-9:[609] at least Western European diacritics are mostly transmitted correctly, but when communicating with Eastern Europe and beyond, data corruption is

---

608 ISO 8859-1
609 ISO 8859-1/-15

inevitable. That has led many Eastern Europeans—so to speak, in anticipatory obedience—to refrain from using Eastern European diacritics for fear of incompatibilities in the e-mail traffic. This has already shown negative effects on the orthographically correct mastery of their mother tongue.[610, 611]

In 2006, some e-mail clients (*Outlook*, *Thunderbird*, etc.) already supported Unicode, but not as a default. Nevertheless, there was an urgent need of a Europe-wide conversion to Unicode (usually UTF-8) as e-mail encoding, because in particular young people often used accounts with free webmail providers the user interfaces of which were generally coded only in Latin-1/-9. These user interfaces rewrote messages in various Unicode formats forcibly to 8-bit character sets, making them partially (see chapter 3.8) or completely illegible (e.g. Cyrillic or Greek texts) and were not even completely compatible with each other, as experiments I conducted showed.[612] Fortunately, most of the messages content can be reconstructed by experienced users by manually changing the page encoding. At this time, the only webmail provider that already consistently used the UTF-8 encoding was Gmail. Still, it was not ideal for a number of reasons: to open a user account you needed an invitation, open security issues, provider GMX does not accept messages from Gmail ("provider wars"). The other operators balked for unknown reasons changing to Unicode.

Today, also Yahoo!,[613] GMX, WEB.DE and others have finally made the turn.

Still, not all is fine. When you want to create an e-mail account with GMX, it produces an error message when you type in an East European diacritic:

---

610 Klara Hola (Czech citizen), personal communication
611 http://sciencev1.orf.at/news/135500.html (2015-02-08)
612 data not shown
613 since about summer 2008

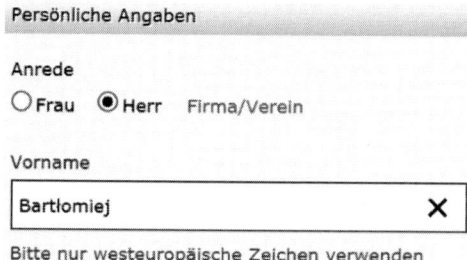

Figure 12.1: **"Please only use Western European characters"**

This "diacritic discrimination" means that if you follow the two rules—give your real name but only use Western European characters—people with Eastern European diacritics can not open an account there!

12.2 Legal Aspects

The starting point was the hypothesis that the prevailing practice of simply removing the diacritics stands in contradiction to the European ideas of *unity is in diversity* and mutual cultural enrichment. In the course of my research, I have found that the arbitrary removal of diacritics from personal names is also discrimination on the basis of language and an unacceptable interference in private and family life and thus a breach of a number of important international treaties or recommendations:

- the *United Nations Charter*,
- the *General Declaration of Human Rights*,
- the *European Convention on Human Rights*,
- the *International Covenant of the United Nations on Civil and Political Rights*,

- the *Helsinki Final Act,*
- the *Document of the Copenhagen Meeting,*
- the *Charter of Paris for a New Europe,*

and in individual cases

- the *UN Declaration on Minority Rights,*
- the *European Charter for Regional or Minority Languages,*
- the *Framework Convention for the Protection of National Minorities,*
- the *Oslo Recommendations Regarding the Linguistic Rights of National Minorities,*
- the CIEC Convention No. 14 *on the indication of surnames and forenames in civil status registers,*
- and the *Treaty between the Federal Republic of Germany and the Republic of Poland on Good-neighbourliness and friendly cooperation* or other bilateral agreements, respectively.

For the German example, authorities are generally obliged by those international laws to use the diacritics belonging to the name of a person. However, in practice *international* treaties do not make very good examples, even though some have the rank of a Federal law under Article 59 of the Basic Law (for example the ECHR and the *European Charter for Regional or Minority Languages*). Also under Article 25 of the Basic Law, the general rules of international law are anyway part of Federal law (that is, proceed the laws, and produce rights and duties for the inhabitants of the federal territory). But crucial to the officers "on the ground" are the concrete service instructions. Accordingly, an obligation to overtake diacritics comes from the ratification of the International Convention *on the on the indication of surnames and forenames in civil status registers,* which translates into § 15 para. 3 *Civil Status Ordinance.* This section provides simultaneously the fulfilment of an obligation of the Federal Republic of Germany under the *European Charter for Regional or Minority Languages.*

For regulatory reporting, an obligation for the complete takeover of diacritics comes from the reference to standards in § 7 para. 2 of the *Second Federal regulatory reporting data transmission ordinance* (standard dataset for reporting, Universal Character Set / Unicode), as of 1 November 2015: § 3 of the new *First* and *Second Federal regulatory reporting data transmission ordinance* (OSCI XMeld and DSMeld will be the standards of data transmission).

The arbitrary removal of diacritics in names of persons by authorities constitutes a violation of the naming rights as moral rights (Article 1-3 of the Basic Law, § 12 Federal Code) and against the *law of the change of family name and first name*, in civil status cases also of the *Civil Status Act*. I have documented ground-breaking Court judgements to appropriate dispute cases.

In principle, the violation of the naming rights as moral rights applies also to wrong spelling of people's names in the media.

- Members of recognized national minorities in Germany (e.g. Sorbs) have additional legal protection: they have the right to carry their names in the form of minority language, also towards authorities (Art. 10 para. 5 of the *European Charter for Regional or Minority Languages*, Art. 11 para. 1 of the *Framework Convention for the Protection of National Minorities*). In case of Polish descent, one can invoke Art. 20 para. 1 and 3, indent 1, of the *Treaty between the Federal Republic of Germany and the Republic of Poland on Good-neighbourliness and friendly cooperation.*

- Foreign nationals, e.g. migrant workers or exchange students, can cite Art. 10 of the *Introductory Act to the Civil Code* for the correct spelling of their name according to *their* national law, i.e. *with* diacritics.

In German authorities daily life, the mentioned treaties, laws and instructions have however proven to be violated again and again. Often it involved lack of inter-cultural competence, incomplete computer skills, cultural chauvinism or pressure for Germanization:[614] the protection in the case of German nationals of foreign origin or with an immigrant background who are not recognized as national minorities (for instance from the former Yugoslavia or Turkey) used to be very weak. German authorities usually too quickly assumed that only the German alphabet was to be applied to their names once these persons changed from foreign into German status. Against this, people had to be very persistent to obtain the correct spelling of their name.

On the other hand, those affected know usually nothing about the mentioned laws that protect the spelling of their names; a formal legal instruction does not take place. During the decade-long dominance of the 8-bit character sets, an unfortunate attitude of toleration has been developed among the affected. In the Unicode era, it will therefore take a while until this is changed. It is only fair that the applicants are now fully informed and aware of their rights. The legal knowledge collected in this book should be therefore made available to those affected by publication in suitable form, to give them an effective tool against authority arbitrariness.

> My Croatian surname contains a so-called hacek over the first letter. I am now 31 years old, but so far it has never been registered in a passport. The entry in the civil status records was present. As with my wedding 2 years ago my wife took my family name, it was said that registration of the diacritic on the identity card would not be possible. Your site[615] was the only

---

614 cf. chapters 9.3.6, 9.3.6.1, 10.2.3, 10.2.4, 9.3.6.1 (Germany), 10.3.1, 10.3.2 (Austria)
615 www.sonderzeichenhilfe.de

one from which I could get that information about it, and that encouraged me to write to the *Bundesdruckerei* directly.

The *Bundesdruckerei* immediately contacted the responsible municipal administration, and the registration was no longer a problem. Right here I hold for the first time our identity cards with the correct spelling of our name in my hands. For your website and the information contained therein, thank you.

A "EU/EEA Diacritics Directive" with a uniform legal basis (instead of a patchwork of inconsistent or even contradictory national rulings), including a common European Norm with Latin diacritics, prepared by the *European Committee for Standardization* (CEN), would be a better solution.

12.3 National implementation

In connection with the question of the future use of a pan-European character set, I initially imagined three possible scenarios:

Scenario 1: "lowest common denominator"

- In the intra-European exchange of information, diacritics are gradually *de facto* abolished (including ä, ö, ü and ß in the case of Germany—cf. ICAO Document 9303 for machine readable spelling).
- The feared loss of cultural identity actually occurs.
- Persistent violation of personal and minority rights.
- Technical innovation is blocked.

Scenario 2: The "European spelling reform"

- Conversion is sloppy and/or implemented over a long period / with high bureaucracy.
- Lack of information causes confusion.
- Resistance in population and business community.
- Ultimately, arbitrariness and inconsistency remain.
- Economic damage, e.g. through incompatible digital files.

Scenario 3: "Setting signs for Europe"

- Uniform regulation will prevail (Union-wide), maybe aided by a EU/EEA Diacritics Directive.
- Increased citizen-friendliness.
- People are sensitized to other cultures and develop respect.
- Trust of the "small" Member States into the EU is growing.
- Increased compatibility promotes the common market and the trans-European networks.

For scenario 1 is to say that it is an obstacle to technical progress to orient one always at the lowest standard (as has been shown by the example of German news agencies). There is no other way that European countries implement the necessary technical steps to convert to Unicode compatibility (and thus to a pan-European Latin repertoire) in public and private sector IT—even in times of tight budgets—if only for legal reasons. Neither delay tactics or half-baked workarounds, mutual recriminations between lawmakers and software manufacturers, ignoring or playing down the problem or even assimilation laws can change that. The only question is whether you still want to grapple yet another decade with the technical problems of migration, or whether the government will promote and co-ordinate the switch, thereby holding duration, burdens and costs of the transition phase as low as possible. The annual damage from data corruption due to incompatible character sets is in Germany alone probably in the millions. Therefore, the rapid, uniform changeover of public and private German administration to consistent Unicode support is of great national economic benefits. For this reason, each nation-state government should be keen to fully support the transition, and they should talk to each other, in order to achieve synergy. The process will take enough time already. The reasons are manifold: transition costs, lack of compatibility of legacy software, the necessary training of employees on the new system, the overall orientation change that is not yet taken throughout, etc.

Parallel to technical change, it has proven to be advantageous that the administration—in a top-down approach—pushes for mandatory rules for the spelling of words with diacritics (i.e. String.Latin in Germany, manual diacritics in Austria, NEN 1888 in the Netherlands, E-nämnden in Sweden...). This is because the administration has legal leverage, whereas international standards organizations and technical consortia can ultimately only make recommendations (and are also subject to a certain communication deficit).

Indispensable prerequisite for the consistent application of the above presented procedures for using and representation of words with the correct diacritics in the public (not only administration, but also media) is an individual and societal learning process. First of all, of course, the decision makers in administration, media, business and politics (senior civil servants, chief editors, CEOs, politicians) must become aware of the problem and become familiar with the necessary procedures. The conversion process may, however, not remain an elite project, but must be completed in a society-wide consensus. The concrete implementation must also be designed efficiently, i.e. foreseeable objections and obstacles need to be addressed in advance. Otherwise threatens scenario 2: embarrassing technical glitches (as with the introduction of German truck toll system), or a provincialism of converters and objectors as already observed with the German spelling reform (several newspaper publishers installed a pick-and-choose 'in-house spelling reform').

To sensitize the society as a whole for the politically, technically and culturally desirable change to the consistent use of a pan-European repertoire, in my view, a well-prepared nationwide information campaign is necessary. A corresponding concept for this could build on the results of this work. Here, relevant social actors should be involved:

- Organizations of stakeholders (e.g. Polish organizations in Germany) can over the media spread specific information about the rights of a person with diacritics in their name.
- Pro-European non-governmental organizations (e.g. Young European Federalists) can raise awareness of the problem with public actions and information events.
- The European information centres can initiate information campaigns, maybe even go into the schools and book German, politics, or computer science lessons to boost European competence.
- Customers can exercise impact on IT companies and webmail providers by suggesting improvement (Unicode as the default, matching fonts, etc.). An increase of comfort and compatibility is also a competitive advantage.
- The competent global, European and national standardization organizations (e.g. W3C, CEN, RFC, ITU-T, DIN) and technical-scientific

associations such as the VDI in Germany can in their publications further highlight the benefits of using Universal Character Set / Unicode and offer assistance for the conversion.

The technical migration in combination with a successful information campaign leads us to scenario 3: the population becomes more aware of other cultures, the uniform scheme to take over diacritics is therefore socially accepted and successful. This will also lead to more citizen-friendliness in the authorities towards persons with names containing diacritics.

12.4 European implementation

If the combination of conversion and information campaign proves successful at a subsequent evaluation, the concept could act even across the EU as a model for national conversion to the consistent use of the Universal Character Set / Unicode. The European Union as a whole would ultimately benefit from it: increased technical compatibility would promote the common market and the trans-European network, the confidence of the Eastern European Member States the into the EU would grow (instead of the self-identification as "other Europe" compared to the "main Europe"), and the EU population would get accustomed to thinking in truly European categories. Approaches have been around:

- Already in 1992, due to a request by the Translation Service of the European Commission, a special working group of the *Comité de Coordination de la Standardisation* adopted an internal document entitled *"Multilingualism – The needs of the Institutions of the European Community"* (Rapporteur: PANAGIOTIS ALEVANTIS). The document includes, among other things, listings of all the considered languages as well as a list of character sets that are needed to support these languages. Quote: "The characters of the répertoire are to be coded according to the ISO 10646 international standard."[616]

- The Interoperability Declaration of Valencia (2006), in which respect is required for the citizens, particularly in relation to private and family life (i.e. also bearing of names). Member States are encouraged to integrate interoperability standards in their laws.[617]

- The Ministerial Declaration of Lisbon on the occasion of the conference *"Reaping the benefits of eGovernment"* (2007), which calls for far-reaching, cross-border interoperable IT solutions, especially for mutual recognition of national electronic ID documents.[618] Comparable Ministerial Declarations were done in in Manchester (2005), Malmö (2009), and Granada (2010).[619]

- The High Level Group on Multilingualism, set up by EU Education Commissioner JÁN FIGEĽ in autumn 2006, published on the European Day of Languages 2007 its final report. It contains the following recommendation:

  > [...] the databases for internal document management and the interfaces of software application and hardware equipment have been built around Unicode, allowing representation of the alphabets of all languages. The Group appeals to those authorities in the Member States and webmail providers who have not yet done so to change over to Unicode in order to avoid

---

616 http://users.skynet.be/p.alevantis//en/MUL9206.pdf (2014-09-13)
617 http://www.sonderzeichenhilfe.de/images/interoperability_declaration_en.pdf (2015-03-14)
618 http://www.ifap.ru/pr/2007/n070921a.pdf (2012-01-29)
619 http://ec.europa.eu/isa/documents/isa_2_proposal_en.pdf (2015-03-14)

continuing discrimination of EU citizens on the grounds of nationality or language.⁶²⁰

- In its Communication of 19 May 2010 *A Digital Agenda for Europe* (DAE), one of the flagship initiatives of its *Europe 2020 Strategy*, the Commission stressed that interoperability is essential to maximise the social and economic potential of ICT and that, consequently, the Digital Agenda can take off only if interoperability is ensured.⁶²¹

- In its Communication of 16 December 2010 *Towards interoperability for European public services*, the Commission introduced the *European Interoperability Strategy* (EIS) and the *European Interoperability Framework* (EIF).⁶²²

The question is: how can European multilingualism, repeatedly requested by the European Commission, be practically realized when European multialphabetism (let alone "multiscriptism") still represents a major technical problem in everyday citizens' life?

Germany is quite advanced in Unicode-compatible e-government. It may build at its perceived role as "advocate of Central Europe" (Krzysztof Skubiszewski)⁶²³ and act as honest broker, also for the small EU Member States, linguistic regions, and linguistic minorities fearing for their cultural identity. Since this is an issue throughout Europe, it should even be thought about a common European Norm (EN). The European Union would have

---

620 http://biblioteca.esec.pt/cdi/ebooks/docs/High_level_report.pdf (2015-06-04)
621 http://ec.europa.eu/isa/documents/isa_2_proposal_en.pdf (2015-03-14)
622 http://ec.europa.eu/isa/documents/isa_2_proposal_en.pdf (2015-03-14)
623 Krzysztof Skubiszewski: *Deutschland: Anwalt Mitteleuropas. Eine polnische Sicht der deutschen Europa-Politik*, in: Angelika Volle und Werner Weidenfeld (Hrsg.): *Europa hat Zukunft. Der Weg ins 21. Jahrhundert*, Verlag für Internationale Politik GmbH, Bonn 1998, ISBN 3-921011-05-1

the jurisdiction (approximation of laws regarding TFEU 170, 171: Trans-European Networks).

As mentioned before, the *European Committee for Standardization* prepared a proposal in 2011 *("define the summary repertoire for use in name writing in European public registers, especially in the light of current and potential future legal requirements")* and tried to secure European Commission co-funding. The European Commission did unfortunately not fund the CEN proposal. Their argumentation was that there was already the overarching Universal Character Set / Unicode standard, not considering that it was highly impractical (113,000 characters and counting, from various scripts), while there was still no legal guarantee for an extended Latin subset (as it had been not defined).

The topic of preparing an European Norm for Latin diacritics might get back on EU level with the *ISA² programme*[624] *("establishing a programme on interoperability solutions for European public administrations, businesses and citizens")*, adopted by the European Commission, but still awaiting adoption by the Council and the European Parliament (probably in summer 2015).[625]

> The bad news is that Maroš Šefčovič, the typographer's least-favourite commissioner, is returning for a second term.[626]
>
> – How surely not to raise Eastern European Member States confidence the into the EU.

---

624 http://ec.europa.eu/isa/documents/isa_2_proposal_en.pdf (2014-12-07)
625 EESC report (5.11, 5.12)
    http://eur-lex.europa.eu/legal-content/EN/TXT/PDF/?uri=CELEX:52014AE4603&from=EN (2015-06-04)
626 EuropeanVoice: Entre Nous / Putting the accent on commissioners' names (2014-09-11)

13 Outlook

The present work is the first that deals in such detail with the topic of handling diacritics. Therefore it was necessary to work out first the extensive technical and legal basis of dealing with diacritics. In addition, I explained the current state of the "diacritic integration" in (mainly) German-speaking countries, using selected examples. These examples could be extended in subsequent studies, such as in areas as television coverage (especially resorts with frequent foreign elements such as politics and sports, e.g. international athletes' names), official letters and company letters, librarianship, a more systematic research on trademarks, and also diacritics in search engines. Also a larger-scale questionnaire would be conceivable.

Points that were not addressed in the present study are for example the use of different male/female forms of the surname (e.g. Ivanov/Ivanova, Krencius/Krencienė/Krenciūtė, see chapter 9.1.10) and the legal right to correction of registry entries written without/with the wrong diacritics. Furthermore, an investigation into the legal situation in other European countries (Greece, Italy, Luxembourg, Turkey, Belgium, Slovenia, Sweden, Liechtenstein, Lithuania, Poland, Denmark, etc.) would be interesting.

In 2006, there was still much in flux in the area of German legislation and in the standards for data transmissions (e.g. XMeld). Therefore it was not possible at that time to come to a final statement. In 2015, the situation is much clearer: the Universal Character Set / Unicode is mandatory for German registration and reporting. Nevertheless, in other countries (Austria, Switzerland, etc.) the topic will remain exciting and relevant and should be continued to be observed scientifically.

Another important issue is the consideration of the nation-state standards from the standpoint of national or European minority protection (cf. RYTIS SATKAUSKAS).[627]

One important area is also education. The aim must be to generate young Europeans for which the competent use of the diacritics of other European countries is a matter of course. To this end, teaching modules must be developed for the subjects of language and computer science, and evaluated in practice.

The switch to diacritics-compatible computer systems, which took place in the German registration and reporting system, is yet to come for some European banks in the course of the SEPA[628] migration. The solution behind, ISO 20022, is an XML standard, i.e. *in principle* Unicode-compatible. Here a Unicode quasi-standard is already in place[629] (the diacritics of the countries participating in SEPA), but the putting into practice is held back by legacy applications. The responsible persons could build on the *technical*

---

627 Use of diacritics: towards a new standard of minority protection? http://www.lvb.lt/primo_library/libweb/action/dlDisplay.do?vid=LDB&docId=TLITLIJ.04~2008~1367164906657&fromSitemap=1&afterPDS=true (2015-03-14)
628 Single European Payment Area
629 SEPA Requirements for an Extended Character Set (UNICODE Subset) - Best Practices
http://www.europeanpaymentscouncil.eu/index.cfm/knowledge-bank/epc-documents/sepa-requirements-for-an-extended-character-set-unicode-subset-best-practices/ (2009-12-21)

experience gained in registration and reporting. This conversion process is certainly worth investigating.

In the time I've spent in Brussels, I realized how important it is to concisely formulate—especially if it is to attract the attention of politicians (the much-cited "elevator pitch").[630] In this sense:

"It must become easier to insert diacritics."

E.g. for weekly magazines, an accented characters menu may suffice, but for daily newspapers even this seems to be a step too much, and even more so for the private (web) communication.

See, for example, the attempt to introduce an international standard orthography for Romani:

> One reason for the reluctance to adopt this standard, according to Canadian Rom RONALD LEE, is that the proposed orthography contains a number of specialized characters not regularly found on European keyboards, such as θ and ʒ. [...] The English-based orthography commonly used in North America is, to a degree, an accommodation of the Pan-Vlax orthography to English-language keyboards, replacing those graphemes with diacritics with digraphs, such as the substitution of ts ch sh zh for c č š ž. This particular orthography seems to have arisen spontaneously as Romani speakers have communicated using email, a medium in which graphemes outside the Latin-1 charset have until recently been difficult to type.[631]

Therefore, I have developed an own input method, which uses only ASCII characters:

---

630 https://en.wikipedia.org/wiki/Elevator_pitch (2015-03-15)
631 http://en.wikipedia.org/wiki/Romani_alphabets#Standardisation (17.03.2012)

14 Development of a practical input method for characters

As the title of the input method I have chosen *Šibboleth*. Background is a passage from the Old Testament (Book of Judges, chapter 12). It reads:

> 5 The Gileadites captured the fords of the Jordan leading to Ephraim, and whenever a survivor of Ephraim said, "Let me cross over," the men of Gilead asked him, "Are you an Ephraimite?" If he replied, "No,"
> 6 they said, "All right, say 'Šibboleth.'" If he said, "Sibboleth," because he could not pronounce the word correctly, they seized him and killed him at the fords of the Jordan.

14.1 Fundamental considerations

1. Existing input methods often work only under certain programs (e.g. MS Word) or only for certain subsets (e.g. Latin-1). There is therefore a need for a *universal* input method that can be used for all Latin characters of modern European languages (at least on MS Windows systems, better yet across platforms).

2. Input methods based on decimal and hexadecimal *numerical* values are not practical because the number of values corresponds by

definition to the number of characters. The average user cannot be expected to retain about 400 numbers in memory or to always have a list of them handy.[632]

3. The execution of all necessary diacritics as *dead keys* (like ˆ ´ `) would require the introduction of at least 14 additional key assignments. These new assignments would have to be *physically* marked on the keyboards. In the long term, existing international standards for keyboard layouts would have to be adjusted accordingly.

   - The Neo keyboard layout,[633] the *Europatastatur*[634] ("European keyboard") and MEEK *(Functional Multilingual Extensions to European keyboard layouts)*[635] are following this approach. The problem is that they are all at least driver-based (if not hardware-based) solutions, i.e. they are not portable.

4. The execution of diacritics as dead keys was a technical necessity of the mechanical typewriter. In the age of electronic text processing, this historically concession is no longer mandatory.

5. Some systems use default escape codes based on existing key assignments. The Ä can be generated e.g. by means of [\\] ["] [A] (TeX source) or [Strg] [⇧] [:] [A] (MS Word).

6. The disadvantage of dead keys and default escape codes is that they are inconsistent with both the manual flow of writing as well as the nomenclature of characters (it is "A with diaeresis", not "diaeresis over A").

---

632 http://unicode.org/charts/PDF/U0100.pdf etc. (2015-07-21)
633 http://de.wikipedia.org/wiki/Neo_%28Tastaturbelegung%29 (2012-01-01)
634 http://www.europatastatur.de/ (2012-01-04)
635 ftp://ftp.cen.eu/CEN/Sectors/List/ICT/CWAs/CWA-16108-2010-MEEK.pdf (2012-01-01)

7. Escape encodings outside the source require a compose function. MS Word, for example, uses the [Strg] key. The disadvantage is that the user must press up to three buttons simultaneously, e.g. [Strg][⇧][:] for a diaeresis.
8. An alternative to keyboard short-cuts is called a *hotstring*, i.e. a string that trigger keyboard events. The string [A][:] would, for example, as hotstring automatically replaced by Ä. The problem is that the replacement would take place also at text positions where a colon was actually desired. Thus, the string must be "armed" by an additional key. This key should be a control button or alternatively a character that is not used in texts (or only rarely). On most keyboards this is the number sign [#] or the plus sign [+].
9. There are two ways of *ordering* a hotstring: [#][A][:] or [A][:][#]. Considering the fact that letters can carry *multiple* diacritics (example Ã), the second variant [A][:][-][#] is preferable because then the end of the escape coding is clear (while [#][A][:][-] could mean both Ã and Ä-).
10. The escape codes should consist exclusively of *ASCII characters* (e.g. characters which are encoded by the vast number of ASCII-derived character sets by the same numerical value) for maximum compatibility and interoperability.
11. The escape codes should be *intuitive*, e.g. their shape should remind of the respective diacritic.

The intuitive combination would be "basic letter + diacritic replacement + compose". They would work for most letters with diacritics and also for ligatures and digraphs.

However, diacritics which can be also set above *and* below would cause a problem. There is therefore a need for a second function key for diacritics that are to be put underneath. Intuitively the underscore ⌴ comes to mind. But in practice, problems occurred when the user assigns file names (and the underscore is used to replace a space). Therefore, we cannot waive the compose key: ⌴#.

Is there a need for a *third* function key, for letters that are *superimposed* by the diacritic? I would simply use the x. So:

1. base letter + diacritic replacement(s) + compose (= standard diacritic)
2. base letter + diacritic replacement + underneath + compose (= diacritic underneath)
3. base letter 1 + base letter 2 + compose (= letter combinations)
4. base letter 1 + base letter 2 + ligature/digraph signal]] + compose (= only dz fi ffi)
5. base letter 1 + base letter 2 + ligature/digraph signal]] + diacritic replacement + compose (= only ǯ dž æ ǽ)
6. basic letter + diacritic replacement + overlay x + compose (= for - and ~)

14.1.1 Potential conflicts

Some cases of conflict must first be resolved:

The combination a e # could principally trigger ä, å, æ and ę. I have chosen the following combinations: a : # = ä, a [e # or ä e # = å, a e # = æ and e & # = ę. These combinations would have a corresponding impact on the generation of œ/ó/ö and ů/ü

The Dutch ligature ij and the Croatian digraphs lj and nj are to be expected more frequent than the ȷ (j without dot, probably only in medieval texts).

Therefore [i][j][#] = ij, [n][j][#] = nj, etc. should get the privilege (= without ligature/digraph signal), and the ȷ should be generated via [j][0][#] instead of [j][#].

Another case of conflict is the combination [d][z][#] that could principally trigger ʒ (ezh) as well as the digraph dz. A further complication is that both ʒ and dz can also occur with a haček (ǯ, dž). If we set [d][z][#] = ʒ, then dz must explicitly generated as digraph via [d][z][]][#], even if this not coherent with lj and nj. It follows [d][z][]][<][#] = ǯ and [d][z][<][]][#] = dž. Both solutions are with five keystrokes comparatively type-intensive, but probably cannot be further optimized. The combination [d][z][h][#] as an alternative would collide with [z][h][#] = ž.

In the same way, [a][e][#] stands for æ but [a][e][]][-][#] / [a][e][]][´][#] for ǣ / ǽ.

The ligature fi is triggered the standard way [f][i][]][#] but ffi is triggered [F][i][]][#] (everything else did not work).

14.2 Escape encodings with diacritics

Taking into consideration escape codes of TEX and MS Word, I have chosen the following assignments:

acute ´	apostrophe [']
double acute ˝	quotation mark ["]
breve ˘	opening parenthesis [(]
inverted breve ˆ	closing parenthesis [)]
broad breve ⌣	two times opening parenthesis [(][(]

broad inverted breve ͡	two times closing parenthesis `))`
breve underneath ̮	closing parenthesis + underscore `)_`
inverted breve underneath ̑	opening parenthesis + underscore `(_`
cedilla ̧	semicolon `;`
descender	digit `4`
gravis `	backslash `\`
double gravis ̏	two times backslash `\\`
haček ̌	less-than sign `<`
haček underneath ̬	less-than sign + underline `<_`
hook ̛	question mark `?`
hook above/underneath	(experimental:) section sign `§` [no ASCII character]
horn ̛	digit `9`
comma ̦	comma `,`
macron ̄	hyphen/minus `-`
macron in centre	hyphen/minus + x `-x`
macron underneath ̱	hyphen/minus + underscore `-_`
double macron underneath ̳	two times hyphen/minus + underscore `--_`
ogonek ̨	& sign `&`
dot ̇ / dot in centre ·	dot `.`
dot underneath ̣ (alternative) [636]	exclamation mark `!`
dash -	equal sign `=`

[636] especially where also one diacritic above exists

ring °	asterisk [*] / degree symbol [°] [no ASCII character]
slash /	slash [/]
tilde ˜	tilde [~]
tilde in centre	tilde + x [~][x]
tilde underneath ˷	tilde + underscore [~][_]
broad tilde ͝	two times tilde [~][~]
trema ¨	colon [:]
top-bar]	closing square bracket []]
circumflex ˆ	greater-than sign [>]
circumflex underneath ˬ	greater-than sign + underscore [>][_]
with long leg |	vertical line [|]
inverted letter |	vertical line [|]
stand-alone diacritic	space + diacritic
combining diacritic	opening square bracket [[] + diacritic

The operation of the program is very easy: enter the basic letter(s), then the diacritic(s), then the number/underscore key.

Examples: [n]['][#] = ń   [u]["][#] = ű   [g][(][#] = ğ   [e][)][#] = ê
[i][)][)][#][a] = îa   [c][;][#] = ç   [n][4][#] = ɲ   [y][\][#] = ỳ   [r][\][\][#] = r̈
[c][<][#] = č   [a][?][#] = å   [z][§][#] = ʒ   [o][9][#] = ơ   [t][,][#] = ţ
[u][-][#] = ū   [o][-][x][#] = ɵ   [e][&][#] = ę   [e][.][#] = ė   [s][!][#] = ş
[z][=][#] = ƶ   [u][°][#] = ů   [o][/][#] = ø   [a][~][#] = ã   [l][~][x][#] = ł
[u][~][_] = ṵ   [x][:][#] = ẍ   [b][]][#] = Ƅ   [y][>][#] = ŷ   [d][>][_] = ḓ

If the basic letter has several diacritics, first the diacritics under the letter and then the diacritics over the letter are entered (ascending).

Examples: [e][!][>][#] = ê̂ [u][:][<][#] = ṳ̆

14.3 Escape encodings *without* diacritics

Some letters are entered directly (without diacritics):

Æ	[A][E] AE ligature
IJ	[I][J] IJ ligature
Œ	[O][E] OE ligature
Đ	[D] Eth
Þ	[T][H] Thorn / Þ [T][H][]][=] Thorn with dash = "that"
İ	[I] Turkish I
Ñ	[N][N] N with tilde (additional)
ß	[S][S] sharp S
ŋ	[N][G] Eng
Ʒ	[D][Z] Ezh / Ʒ [D][Z][]][<]
ə	[Ä] Schwa (additional) [no ASCII character], [A][:][]]
DZ	[D][Z][]] DZ digraph / DŽ [D][Z][<][]] DŽ digraph
LJ	[L][J] LJ digraph
NJ	[N][J] NJ digraph
Q	[K][V] (additional)
W	[V][V] (additional)
X	[K][S] (additional)
Å	[A][A] (additional)

Θ	[T][0]	Greek Theta (for Romani)
ſ	[s][] long s / [s][][t][] ft ligature	
Ǻ	[Ä][e]	over-set e set in early forms of Ä (additional) [no ASCII character]
ƿ	[W]	Wynn
ȝ	[G][H]	Yogh
ƒ	[f]	florin (guilder)
ĸ	[k]	kra (the capital letter is K', i.e. K + singular quotation marks above)
Ɋ	[Q]	Gha
ө	[Ö]	(additional) [no ASCII character]
Ƕ	[H][V]	Hwair, for transcription of the letter ⌧ from the Gothic script
ŋ	[N][]	N with extended right leg
Ʀ	[Y][R]	for transcription of the Norse rune *elhaz* ⌧
8	[O][U]	OU ligature, in Indian languages
Ⱶ	[/][H]	claudianic *Sonus medius*
Ↄ	[B][S], [P][S]	claudianic *Antisigma*
I	[I][/][], [I][], [I][]	Latin *I longa* (aus Í)
Ɯ	[M][M]	Latin archaic M
ȷ	[j][0]	j without dot
ǂ	[][=][=]	alveolar click
!	[!][]	retroflex click
Ỻ	[L][L][]	middle-Welsh LL

AA   A A] AA digraph
AO   A O] AO digraph
AJ   A U] AU digraph
AV   A V] AV digraph / AV A V] - AV digraph with dash
AY   A Y] AY digraph
OO   O O] OO digraph
VY   V Y] VY digraph

For the other characters I have chosen the following assignments:

‰   % promille
@   a t at sign
¤   i c s international currency symbol
0ª... 9ª   0 a ... 9 a numbers, female
0°... 9°   0 o ... 9 o numbers, male
¬   N O T NOT sign
°   d e g degree symbol
·   . stand-alone dot in the middle
¼   space 1 / 4
             ½ – space 1 / 2
             ¾ – space 3 / 4
             ⅓ – space 1 / 3
             ⅔ – space 2 / 3
             ⅕ – space 1 / 5
             ⅖ – space 2 / 5
             ⅗ – space 3 / 5
             ⅘ – space 4 / 5

	⅙ – space [1] [/] [6]
	⅚ – space [5] [/] [6]
	⅛ – space [1] [/] [8]
	⅜ – space [3] [/] [8]
	⅝ – space [5] [/] [8]
	⅞ – space [7] [/] [8]
	⅟ – space [1] [/]
″	space ['] ['] space – inch
‽	[?] [!] interrobang
℀	[a] [/] [c] account of ...
℁	[a] [/] [s] addressed to the subject ...
℅	[c] [/] [o] care of ...
℆	[c] [/] [u] *cada una* (each piece)
℃	[°] [C], [d] [C] degrees Celsius
℉	[°] [F], [d] [F] degrees Fahrenheit
™	[T] [M] trademark sign
☺	[:] [)] Smiley
☹	[:] [(] Frowny
⅍	[A] [/] [S] *Aktieselskab* (Danish for company)
¦	space [|] broken bar
→	[-] [-] [>] arrow
↛	[-] [/] [-] [>] arrow struck through
↔	[<] [-] [>] arrow with two heads
⇒	[=] [=] [>] thick arrow
⇔	[<] [=] [>] thick arrow with two heads
∑	[s] [u] [m] sum sign

№   [N][o] number sign
⊕   [(][+][)] circled plus sign
⊖   [(][-][)] circled minus sign
⌀   [0][/] diameter
☧   [x][p] chi-rho
卐   [x][x] right-wing Swastika
☭   [*][)] hammer and sickle
☪   [(][*] crescent and star
☯   [Y][Y] yin-yang

‖ Do not forget to add [#]! ‖

14.4 Underscore

With only an underscore [_], the following characters are made:

¡   [!][_] Spanish inverted exclamation mark
¿   [?][_] Spanish inverted question mark
ɯ   [M][]][_]
| [|][_] dental click
‖   [|][!][_] lateral click

With underscore [_] plus compose key [#], the following characters are made:

ɔ   [C][_] African O
ⅎ   [F][_] claudian *Digamma inversum*

and other reverse letters ([A][_], etc.)

∞   [8][_] infinity symbol

"Underscore plus compose key" instead of simply an underscore became necessary as field testing revealed that people frequently name files with an underscore between letters.

14.5 Other characters (no compose key)

„ "	space[„][„] ... ["]["]space	exclamation marks (default German)
» «	space[>][>] ... [<][<]space	*guillemets*
–	space[-][-]space	n-dash
—	space[-][-][-]space	m-dash
±	[+][-]space	plus or minus
−	[-]	real minus sign (on numeric keypad)
×	space[*][*]	real multiplication sign
÷	space[/][/]	real division sign
≥	[>][=]	greater than or equal to
≤	[<][=]	less than or equal to
≠	[=][/]	not equal
≙	[=][>]	corresponds to
≈	[=][~]	almost equal
⇌	[<][>]	chemical equilibrium
†	[+][|]	dagger
‡	[+][+]	double dagger
...	[.][.][.]	ellipse
♥	[<][3]	heart
⁊	[&][&]	Tironian et

Currency symbols: $ + ISO 4217 code [637] (if there is a currency symbol)

₴   [s] [u] [a] [h] Ukrainian Hryvnia

14.6 Dead keys

The scope of the dead keys was extended. Now it is possible to enter all the letters with ´ ` ˛ ¨ directly (also in combinations).

I used the scripting language *AutoHotkey_L* for MS Window [638] to realize the above presented escape codes (and some others). The result is the commercial program *Šibboleth*. [639]

IronAHK, a rewritten *AutoHotkey* for .NET and Mono for the purpose of cross-platform application (Unix, Mac) has unfortunately moved into permanent hibernation, it seems. [640]

> You have found a mistake in this book,
> want to send me an idea, an image etc.?
> bernd.kappenberg@gmx.de

---

637 https://en.wikipedia.org/wiki/ISO_4217 (2015-08-06)
638 free of charge: http://l.autohotkey.net/ (03.01.2012)
639 www.sonderzeichenhilfe.de
640 http://www.autohotkey.com/board/topic/50354-ironahk-alpha-cross-platform-net-rewrite-of-autohotkey/page-39

Further readings

Alevantis, Panagiotis (1992). *Multilingualism. The needs of the Institutions of the European Community*. Tech. rep. D/466. Version 4. Commission des Communautés Européennes / Service de traduction / Informatique. URL: http://users.skynet.be/p.alevantis//en/MUL9206.pdf.

Peruginelli, Susanna, Giovanni Bergamin, and Pino Ammendola (1992). "Character sets: towards a standard solution?" In: *Program* 26.3, pp. 215–223. DOI: 10.1108/eb047115. URL: http://www.emeraldinsight.com/doi/abs/10.1108/eb047115.

British Library and Biblioteca Nazionale (1993). *Definition of a Basic European Character Set: Final Report: Public Version*. British Library. URL: http://books.google.be/books?id=j843twAACAAJ.

Byrum, J.D. et al. (1998). *Multi-script, multilingual, multi-character issues for the online environment: proceedings of a workshop sponsored by the IFLA Section on Cataloguing, Istanbul, Turkey, August 24, 1995*. IFLA publications. K.G. Saur. ISBN: 9783598218149. URL: http://books.google.be/books?id=RNzgAAAAMAAJ.

Satkauskas, Rytis (2008). "Use of diacritics: towards a new standard of minority protection?" In: *Lithuanian foreign policy review* 21, pp. 112–135. ISSN: 1392-5504. URL: http://www.lfpr.lt/uploads/File/2008-21/Satkauskas_ENG.pdf.

SOVIET AND POST-SOVIET POLITICS AND SOCIETY

Edited by Dr. Andreas Umland

ISSN 1614-3515

1   *Андреас Умланд (ред.)*
    Воплощение Европейской
    конвенции по правам человека в
    России
    Философские, юридические и
    эмпирические исследования
    ISBN 3-89821-387-0

2   *Christian Wipperfürth*
    Russland – ein vertrauenswürdiger
    Partner?
    Grundlagen, Hintergründe und Praxis
    gegenwärtiger russischer Außenpolitik
    Mit einem Vorwort von Heinz Timmermann
    ISBN 3-89821-401-X

3   *Manja Hussner*
    Die Übernahme internationalen Rechts
    in die russische und deutsche
    Rechtsordnung
    Eine vergleichende Analyse zur
    Völkerrechtsfreundlichkeit der Verfassungen
    der Russländischen Föderation und der
    Bundesrepublik Deutschland
    Mit einem Vorwort von Rainer Arnold
    ISBN 3-89821-438-9

4   *Matthew Tejada*
    Bulgaria's Democratic Consolidation
    and the Kozloduy Nuclear Power Plant
    (KNPP)
    The Unattainability of Closure
    With a foreword by Richard J. Crampton
    ISBN 3-89821-439-7

5   *Марк Григорьевич Меерович*
    Квадратные метры, определяющие
    сознание
    Государственная жилищная политика в
    СССР. 1921 – 1941 гг
    ISBN 3-89821-474-5

6   *Andrei P. Tsygankov, Pavel
    A.Tsygankov (Eds.)*
    New Directions in Russian
    International Studies
    ISBN 3-89821-422-2

7   *Марк Григорьевич Меерович*
    Как власть народ к труду приучала
    Жилище в СССР – средство управления
    людьми. 1917 – 1941 гг.
    С предисловием Елены Осокиной
    ISBN 3-89821-495-8

8   *David J. Galbreath*
    Nation-Building and Minority Politics
    in Post-Socialist States
    Interests, Influence and Identities in Estonia
    and Latvia
    With a foreword by David J. Smith
    ISBN 3-89821-467-2

9   *Алексей Юрьевич Безугольный*
    Народы Кавказа в Вооруженных
    силах СССР в годы Великой
    Отечественной войны 1941-1945 гг.
    С предисловием Николая Бугая
    ISBN 3-89821-475-3

10 *Вячеслав Лихачев и Владимир
    Прибыловский (ред.)*
    Русское Национальное Единство,
    1990-2000. В 2-х томах
    ISBN 3-89821-523-7

11 *Николай Бугай (ред.)*
    Народы стран Балтии в условиях
    сталинизма (1940-е – 1950-е годы)
    Документированная история
    ISBN 3-89821-525-3

12 *Ingmar Bredies (Hrsg.)*
    Zur Anatomie der Orange Revolution
    in der Ukraine
    Wechsel des Elitenregimes oder Triumph des
    Parlamentarismus?
    ISBN 3-89821-524-5

13 *Anastasia V. Mitrofanova*
    The Politicization of Russian
    Orthodoxy
    Actors and Ideas
    With a foreword by William C. Gay
    ISBN 3-89821-481-8

14 Nathan D. Larson
    Alexander Solzhenitsyn and the
    Russo-Jewish Question
    ISBN 3-89821-483-4

15 Guido Houben
    Kulturpolitik und Ethnizität
    Staatliche Kunstförderung im Russland der
    neunziger Jahre
    Mit einem Vorwort von Gert Weisskirchen
    ISBN 3-89821-542-3

16 Leonid Luks
    Der russische „Sonderweg"?
    Aufsätze zur neuesten Geschichte Russlands
    im europäischen Kontext
    ISBN 3-89821-496-6

17 Евгений Мороз
    История «Мёртвой воды» – от
    страшной сказки к большой
    политике
    Политическое неоязычество в
    постсоветской России
    ISBN 3-89821-551-2

18 Александр Верховский и Галина
    Кожевникова (ред.)
    Этническая и религиозная
    интолерантность в российских СМИ
    Результаты мониторинга 2001-2004 гг.
    ISBN 3-89821-569-5

19 Christian Ganzer
    Sowjetisches Erbe und ukrainische
    Nation
    Das Museum der Geschichte des Zaporoger
    Kosakentums auf der Insel Chortycja
    Mit einem Vorwort von Frank Golczewski
    ISBN 3-89821-504-0

20 Эльза-Баир Гучинова
    Помнить нельзя забыть
    Антропология депортационной травмы
    калмыков
    С предисловием Кэролайн Хамфри
    ISBN 3-89821-506-7

21 Юлия Лидерман
    Мотивы «проверки» и «испытания»
    в постсоветской культуре
    Советское прошлое в российском
    кинематографе 1990-х годов
    С предисловием Евгения Марголита
    ISBN 3-89821-511-3

22 Tanya Lokshina, Ray Thomas, Mary
    Mayer (Eds.)
    The Imposition of a Fake Political
    Settlement in the Northern Caucasus
    The 2003 Chechen Presidential Election
    ISBN 3-89821-436-2

23 Timothy McCajor Hall, Rosie Read
    (Eds.)
    Changes in the Heart of Europe
    Recent Ethnographies of Czechs, Slovaks,
    Roma, and Sorbs
    With an afterword by Zdeněk Salzmann
    ISBN 3-89821-606-3

24 Christian Autengruber
    Die politischen Parteien in Bulgarien
    und Rumänien
    Eine vergleichende Analyse seit Beginn der
    90er Jahre
    Mit einem Vorwort von Dorothée de Nève
    ISBN 3-89821-476-1

25 Annette Freyberg-Inan with Radu
    Cristescu
    The Ghosts in Our Classrooms, or:
    John Dewey Meets Ceauşescu
    The Promise and the Failures of Civic
    Education in Romania
    ISBN 3-89821-416-8

26 John B. Dunlop
    The 2002 Dubrovka and 2004 Beslan
    Hostage Crises
    A Critique of Russian Counter-Terrorism
    With a foreword by Donald N. Jensen
    ISBN 3-89821-608-X

27 Peter Koller
    Das touristische Potenzial von
    Kam''janec'–Podil's'kyj
    Eine fremdenverkehrsgeographische
    Untersuchung der Zukunftsperspektiven und
    Maßnahmenplanung zur
    Destinationsentwicklung des „ukrainischen
    Rothenburg"
    Mit einem Vorwort von Kristiane Klemm
    ISBN 3-89821-640-3

28 Françoise Daucé, Elisabeth Sieca-
    Kozlowski (Eds.)
    Dedovshchina in the Post-Soviet
    Military
    Hazing of Russian Army Conscripts in a
    Comparative Perspective
    With a foreword by Dale Herspring
    ISBN 3-89821-616-0

29 Florian Strasser
    Zivilgesellschaftliche Einflüsse auf die
    Orange Revolution
    Die gewaltlose Massenbewegung und die
    ukrainische Wahlkrise 2004
    Mit einem Vorwort von Egbert Jahn
    ISBN 3-89821-648-9

30 Rebecca S. Katz
    The Georgian Regime Crisis of 2003-
    2004
    A Case Study in Post-Soviet Media
    Representation of Politics, Crime and
    Corruption
    ISBN 3-89821-413-3

31 Vladimir Kantor
    Willkür oder Freiheit
    Beiträge zur russischen Geschichtsphilosophie
    Ediert von Dagmar Herrmann sowie mit
    einem Vorwort versehen von Leonid Luks
    ISBN 3-89821-589-X

32 Laura A. Victoir
    The Russian Land Estate Today
    A Case Study of Cultural Politics in Post-
    Soviet Russia
    With a foreword by Priscilla Roosevelt
    ISBN 3-89821-426-5

33 Ivan Katchanovski
    Cleft Countries
    Regional Political Divisions and Cultures in
    Post-Soviet Ukraine and Moldova
    With a foreword by Francis Fukuyama
    ISBN 3-89821-558-X

34 Florian Mühlfried
    Postsowjetische Feiern
    Das Georgische Bankett im Wandel
    Mit einem Vorwort von Kevin Tuite
    ISBN 3-89821-601-2

35 Roger Griffin, Werner Loh, Andreas
    Umland (Eds.)
    Fascism Past and Present, West and
    East
    An International Debate on Concepts and
    Cases in the Comparative Study of the
    Extreme Right
    With an afterword by Walter Laqueur
    ISBN 3-89821-674-8

36 Sebastian Schlegel
    Der „Weiße Archipel"
    Sowjetische Atomstädte 1945-1991
    Mit einem Geleitwort von Thomas Bohn
    ISBN 3-89821-679-9

37 Vyacheslav Likhachev
    Political Anti-Semitism in Post-Soviet
    Russia
    Actors and Ideas in 1991-2003
    Edited and translated from Russian by Eugene
    Veklerov
    ISBN 3-89821-529-6

38 Josette Baer (Ed.)
    Preparing Liberty in Central Europe
    Political Texts from the Spring of Nations
    1848 to the Spring of Prague 1968
    With a foreword by Zdeněk V. David
    ISBN 3-89821-546-6

39 Михаил Лукьянов
    Российский консерватизм и
    реформа, 1907-1914
    С предисловием Марка Д. Стейнберга
    ISBN 3-89821-503-2

40 Nicola Melloni
    Market Without Economy
    The 1998 Russian Financial Crisis
    With a foreword by Eiji Furukawa
    ISBN 3-89821-407-9

41 Dmitrij Chmelnizki
    Die Architektur Stalins
    Bd. 1: Studien zu Ideologie und Stil
    Bd. 2: Bilddokumentation
    Mit einem Vorwort von Bruno Flierl
    ISBN 3-89821-515-6

42 Katja Yafimava
    Post-Soviet Russian-Belarussian
    Relationships
    The Role of Gas Transit Pipelines
    With a foreword by Jonathan P. Stern
    ISBN 3-89821-655-1

43 Boris Chavkin
    Verflechtungen der deutschen und
    russischen Zeitgeschichte
    Aufsätze und Archivfunde zu den
    Beziehungen Deutschlands und der
    Sowjetunion von 1917 bis 1991
    Ediert von Markus Edlinger sowie mit einem
    Vorwort versehen von Leonid Luks
    ISBN 3-89821-756-6

44 Anastasija Grynenko in
Zusammenarbeit mit Claudia Dathe
Die Terminologie des Gerichtswesens
der Ukraine und Deutschlands im
Vergleich
Eine übersetzungswissenschaftliche Analyse
juristischer Fachbegriffe im Deutschen,
Ukrainischen und Russischen
Mit einem Vorwort von Ulrich Hartmann
ISBN 3-89821-691-8

45 Anton Burkov
The Impact of the European
Convention on Human Rights on
Russian Law
Legislation and Application in 1996-2006
With a foreword by Françoise Hampson
ISBN 978-3-89821-639-5

46 Stina Torjesen, Indra Overland (Eds.)
International Election Observers in
Post-Soviet Azerbaijan
Geopolitical Pawns or Agents of Change?
ISBN 978-3-89821-743-9

47 Taras Kuzio
Ukraine – Crimea – Russia
Triangle of Conflict
ISBN 978-3-89821-761-3

48 Claudia Šabić
"Ich erinnere mich nicht, aber L'viv!"
Zur Funktion kultureller Faktoren für die
Institutionalisierung und Entwicklung einer
ukrainischen Region
Mit einem Vorwort von Melanie Tatur
ISBN 978-3-89821-752-1

49 Marlies Bilz
Tatarstan in der Transformation
Nationaler Diskurs und Politische Praxis
1988-1994
Mit einem Vorwort von Frank Golczewski
ISBN 978-3-89821-722-4

50 Марлен Ларюэль (ред.)
Современные интерпретации
русского национализма
ISBN 978-3-89821-795-8

51 Sonja Schüler
Die ethnische Dimension der Armut
Roma im postsozialistischen Rumänien
Mit einem Vorwort von Anton Sterbling
ISBN 978-3-89821-776-7

52 Галина Кожевникова
Радикальный национализм в России
и противодействие ему
Сборник докладов Центра «Сова» за 2004-
2007 гг.
С предисловием Александра Верховского
ISBN 978-3-89821-721-7

53 Галина Кожевникова и Владимир
Прибыловский
Российская власть в биографиях I
Высшие должностные лица РФ в 2004 г.
ISBN 978-3-89821-796-5

54 Галина Кожевникова и Владимир
Прибыловский
Российская власть в биографиях II
Члены Правительства РФ в 2004 г.
ISBN 978-3-89821-797-2

55 Галина Кожевникова и Владимир
Прибыловский
Российская власть в биографиях III
Руководители федеральных служб и
агентств РФ в 2004 г.
ISBN 978-3-89821-798-9

56 Ileana Petroniu
Privatisierung in
Transformationsökonomien
Determinanten der Restrukturierungs-
Bereitschaft am Beispiel Polens, Rumäniens
und der Ukraine
Mit einem Vorwort von Rainer W. Schäfer
ISBN 978-3-89821-790-3

57 Christian Wipperfürth
Russland und seine GUS-Nachbarn
Hintergründe, aktuelle Entwicklungen und
Konflikte in einer ressourcenreichen Region
ISBN 978-3-89821-801-6

58 Togzhan Kassenova
From Antagonism to Partnership
The Uneasy Path of the U.S.-Russian
Cooperative Threat Reduction
With a foreword by Christoph Bluth
ISBN 978-3-89821-707-1

59 Alexander Höllwerth
Das sakrale eurasische Imperium des
Aleksandr Dugin
Eine Diskursanalyse zum postsowjetischen
russischen Rechtsextremismus
Mit einem Vorwort von Dirk Uffelmann
ISBN 978-3-89821-813-9

60 *Олег Рябов*
«Россия-Матушка»
Национализм, гендер и война в России XX века
С предисловием Елены Гощило
ISBN 978-3-89821-487-2

61 *Ivan Maistrenko*
Borot'bism
A Chapter in the History of the Ukrainian Revolution
With a new introduction by Chris Ford
Translated by George S. N. Luckyj with the assistance of Ivan L. Rudnytsky
ISBN 978-3-89821-697-5

62 *Maryna Romanets*
Anamorphosic Texts and Reconfigured Visions
Improvised Traditions in Contemporary Ukrainian and Irish Literature
ISBN 978-3-89821-576-3

63 *Paul D'Anieri and Taras Kuzio (Eds.)*
Aspects of the Orange Revolution I
Democratization and Elections in Post-Communist Ukraine
ISBN 978-3-89821-698-2

64 *Bohdan Harasymiw in collaboration with Oleh S. Ilnytzkyj (Eds.)*
Aspects of the Orange Revolution II
Information and Manipulation Strategies in the 2004 Ukrainian Presidential Elections
ISBN 978-3-89821-699-9

65 *Ingmar Bredies, Andreas Umland and Valentin Yakushik (Eds.)*
Aspects of the Orange Revolution III
The Context and Dynamics of the 2004 Ukrainian Presidential Elections
ISBN 978-3-89821-803-0

66 *Ingmar Bredies, Andreas Umland and Valentin Yakushik (Eds.)*
Aspects of the Orange Revolution IV
Foreign Assistance and Civic Action in the 2004 Ukrainian Presidential Elections
ISBN 978-3-89821-808-5

67 *Ingmar Bredies, Andreas Umland and Valentin Yakushik (Eds.)*
Aspects of the Orange Revolution V
Institutional Observation Reports on the 2004 Ukrainian Presidential Elections
ISBN 978-3-89821-809-2

68 *Taras Kuzio (Ed.)*
Aspects of the Orange Revolution VI
Post-Communist Democratic Revolutions in Comparative Perspective
ISBN 978-3-89821-820-7

69 *Tim Bohse*
Autoritarismus statt Selbstverwaltung
Die Transformation der kommunalen Politik in der Stadt Kaliningrad 1990-2005
Mit einem Geleitwort von Stefan Troebst
ISBN 978-3-89821-782-8

70 *David Rupp*
Die Rußländische Föderation und die russischsprachige Minderheit in Lettland
Eine Fallstudie zur Anwaltspolitik Moskaus gegenüber den russophonen Minderheiten im „Nahen Ausland" von 1991 bis 2002
Mit einem Vorwort von Helmut Wagner
ISBN 978-3-89821-778-1

71 *Taras Kuzio*
Theoretical and Comparative Perspectives on Nationalism
New Directions in Cross-Cultural and Post-Communist Studies
With a foreword by Paul Robert Magocsi
ISBN 978-3-89821-815-3

72 *Christine Teichmann*
Die Hochschultransformation im heutigen Osteuropa
Kontinuität und Wandel bei der Entwicklung des postkommunistischen Universitätswesens
Mit einem Vorwort von Oskar Anweiler
ISBN 978-3-89821-842-9

73 *Julia Kusznir*
Der politische Einfluss von Wirtschaftseliten in russischen Regionen
Eine Analyse am Beispiel der Erdöl- und Erdgasindustrie, 1992-2005
Mit einem Vorwort von Wolfgang Eichwede
ISBN 978-3-89821-821-4

74 *Alena Vysotskaya*
Russland, Belarus und die EU-Osterweiterung
Zur Minderheitenfrage und zum Problem der Freizügigkeit des Personenverkehrs
Mit einem Vorwort von Katlijn Malfliet
ISBN 978-3-89821-822-1

75 Heiko Pleines (Hrsg.)
    Corporate Governance in post-
    sozialistischen Volkswirtschaften
    ISBN 978-3-89821-766-8

76 Stefan Ihrig
    Wer sind die Moldawier?
    Rumänismus versus Moldowanismus in
    Historiographie und Schulbüchern der
    Republik Moldova, 1991-2006
    Mit einem Vorwort von Holm Sundhaussen
    ISBN 978-3-89821-466-7

77 Galina Kozhevnikova in collaboration
    with Alexander Verkhovsky and
    Eugene Veklerov
    Ultra-Nationalism and Hate Crimes in
    Contemporary Russia
    The 2004-2006 Annual Reports of Moscow's
    SOVA Center
    With a foreword by Stephen D. Shenfield
    ISBN 978-3-89821-868-9

78 Florian Küchler
    The Role of the European Union in
    Moldova's Transnistria Conflict
    With a foreword by Christopher Hill
    ISBN 978-3-89821-850-4

79 Bernd Rechel
    The Long Way Back to Europe
    Minority Protection in Bulgaria
    With a foreword by Richard Crampton
    ISBN 978-3-89821-863-4

80 Peter W. Rodgers
    Nation, Region and History in Post-
    Communist Transitions
    Identity Politics in Ukraine, 1991-2006
    With a foreword by Vera Tolz
    ISBN 978-3-89821-903-7

81 Stephanie Solywoda
    The Life and Work of
    Semen L. Frank
    A Study of Russian Religious Philosophy
    With a foreword by Philip Walters
    ISBN 978-3-89821-457-5

82 Vera Sokolova
    Cultural Politics of Ethnicity
    Discourses on Roma in Communist
    Czechoslovakia
    ISBN 978-3-89821-864-1

83 Natalya Shevchik Ketenci
    Kazakhstani Enterprises in Transition
    The Role of Historical Regional Development
    in Kazakhstan's Post-Soviet Economic
    Transformation
    ISBN 978-3-89821-831-3

84 Martin Malek, Anna Schor-
    Tschudnowskaja (Hrsg.)
    Europa im Tschetschenienkrieg
    Zwischen politischer Ohnmacht und
    Gleichgültigkeit
    Mit einem Vorwort von Lipchan Basajewa
    ISBN 978-3-89821-676-0

85 Stefan Meister
    Das postsowjetische Universitätswesen
    zwischen nationalem und
    internationalem Wandel
    Die Entwicklung der regionalen Hochschule
    in Russland als Gradmesser der
    Systemtransformation
    Mit einem Vorwort von Joan DeBardeleben
    ISBN 978-3-89821-891-7

86 Konstantin Sheiko in collaboration
    with Stephen Brown
    Nationalist Imaginings of the
    Russian Past
    Anatolii Fomenko and the Rise of Alternative
    History in Post-Communist Russia
    With a foreword by Donald Ostrowski
    ISBN 978-3-89821-915-0

87 Sabine Jenni
    Wie stark ist das „Einige Russland"?
    Zur Parteibindung der Eliten und zum
    Wahlerfolg der Machtpartei
    im Dezember 2007
    Mit einem Vorwort von Klaus Armingeon
    ISBN 978-3-89821-961-7

88 Thomas Borén
    Meeting-Places of Transformation
    Urban Identity, Spatial Representations and
    Local Politics in Post-Soviet St Petersburg
    ISBN 978-3-89821-739-2

89 Aygul Ashirova
    Stalinismus und Stalin-Kult in
    Zentralasien
    Turkmenistan 1924-1953
    Mit einem Vorwort von Leonid Luks
    ISBN 978-3-89821-987-7

90   *Leonid Luks*
Freiheit oder imperiale Größe?
Essays zu einem russischen Dilemma
ISBN 978-3-8382-0011-8

91   *Christopher Gilley*
The 'Change of Signposts' in the Ukrainian Emigration
A Contribution to the History of Sovietophilism in the 1920s
With a foreword by Frank Golczewski
ISBN 978-3-89821-965-5

92   *Philipp Casula, Jeronim Perovic (Eds.)*
Identities and Politics During the Putin Presidency
The Discursive Foundations of Russia's Stability
With a foreword by Heiko Haumann
ISBN 978-3-8382-0015-6

93   *Marcel Viëtor*
Europa und die Frage nach seinen Grenzen im Osten
Zur Konstruktion ‚europäischer Identität' in Geschichte und Gegenwart
Mit einem Vorwort von Albrecht Lehmann
ISBN 978-3-8382-0045-3

94   *Ben Hellman, Andrei Rogachevskii*
Filming the Unfilmable
Casper Wrede's 'One Day in the Life of Ivan Denisovich'
Second, Revised and Expanded Edition
ISBN 978-3-8382-0044-6

95   *Eva Fuchslocher*
Vaterland, Sprache, Glaube
Orthodoxie und Nationenbildung am Beispiel Georgiens
Mit einem Vorwort von Christina von Braun
ISBN 978-3-89821-884-9

96   *Vladimir Kantor*
Das Westlertum und der Weg Russlands
Zur Entwicklung der russischen Literatur und Philosophie
Ediert von Dagmar Herrmann
Mit einem Beitrag von Nikolaus Lobkowicz
ISBN 978-3-8382-0102-3

97   *Kamran Musayev*
Die postsowjetische Transformation im Baltikum und Südkaukasus
Eine vergleichende Untersuchung der politischen Entwicklung Lettlands und Aserbaidschans 1985-2009
Mit einem Vorwort von Leonid Luks
Ediert von Sandro Henschel
ISBN 978-3-8382-0103-0

98   *Tatiana Zhurzhenko*
Borderlands into Bordered Lands
Geopolitics of Identity in Post-Soviet Ukraine
With a foreword by Dieter Segert
ISBN 978-3-8382-0042-2

99   *Кирилл Галушко, Лидия Смола (ред.)*
Пределы падения – варианты украинского будущего
Аналитико-прогностические исследования
ISBN 978-3-8382-0148-1

100   *Michael Minkenberg (ed.)*
Historical Legacies and the Radical Right in Post-Cold War Central and Eastern Europe
With an afterword by Sabrina P. Ramet
ISBN 978-3-8382-0124-5

101   *David-Emil Wickström*
Rocking St. Petersburg
Transcultural Flows and Identity Politics in the St. Petersburg Popular Music Scene
With a foreword by Yngvar B. Steinholt
Second, Revised and Expanded Edition
ISBN 978-3-8382-0100-9

102   *Eva Zabka*
Eine neue „Zeit der Wirren"?
Der spät- und postsowjetische Systemwandel 1985-2000 im Spiegel russischer gesellschaftspolitischer Diskurse
Mit einem Vorwort von Margareta Mommsen
ISBN 978-3-8382-0161-0

103   *Ulrike Ziemer*
Ethnic Belonging, Gender and Cultural Practices
Youth Identitites in Contemporary Russia
With a foreword by Anoop Nayak
ISBN 978-3-8382-0152-8

104 Ksenia Chepikova
‚Einiges Russland' - eine zweite KPdSU?
Aspekte der Identitätskonstruktion einer postsowjetischen „Partei der Macht"
Mit einem Vorwort von Torsten Oppelland
ISBN 978-3-8382-0311-9

105 Леонид Люкс
Западничество или евразийство? Демократия или идеократия?
Сборник статей об исторических дилеммах России
С предисловием Владимира Кантора
ISBN 978-3-8382-0211-2

106 Anna Dost
Das russische Verfassungsrecht auf dem Weg zum Föderalismus und zurück
Zum Konflikt von Rechtsnormen und -wirklichkeit in der Russländischen Föderation von 1991 bis 2009
Mit einem Vorwort von Alexander Blankenagel
ISBN 978-3-8382-0292-1

107 Philipp Herzog
Sozialistische Völkerfreundschaft, nationaler Widerstand oder harmloser Zeitvertreib?
Zur politischen Funktion der Volkskunst im sowjetischen Estland
Mit einem Vorwort von Andreas Kappeler
ISBN 978-3-8382-0216-7

108 Marlène Laruelle (ed.)
Russian Nationalism, Foreign Policy, and Identity Debates in Putin's Russia
New Ideological Patterns after the Orange Revolution
ISBN 978-3-8382-0325-6

109 Michail Logvinov
Russlands Kampf gegen den internationalen Terrorismus
Eine kritische Bestandsaufnahme des Bekämpfungsansatzes
Mit einem Geleitwort von Hans-Henning Schröder
und einem Vorwort von Eckhard Jesse
ISBN 978-3-8382-0329-4

110 John B. Dunlop
The Moscow Bombings of September 1999
Examinations of Russian Terrorist Attacks at the Onset of Vladimir Putin's Rule
Second, Revised and Expanded Edition
ISBN 978-3-8382-0388-1

111 Андрей А. Ковалёв
Свидетельство из-за кулис российской политики I
Можно ли делать добро из зла?
(Воспоминания и размышления о последних советских и первых послесоветских годах)
With a foreword by Peter Reddaway
ISBN 978-3-8382-0302-7

112 Андрей А. Ковалёв
Свидетельство из-за кулис российской политики II
Угроза для себя и окружающих
(Наблюдения и предостережения относительно происходящего после 2000 г.)
ISBN 978-3-8382-0303-4

113 Bernd Kappenberg
Zeichen setzen für Europa
Der Gebrauch europäischer lateinischer Sonderzeichen in der deutschen Öffentlichkeit
Mit einem Vorwort von Peter Schlobinski
ISBN 978-3-89821-749-1

114 Ivo Mijnssen
The Quest for an Ideal Youth in Putin's Russia I
Back to Our Future! History, Modernity, and Patriotism according to Nashi, 2005-2013
With a foreword by Jeronim Perović
Second, Revised and Expanded Edition
ISBN 978-3-8382-0368-3

115 Jussi Lassila
The Quest for an Ideal Youth in Putin's Russia II
The Search for Distinctive Conformism in the Political Communication of Nashi, 2005-2009
With a foreword by Kirill Postoutenko
Second, Revised and Expanded Edition
ISBN 978-3-8382-0415-4

116 Valerio Trabandt
Neue Nachbarn, gute Nachbarschaft?
Die EU als internationaler Akteur am Beispiel ihrer Demokratieförderung in Belarus und der Ukraine 2004-2009
Mit einem Vorwort von Jutta Joachim
ISBN 978-3-8382-0437-6

117 Fabian Pfeiffer
Estlands Außen- und Sicherheitspolitik I
Der estnische Atlantizismus nach der
wiedererlangten Unabhängigkeit 1991-2004
Mit einem Vorwort von Helmut Hubel
ISBN 978-3-8382-0127-6

118 Jana Podßuweit
Estlands Außen- und Sicherheitspolitik II
Handlungsoptionen eines Kleinstaates im
Rahmen seiner EU-Mitgliedschaft (2004-2008)
Mit einem Vorwort von Helmut Hubel
ISBN 978-3-8382-0440-6

119 Karin Pointner
Estlands Außen- und Sicherheitspolitik III
Eine gedächtnispolitische Analyse estnischer
Entwicklungskooperation 2006-2010
Mit einem Vorwort von Karin Liebhart
ISBN 978-3-8382-0435-2

120 Ruslana Vovk
Die Offenheit der ukrainischen
Verfassung für das Völkerrecht und
die europäische Integration
Mit einem Vorwort von Alexander
Blankenagel
ISBN 978-3-8382-0481-9

121 Mykhaylo Banakh
Die Relevanz der Zivilgesellschaft
bei den postkommunistischen
Transformationsprozessen in mittel-
und osteuropäischen Ländern
Das Beispiel der spät- und postsowjetischen
Ukraine 1986-2009
Mit einem Vorwort von Gerhard Simon
ISBN 978-3-8382-0499-4

122 Michael Moser
Language Policy and the Discourse on
Languages in Ukraine under President
Viktor Yanukovych (25 February
2010–28 October 2012)
ISBN 978-3-8382-0497-0 (Paperback edition)
ISBN 978-3-8382-0507-6 (Hardcover edition)

123 Nicole Krome
Russischer Netzwerkkapitalismus
Restrukturierungsprozesse in der
Russischen Föderation am Beispiel des
Luftfahrtunternehmens "Aviastar"
Mit einem Vorwort von Petra Stykow
ISBN 978-3-8382-0534-2

124 David R. Marples
'Our Glorious Past'
Lukashenka's Belarus and
the Great Patriotic War
ISBN 978-3-8382-0574-8 (Paperback edition)
ISBN 978-3-8382-0675-2 (Hardcover edition)

125 Ulf Walther
Russlands "neuer Adel"
Die Macht des Geheimdienstes von
Gorbatschow bis Putin
Mit einem Vorwort von Hans-Georg Wieck
ISBN 978-3-8382-0584-7

126 Simon Geissbühler (Hrsg.)
Kiew – Revolution 3.0
Der Euromaidan 2013/14 und die
Zukunftsperspektiven der Ukraine
ISBN 978-3-8382-0581-6 (Paperback edition)
ISBN 978-3-8382-0681-3 (Hardcover edition)

127 Andrey Makarychev
Russia and the EU
in a Multipolar World
Discourses, Identities, Norms
With a foreword by Klaus Segbers
ISBN 978-3-8382-0629-5

128 Roland Scharff
Kasachstan als postsowjetischer
Wohlfahrtsstaat
Die Transformation des sozialen
Schutzsystems
Mit einem Vorwort von Joachim Ahrens
ISBN 978-3-8382-0622-6

129 Katja Grupp
Bild Lücke Deutschland
Kaliningrader Studierende sprechen über
Deutschland
Mit einem Vorwort von Martin Schulz
ISBN 978-3-8382-0552-6

130 Konstantin Sheiko, Stephen Brown
History as Therapy
Alternative History and Nationalist
Imaginings in Russia, 1991-2014
ISBN 978-3-8382-0665-3

131   Elisa Kriza
      Alexander Solzhenitsyn: Cold War
      Icon, Gulag Author, Russian
      Nationalist?
      A Study of the Western Reception of his
      Literary Writings, Historical Interpretations,
      and Political Ideas
      With a foreword by Andrei Rogatchevski
      ISBN 978-3-8382-0589-2 (Paperback edition)
      ISBN 978-3-8382-0690-5 (Hardcover edition)

132   Serghei Golunov
      The Elephant in the Room
      Corruption and Cheating in Russian
      Universities
      ISBN 978-3-8382-0570-0

133   Manja Hussner, Rainer Arnold (Hgg.)
      Verfassungsgerichtsbarkeit in
      Zentralasien I
      Sammlung von Verfassungstexten
      ISBN 978-3-8382-0595-3

134   Nikolay Mitrokhin
      Die "Russische Partei"
      Die Bewegung der russischen Nationalisten in
      der UdSSR 1953-1985
      Aus dem Russischen übertragen von einem
      Übersetzerteam unter der Leitung von Larisa Schippel
      ISBN 978-3-8382-0024-8

135   Manja Hussner, Rainer Arnold (Hgg.)
      Verfassungsgerichtsbarkeit in
      Zentralasien II
      Sammlung von Verfassungstexten
      ISBN 978-3-8382-0597-7

136   Manfred Zeller
      Das sowjetische Fieber
      Fußballfans im poststalinistischen
      Vielvölkerreich
      Mit einem Vorwort von Nikolaus Katzer
      ISBN 978-3-8382-0757-5

137   Kristin Schreiter
      Stellung und Entwicklungspotential
      zivilgesellschaftlicher Gruppen in
      Russland
      Menschenrechtsorganisationen im Vergleich
      ISBN 978-3-8382-0673-8

138   David R. Marples, Frederick V. Mills
      (Eds.)
      Ukraine's Euromaidan
      Analyses of a Civil Revolution
      ISBN 978-3-8382-0660-8

139   Bernd Kappenberg
      Setting Signs for Europe
      Why Diacritics Matter for
      European Integration
      With a foreword by Peter Schlobinski
      ISBN 978-3-8382-0663-9

140   René Lenz
      Internationalisierung, Kooperation
      und Transfer
      Externe bildungspolitische Akteure in der
      Russischen Föderation
      Mit einem Vorwort von Frank Ettrich
      ISBN 978-3-8382-0751-3

141   Juri Plusnin, Yana Zausaeva, Natalia
      Zhidkevich, Artemy Pozanenko
      Wandering Workers
      Mores, Behavior, Way of Life, and Political
      Status of Domestic Russian Labor Migrants
      Translated by Julia Kazantseva
      ISBN 978-3-8382-0653-0

142   Matthew Kott, David J. Smith (eds.)
      Latvia – A Work in Progress?
      100 Years of State- and Nation-building
      ISBN 978-3-8382-0648-6

143   Инна Чувычкина (ред.)
      Экспортные нефте- и газопроводы
      на постсоветском пространстве
      Анализ трубопроводной политики в свете
      теории международных отношений
      ISBN 978-3-8382-0822-0

144   Johann Zajaczkowski
      Russland – eine pragmatische
      Großmacht?
      Eine rollentheoretische Untersuchung
      russischer Außenpolitik am Beispiel der
      Zusammenarbeit mit den USA nach 9/11 und
      des Georgienkrieges von 2008
      Mit einem Vorwort von Siegfried Schieder
      ISBN 978-3-8382-0837-4

145   Boris Popivanov
      Changing Images of the Left in
      Bulgaria
      The Challenge of Post-Communism in the
      Early 21st Century
      ISBN 978-3-8382-0667-7

146   Lenka Krátká
      A History of the Czechoslovak Ocean
      Shipping Company 1948-1989
      How a Small, Landlocked Country Ran
      Maritime Business During the Cold War
      ISBN 978-3-8382-0666-0

***ibidem*-**Verlag

Melchiorstr. 15

D-70439 Stuttgart

info@ibidem-verlag.de

www.ibidem-verlag.de
www.ibidem.eu
www.edition-noema.de
www.autorenbetreuung.de